Dr. Noëlle O'Connor
Dr Sheila Flanagan
Prof. David Gilbert

A Film Marketing Action Plan for Film Induced Tourism Destinations

Dr. Noëlle O'Connor
Dr Sheila Flanagan
Prof. David Gilbert

A Film Marketing Action Plan for Film Induced Tourism Destinations

Using Yorkshire as a case study

Lambert Academic Publishing

Impressum/Imprint (nur für Deutschland/ only for Germany)

Bibliografische Information der Deutschen Nationalbibliothek: Die Deutsche Nationalbibliothek verzeichnet diese Publikation in der Deutschen Nationalbibliografie; detaillierte bibliografische Daten sind im Internet über http://dnb.d-nb.de abrufbar.

Alle in diesem Buch genannten Marken und Produktnamen unterliegen warenzeichen-, marken- oder patentrechtlichem Schutz bzw. sind Warenzeichen oder eingetragene Warenzeichen der jeweiligen Inhaber. Die Wiedergabe von Marken, Produktnamen, Gebrauchsnamen, Handelsnamen, Warenbezeichnungen u.s.w. in diesem Werk berechtigt auch ohne besondere Kennzeichnung nicht zu der Annahme, dass solche Namen im Sinne der Warenzeichen- und Markenschutzgesetzgebung als frei zu betrachten wären und daher von jedermann benutzt werden dürften.

Verlag: Lambert Academic Publishing AG & Co. KG
Dudweiler Landstr. 99, 66123 Saarbrücken, Deutschland
Telefon +49 681 3720-310, Telefax +49 681 3720-3109, Email: info@lap-publishing.com

Herstellung in Deutschland:
Schaltungsdienst Lange o.H.G., Berlin
Books on Demand GmbH, Norderstedt
Reha GmbH, Saarbrücken
Amazon Distribution GmbH, Leipzig
ISBN: 978-3-8383-2018-2

Imprint (only for USA, GB)

Bibliographic information published by the Deutsche Nationalbibliothek: The Deutsche Nationalbibliothek lists this publication in the Deutsche Nationalbibliografie; detailed bibliographic data are available in the Internet at http://dnb.d-nb.de.

Any brand names and product names mentioned in this book are subject to trademark, brand or patent protection and are trademarks or registered trademarks of their respective holders. The use of brand names, product names, common names, trade names, product descriptions etc. even without a particular marking in this works is in no way to be construed to mean that such names may be regarded as unrestricted in respect of trademark and brand protection legislation and could thus be used by anyone.

Publisher:
Lambert Academic Publishing AG & Co. KG
Dudweiler Landstr. 99, 66123 Saarbrücken, Germany
Phone +49 681 3720-310, Fax +49 681 3720-3109, Email: info@lap-publishing.com

Printed in the U.S.A.
Printed in the U.K. by (see last page)
ISBN: 978-3-8383-2018-2

A FILM MARKETING ACTION PLAN (FMAP) FOR FILM INDUCED TOURISM DESTINATIONS

Dr Noëlle O'Connor,
Senior Lecturer in Tourism and Hospitality,
Department of Humanities,
School of Business and Humanities,
Limerick Institute of Technology,
Ireland.
Tel: + 353 61 490166
Email: noelle.oconnor@lit.ie

Dr. Sheila Flanagan,
Head of School,
School of Hospitality Management and Tourism,
Faculty of Tourism and Food,
Dublin Institute of Technology,
Cathal Brugha Street,
Dublin 1, Ireland.
Tel: +353 1 4024380
Email: sheila.flanagan@dit.ie

Prof. David Gilbert,
Professor of Marketing
School of Management,
University of Surrey,
Guildford,
Surrey,
GU2 7XH,
U.K.
Tel: +44 1483 689347
Email: d.gilbert@surrey.ac.uk

SUMMARY

This research study examines the impact of film induced tourism and destination branding on locations featured in popular films and television series. It also investigates the characteristics of film induced tourism and determines if the key film and tourism stakeholders support the integration of film into Yorkshire's (UK) tourism product.

Yorkshire was selected as the case study area, as it has been the film location for many popular television series and is the subject of much location research within the tourism discipline. The need for a thorough investigation into the film induced tourism phenomenon was particularly evident from the literature review undertaken, as it showed that there was a significant research gap in the successful integration of this phenomenon and destination marketing. In response to this gap, a two phased approach was adopted; the first involved a tourist survey regarding the film induced tourist, while the second phase consisted of strategic conversations with the key stakeholders behind the Yorkshire brand. The issues evolving from these and also the literature review, highlight a number of implications for the future development of such destinations, namely the successful use of destination branding in the promotion of a film location. These issues also facilitated the creation of the Film Marketing Action Plan (FMAP), as it has become apparent that most of the film induced tourism models investigated were inadequate in explaining the relationship between film induced tourism and destination branding. Thus, a new model that is more reflective of the process was developed, using the main concepts and themes that arose from the research findings. Overall, film induced tourism is not widely welcomed by the stakeholders and the implications for retaining a clear balance between Yorkshire's current tourism product and making the most of the opportunities that could arise, may be the most appropriate way forward.

2

ABBREVIATION LIST

ATC	Australian Tourism Commission
ATP	Area Tourism Partnerships
BTA	British Tourist Authority
CAUTHE	Council for Australian University Tourism and Hospitality Education
CHRIE	Council on Hotel, Restaurant and Institutional Education
DCMS	Department of Culture, Media and Sport
DMO	Destination Marketing Organization
DMS	Destination Marketing Strategy
EU	European Union
FECTO	Federation of European Cities Tourist Offices
FMAP	Film Marketing Action Plan
FMD	Foot and Mouth Disease
FNZ	Film New Zealand
GDP	Gross Domestic Product
ICT	Information and Communications Technology
ITAM	International Tourism and Media Conference
LA	Local Authority
NPA	National Park Authority
NTA	National Tourism Authority
NTO	National Tourism Organisation
NWRDA	North West Regional Development Authority
NYMNP	North York Moors National Park
OECD	Organisation for Economic Co-operation and Development
PPE	Post Production Effect
RDA	Regional Development Authorities
RIFE	Regional Investment Fund for England
RSA	Regional Screen Agencies
RTA	Regional Tourism Authorities
STG	Sterling
TAT	Tourism Authority of Thailand
TIC	Tourism Information Centre
TIL	Tourism Ireland Limited
TNZ	Tourism New Zealand
TTRA	Travel and Tourism Research Association

UK	United Kingdom
USA	United States of America
USP	Unique Selling Point
WTO	World Tourism Organization
WTTC	World Travel and Tourism Council
YTB	Yorkshire Tourist Board

LIST OF TABLES

LIST OF FIGURES

TABLE OF CONTENTS

Chapter 3: Literature review II – Film induced tourism

Chapter 4: Research methodology

Chapter 5: Survey Results and Detailed Analysis of Strategic conversations with tourism and film stakeholders in Yorkshire

Chapter 6: The Film Marketing Action Plan (FMAP)

Chapter 7: Conclusions and recommendations

CHAPTER 1

INTRODUCTION

1.1 Introduction

Chapter 1 provides a background to this research study – *A Film Marketing Action Plan (FMAP) for Film Induced Tourism Destinations, Using Yorkshire (UK) as the Case Study Area.* Film induced tourism is *the collective term used for the study of tourist visits to a destination or attraction as a result of the destination being featured on the cinema screen, DVD, television or on video* (Hudson and Ritchie 2006a: 256). It introduces the rationale for studying the literature associated with destination branding, destination imagery and film induced tourism. Chapter 1 also identifies the relevance of the study and examines the research questions and objectives (see Table 1.1) which form the basis of this research. Finally, the organization of this research study is elaborated upon and is supported by the use of a model, which gives the reader an insight into the logic of this research.

1.2 Rationale for Studying Destination Branding, Destination Imagery and Film Induced Tourism in Yorkshire, UK

Beeton (2005: 17–18) implies that much of the latest academic literature has not particularly added to the body of research on film induced tourism as it tends to concentrate on replicating and supporting these earlier studies looking predominantly at the promotional importance of film in relation to tourism. Other than the fact that this has reinforced the outcomes of previous research, little new material has been added to the literature on film induced tourism. Every paper published concludes by asserting the necessity for additional research but the minority have followed their own recommendations leaving the feeling that such proclamations are simply escape clauses for those taking on interim or solitary research assignments. If destinations are to successfully make the most of their own popularity, but within a sustainable framework, the various stakeholders' interests should find a compromise in setting suitable objectives to capitalize on the benefits and reduce costs of such tourism (Beeton 2005: 17–18).

This research study examines the impact of film induced tourism and destination branding on locations featured in popular films and television series. It also investigates the nature the of film induced tourism concept and determines if the key film and tourism stakeholders support the integration of film into Yorkshire's (See Figure 1.1) tourism product.

Figure 1.1

Location Map of Yorkshire, UK

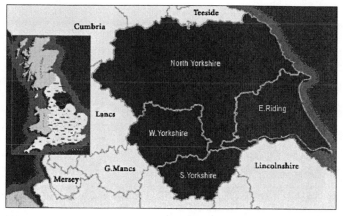

(Source: Pictures of England 2009)

Yorkshire was selected as the case study area as it has been the film location for many popular television series and films (See Table 1.1). It is also the subject of much location research within the tourism discipline (see Beeton 2000, 2005; Mordue 1999, 2001; O'Connor *et al.* 2005, 2006, 2008). The need for a thorough investigation into the film induced tourism phenomenon was particularly evident from the literature review undertaken, as it showed that there was a significant research gap in the successful integration of this phenomenon and destination marketing.

Table 1.1

Yorkshire Based Film and Television Series (1960s to 2001)

Year	Television Series	Film
1960s	*This Sporting Life*	
1967	*The Railway Children*	
1970		*Jane Eyre*
1970		*The Railway Children*
1970 & 1992		*Wuthering Heights*
1972	*The Darling Buds of May*	
1972–	*Emmerdale (Farm)*	
1973–	*Last of the Summer Wine*	
1978–1990	*All Creatures Great and Small*	
1980s	*A Woman of Substance, Hold the Dream, Act of Will*	
1981	*Brideshead Revisited*	
1985		*Wetherby*
1986		*Rita, Sue and Bob Too*
1989	*A Bit of a Do*	
1991		*Robin Hood – Prince of Thieves*
1993		*The Secret Garden*
1992–	*Heartbeat*	
1995	*Band of Gold*	
1996		*Brassed Off*
1996		*When Saturday Comes*
1996–2006	*Where the Heart Is*	
1997		*The Full Monty*
1998		*Elizabeth*
1998		*Little Voice*
1998	*Playing the Field*	
2001		*Harry Potter and the Philosopher's Stone*
2001	*The Inspector Linley Mysteries*	

(Adapted from YTB 2001/2002)

The fundamental issues in this case study (Yorkshire) are of international significance, providing a revelatory case for the application of the concepts summarized in other film induced tourism destinations. This case study can assist destinations in planning the best possible levels of tourist numbers and revenue, in conjunction with film induced tourism. It may also be utilized in regional tourism policy development. Tourist numbers are influenced through policy decisions, which may affect the tourist influx to a rural community, or other recreational policies might affect the level of development or income (Beeton 2001a: 24).

1.3 Relevance of the Study

Film induced tourism has the potential to offer fantastic opportunities but also creates many drawbacks, which are demonstrated in **Chapters 3 and 5.** The concept of film induced tourism is not widely welcomed by the tourism and film stakeholders in Yorkshire and the challenge is to retain a transparent balance between Yorkshire's current tourism product and making the most of the opportunities that arise in new markets which may be the most appropriate way forward (Connell 2005a: 774). Investigating this balance has aided the development of the FMAP **(see Figure 6.2),** which is a model to be used as a best practice framework for the successful integration of film induced tourism in a destinations marketing strategy. This has not previously been undertaken.

1.4 Research Questions and Objectives

The main objective of this research is *to develop a model to be used as a best practice framework for the successful integration of film induced tourism in a Destinations Marketing Strategy* (DMS). To collect the views and perspective, which allow for informed interpretations to be made, it is vital that the gathered data are collected in a well thought-out manner. To establish if film induced tourism can bring significant benefits to the development of a destination, it is necessary to establish a framework for research completion. This will put in place the appropriate data collection methods, which are illustrated in more detail in **Table 1.2.** The key research questions (which will be elaborated on further in Chapter 4) in this work are:

- What are the film induced images that tourists presently have of Yorkshire? **(See Research Objective 1.)**
- What are the current and future tourism and marketing objectives and priorities of Yorkshire's key tourism and film stakeholders? **(See Research Objective 2.)**
- Are these stakeholders who are involved in the development of Yorkshire embracing the film tourism concept? **(See Research Objective 2.)**

- If so, is the film induced tourism concept successfully integrated into their destination marketing campaign? **(See Research Objective 2.)**
- Is the film induced tourism brand currently subsumed within Yorkshire's overall tourism brand? **(See Research Objective 2.)**
- Do the tourism and film stakeholders work in tandem? **(See Research Objective 2.)**
- What conclusions and recommendations emerge based on the research findings? **(See Research Objective 3.)**

Table 1.2   Framework for Research Completion

Research Questions	Research Objectives	Data Collection Methods	Expected Outcomes
What are the film induced images that tourists presently have of Yorkshire?	1. Identify the film induced images that tourists presently have of Yorkshire. ▪ Evaluate the level of imagery that Yorkshire has in the mind of the tourist. ▪ Identify if tourists are aware of Yorkshire based television series. ▪ Discover the images, if any that tourists associate with the three Yorkshire based television series under review. ▪ Ascertain tourist awareness in relation to the three television associated marketing brands that are used by the Yorkshire Tourist Board to promote the county. ▪ Highlight the key success factors of the Yorkshire tourism product.	Secondary research (literature review: destination branding, destination imagery and film induced tourism) complemented by a tourist survey. **(See Chapters 2, 3, 4, 5, 6 and 7.)**	Develop an initial understanding of the film induced tourism concept as applied to Yorkshire from the tourist's perspective.
What are the current and future tourism and marketing objectives and priorities of	2. Determine if key tourism and film stakeholders support the integration of film into Yorkshire's	Secondary research complemented by strategic conversations with	Determine if film induced tourism is a future priority for the

19

Yorkshire's key tourism and television stakeholders?	tourism product.	tourism and film stakeholders in Yorkshire. **(See Chapters 2, 3, 4, 5, 6 and 7.)**	stakeholders.
Are these stakeholders who are involved in the development of Yorkshire, embracing the film tourism concept?	2. Determine if key tourism and film stakeholders support the integration of film into Yorkshire's tourism product.	Strategic conversations. **(See Chapters 4, 5, 6 and 7.)**	Identify if the stakeholders accept that film induced tourism is a viable tourism product.
If so, is the film induced tourism concept successfully integrated into their destination marketing campaign?	2. Determine if key tourism and film stakeholders support the integration of film into Yorkshire's tourism product.	Secondary research complemented by strategic conversations. **(See Chapters 2, 3, 4, 5, 6 and 7.)**	Discover to what extent the integration of film and tourism has actually occurred in Yorkshire.
Is the film induced tourism brand currently subsumed within Yorkshire's overall tourism brand?	2. Determine if key tourism and film stakeholders support the integration of film into Yorkshire's tourism product.	Strategic conversations. **(See Chapters 4, 5, 6 and 7.)**	See if film induced tourism can be used as a stand alone destination brand.
Do the tourism and film stakeholders work in tandem?	2. Determine if key tourism and film stakeholders support the integration of film into Yorkshire's tourism product.	Strategic conversations. **(See Chapters 4, 5, 6 and 7.)**	Detect if the stakeholders work together.
What conclusions and recommendations emerge based on the research findings?	3. Develop a model to be used as a best practice framework for the successful integration of film induced tourism into a destinations marketing strategy.	Secondary research complemented by a tourist survey and strategic conversations. **(See Chapters 2, 3 4, 5, 6 and 7.)**	Recommend a final course of action through the creation of an FMAP.

1.5   Organization of this Research

This research study consists of seven chapters which are illustrated in Figure 1.2.

Figure 1.2   Organization of this Research

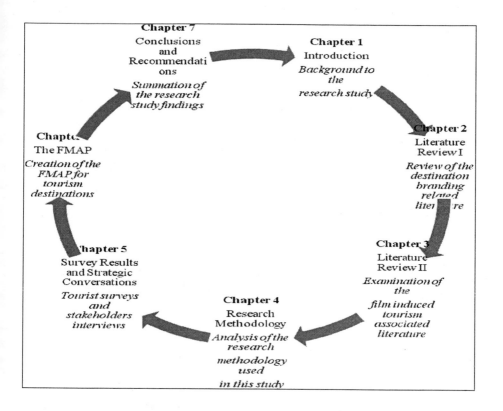

Chapter 2 is a literature review of the theoretical concepts of investigating a film induced tourism destination such as Yorkshire. This chapter reviews the impact of film related branding on a destination, by examining the current theoretical and applied branding literature with special emphasis on destination branding, destination imagery and film induced destination branding.

Chapter 3 examines this evolving research area by studying the background and theoretical context of the film induced tourism phenomenon. An understanding of this concept and its emergence as a research discipline within the tourism area will also be examined. Furthermore, this chapter will look at both the negative and positive impacts that film induced tourism can have on a destination.

Chapter 4 describes the methodology used for this research study. The chapter commences with an introduction to the background of the study. The aim of this two-phase, sequential mixed methods study is to acquire statistical quantitative results (tourist survey) from a sample, and subsequently to follow up with individuals to investigate those results in more depth. In the second phase, qualitative interviews (strategic conversations) with key tourism and film stakeholders in Yorkshire will be undertaken to explore the emergent themes and issues from the first phase. Chapter 4 concludes with an investigation into the data analysis used and the research limitations met during the course of the study. **(See Research Objectives 1 and 2.)**

Chapter 5 identifies the findings of the tourist survey and the issues which emerged from the literature review. A number of implications for the future development of such destinations are highlighted, for instance, the many positive and negative impacts of filming the various television series in Yorkshire and the use of destination branding in the promotion of a film destination. To proceed to the next stage of research, the key tourism and film stakeholders behind the Yorkshire brand were interviewed, as the main objective of this research is *to develop a model to be used as a best practice framework for the successful integration of film induced tourism in a destinations marketing strategy*, which in turn could possibly be implemented by these stakeholders. **(See Research Objectives 1 and 2.)**

The primary focus of Chapter 6 is to design a model (the FMAP) for film induced tourism as a result of this research study. **(See Research Objective 3.)** The other purpose of this chapter is to draw together the crucial findings of the research, which address the main objectives of the **study.** To support the main objective stated previously, a model will be devised through the creation of an FMAP.

Chapter 7 provides an overall discussion on the conclusions and recommendations of the outputs from the previous chapters and makes suggestions for future research in this discipline as well as summarizing how these conclusions and suggestions came into place. **(See Research Objectives 1, 2 and 3.)**

CHAPTER 2

LITERATURE REVIEW I
DESTINATION BRANDING

2.1   Introduction

Chapter 2 (see also **Chapters 3 and 4**) presents the academic foundation for this research study's main objectives **(See Table 1.2)**. It identifies the role of branding in tourism destinations that have become popular due to being featured in a well-liked film or television series. The main objective of this research is *to develop a model to be used as a best practice framework for the successful integration of film induced tourism in a destinations marketing strategy.* As a result, Chapter 2 will examine the impact of film induced branding on a destination by reviewing the current theoretical and empirical branding literature with special emphasis on destination branding, destination image and film induced destination branding.

2.2   Branding

Xiang (2006: 37) claims that destination branding has attracted widespread attention in recent years (see also Cai 2002; Morgan, Pritchard and Piggott 2003; Morgan, Pritchard and Pride 2004). The American Marketing Association characterizes a brand as '*a name, term, sign, symbol, design or a combination of these intended to identify the goods or services of one seller or group of sellers and to differentiate them from those of competition*' (Kotler and Armstrong 1999: 249). Thus, branding is made up of the combined '*efforts to create, maintain, protect and enhance one particular brand to secure a sustainable competitive advantage*' (Kotler and Armstrong 1999: 301). Xiang (2006: 37) suggests that for a time, marketing researchers have emphasized the importance of branding (citing Allison and Uhl 1964; Dichter 1964; Gardner and Levy 1955; Haire 1950; Levy 1959).

A tourism marketing brand signifies a distinctive amalgamation of product and service characteristics. Evidently, it is an appealing idea with its distinct image and superficial competitive advantage, which offers added value to a product and/or service beyond its standard physical features. Prominent brands such as Coca Cola and Nike are globally recognizable. McDonalds and Shell are two of the world's leading brands, familiar to nearly 90% of the world's inhabitants. These are surpassed only by the rings symbol of the Olympic association (Morgan and Pritchard 1998: 140). Sony almost certainly spends more on its annual advertising budget than the combined totals of many of the world's National Tourism Organizations (NTO)[1] (Morgan and Pritchard 1998: 13). Popular tourism destinations like Croatia, France and Thailand have to compete with these companies for consumer mind share in a packed environment which is very much influenced by spiraling media costs (Morgan and Pritchard 1998: 140).

---

1 NTO is generally the government body responsible for tourism at national level.

Middleton and Clarke (2001: 133) contend that tourism destinations are very susceptible to environmental disasters, international economics, politics and terrorism. Consequently, there are many characteristics of the tourism industry, which mean that specific benefits may be obtained from successful destination branding, for instance:

- The reduction of the unpredictable external events that affect the tourism industry such as the terrorist attacks in the Bali, Madrid, Saudi Arabia, Turkey and the United States of America (USA), the hurricanes in the Caribbean and the USA. These are just some of the recent events that have slowed down the successful promotion of destinations;
- Reducing the risks for the tourist prior to their arrival at the destination by highlighting the expected quality and performance of an intangible product;
- The facilitation of precise marketing segmentation by attracting some consumer segments and discouraging others. The British tour operator *Club 18–30* attracts certain segments of the youth holiday market while discouraging others;
- The use of branding as a strategic tool for long-term tourism planning, for example, that employed by British Airways in its lucrative repositioning as a major international airline (Middleton and Clarke 2001: 133).

Many see clearly recognized global branding as a fundamental precursor to the productive use of business communications and distribution on the internet (Middleton and Clarke 2001: 134). The biggest dilemma that destinations face, however, is that the message portrayed is not always the message that the tourist receives, though this can be offset by way of an effective destination branding strategy **(see 2.3.1).**

2.3   Destination Branding

Recently, branding has been used by destination marketers who believe that the concept is as applicable to destinations as it is to airlines, attractions, hotels and restaurants (Seaton and Bennett 1996: 130). Many tourism researchers (Chambers 1989; Nasser 2003) consider that tourism destinations can improve their success levels by forming a resilient brand strategy which enhances their market share as seen in the *I♥NY* (1983) and *Glasgow's Miles Better* (1977) campaigns, irrespective of where destinations are in the life cycle. Destination Marketing Organizations[2] (DMO) face specific branding challenges as referred to earlier (Gibson and Nielson 2000: 223) and

---

2 A DMO is an organization at any level which is responsible for the marketing of an identifiable destination. Therefore, this excludes separate government departments that are responsible for planning and policy (Pike 2004: 14).

also have restricted budgets, nevertheless they have to market internationally, competing not just with other destinations but also with other universal brands (Morgan, Pritchard and Pride 2002: 62).

A tourism brand is considered to represent an exclusive amalgamation of product characteristics and added values, which have taken on a relevant meaning connected to brand awareness that may be conscious or intuitive (Morgan and Pritchard 1999). In recent years, the marketing of destinations has grown to be extremely competitive and as the stakes are raised, public sector marketing strategies are becoming increasingly sophisticated (Morgan and Pritchard 1998: 145). With the emergence of new destinations, branding strategies need to highlight product differentiation. In particular, these up-and-coming new destinations are trying to cultivate a niche and create images which underline the distinctiveness of their product. To a greater extent, destinations are now pursuing a more focused communications strategy to which branding plays a central role to facilitate overcoming the media chaos of the tourism marketing world (Seaton and Bennett 1996).

The World Tourism Organization (WTO)3 estimates that the world's governments spend around 50% of the marketing budgets of the NTOs on destination marketing. Brand advantage can be obtained through image building campaigns, which emphasize the explicit benefits of a product, concluding with an overall impression of an exceptional brand. Whether, destination branding is economically effective or not, is hard to quantify due to the lack of empirical research in this area (WTO 1979).

O'Regan (2000) argues that tourist product positioning is one of the many challenges confronting tourism marketers. Each year airlines and countries splurge billions of Euros in an effort to shape favourable travel images, whether true or not, representing a reality to potential tourists when selecting a holiday destination (Ruddy and Flanagan 2000: 6). As a result, the image of a destination is a decisive factor in a tourist's destination choice process. Productive destination marketing depends fundamentally on the way tourists perceive the product and the marketing incentives intended to promote the product. Destination marketing is used to distinguish destinations from those of their competitors, meaning those with strong images are more predisposed to being selected in the travel decision process. Prospective tourists are possibly aware of the available destinations and may just contemplate a limited set of their products and services.

---

3 The WTO is a specialized agency of the United Nations and is the leading international organization in the field of tourism. It serves as a global forum for tourism policy issues and as a practical source of tourism know-how.

As a result, tourists rely very much on the destination image in deciding on which destination to visit next (Ruddy and Flanagan 2000: 6).

Slater (2004) states that the tourism industry is presently using branding as a means of accentuating the feel of the destination and creating a personality which differentiates it, since the branded destination is an experience, not just a place to go (Anon. 1996). This branding outlook has been noted in many recent campaigns; for Australia *Come and Say G'Day* (1994) and New Zealand's *100% Pure New Zealand* (1999). The Travel Industry Association of America (2003) estimates that the USA state government spent €715 million in 2002–2003 in tourism promotion for the fifty states (Morgan *et al.* 2004: 227).

2.3.1   Successful destination branding strategies

Tourism destinations are in all probability one of the toughest products to sell as they involve many stakeholders and also a brand image over which a destination marketer more often than not has very little control. The range and complexity of tourism destinations has been well acknowledged (Leiper 1996), which makes brand development very difficult for national, regional and local tourism organizations. Destination branding inevitably involves the focused attention of all tourism stakeholders in the destination and this can create an immense challenge in creating a consistent theme (Palmer 2004: 128) also if the name of the destination appears in a communications strategy, it does not necessarily mean that it is a branding strategy.

Anholt (2004: 27) recognizes that those destination brands which have emerged to achieve instant stardom are not surprisingly the world's top ten destination brands; Britain, France, Germany, Italy, Japan, Scandinavia, South Korea, Spain, Switzerland and the USA. Anholt (2004: 27) also maintains that Germany and the USA are the leading global destination brands, to a certain extent because they have been so carefully marketed worldwide. Brand status is also often due as the result of long-term cultural, economic, political and social factors. There have been many notable successes in developing strong tourist development brands such as in Glasgow, New York and Spain (Morgan and Pritchard 2002: 36–37).

In their research, Morgan and Pritchard (2002: 36–37) highlight the success of countries like Spain. This they suggest indicates that destination brands can become fashionable and can remain popular over a long period of time. However, this does not mean that a strong place brand is easy to sustain. It takes perseverance to establish brand reputations and creating a strong destination brand is a long-term effort, which can generate incremental results (Morgan and Pritchard 2002: 36–37).

For a brand to be truly successful the vision also has to be reproduced in the product and service on offer, as the marketing of a destination can have a significant impact on its development. In the case of Spain, this meant creating a public–private partnership to reposition the country internationally. In 1992, Barcelona hosted the Olympics; Seville the World Expo, and the Guggenheim Museum was opened in Bilbao in 1997, while decomposing beachfronts were refurbished in the main tourist resorts from Benidorm to Majorca (Morgan and Pritchard 1998: 282). Spain is also one of the best examples of successful destination branding as it continues to build on what actually exists. Its branding efforts integrate many activities under one 'umbrella' to drive an adaptable approach (Preston 1999).

Canada's *The World Next Door* (1990) brand associates their destination with a very identifiable label. Middleton and Clarke (2001: 336–337) are impressed by these examples as they would have taken the following into consideration prior to their development. They would have to

- Be based on authentic product values and characteristics that can be delivered and that tourists appreciate as legitimate;
- Be promptly recognized by tourists at the point of purchase;
- Involve at least the principal stakeholders in the commercial sector;
- Be integrated into the marketing efforts of a destination's regions and resorts;
- Be maintained over many years if they are to overcome any communication impediments;
- Target tourists on arrival at the destination, as well as potential tourists in countries of origin through sales promotion and customer servicing techniques (Middleton and Clarke 2001: 336–337).

A destination can become stronger through effective branding but the previous issues should be taken into consideration. Aaker (1996) and Middleton and Clarke (2001) both found that if the key factors necessary to create a successful destination brand are considered, a strengthened destination brand strategy can be put into place. This is evident in Aaker's (1996) study of the State of Louisiana brand management team. They invested significantly in the brand, as they acknowledged that a well-planned tourism destination branding campaign could be very productive for their tourism destination (Slater 2004: 227–228).

According to Aaker (1996), the Louisiana brand involves the following factors which can be identified with a strong brand:

- A brand identity with an associated competitive advantage has been created. The brand identity directs the brand association of Louisiana as an culinary, cultural, exclusive, historical and musical experience.
- It has achieved brand awareness through extensive exposure of its resilient and consistent message.
- The brand has a perceived quality, in that tourists believe what they hear, read and see about the state and those expectations are satisfied once the visit has been undertaken.
- The brand delivers on its promise by offering something that is unavailable elsewhere.
- There is brand loyalty evidenced in repeat tourists and the state does a good job in providing tourists with a reason to return, such as the *Louisiana Purchase Celebration* (2003) (Slater 2004: 239–240).

According to Davies (2003), the strongest tourism motivator is the destination brand image; this creates an emotional appeal, which enhances that destination's chances of being selected. For example, in 1998, research financed by the Malaysian Tourism Promotion Board, showed that Singapore was viewed by many tourists and tourist agents from Australia, Germany, India, Japan, Sweden, the UK and the USA as *clean, modern and safe*. China's dominant image was *culture*. Malaysia was seen as *multicultural with many beaches* and Thailand had a brand image of *exotic, fun, and friendly people* (Davies 2003). These images in turn can lead to brand success, if they are a genuine reflection of the destination. Vellas and Bécherel (1999: 190–191) argue that destination marketers select the name for the destination from tourist associations and perceptions (both positive and negative). The marketers usually then have to adapt the inherited brand name to publicize the most effective positive message (Vellas and Bécherel 1999: 190–191).

2.3.2   Destination brand name

The concept of a brand name can also extend to a tourist destination, e.g. Acapulco, the French Riviera and Palm Springs, which have developed solid reputations, consumer perceptions and expectations. In similar ways; Florence (Italy) based on the *Centre of the Renaissance*, Greece on the *Birthplace of Democracy*, Niagara Falls (USA/Canada) on *Romance*, Mississippi (USA) on the *Heart of Dixie* and Virginia (USA) builds on the *Birthplace of Presidents*. Such positioning makes particular attractions interesting and is a platform for building on a destination image (Morgan and Pritchard 1998: 146–147). One example of the exception to this is *EuroDisney*, where a totally new destination was created and branded. Ironically, the operators got their initial branding wrong.

They had to undertake expensive rebranding and *EuroDisney* was re-launched as *Disneyland Europe*. Rebranding is something marketers need to reflect upon before they commence their brand campaign (Vellas and Bécherel 1999: 191).

Torbay (UK) which combines the three towns of Brixham, Paignton and Torquay, has successfully created its brand. The three distinctively different towns keep their identity as a sub-title to Torbay. This brand uses the cheeky slogan; *The English Riviera*, which positions Torbay as trendy and blessed with good weather. This last point is highlighted by the use of a palm tree as a logo. Seasonality is an ongoing problem for Torbay, which has tried to lengthen its tourist season by showing palm trees decked out in Christmas lights to create the illusion of Torbay as a year round destination (Vellas and Bécherel 1999: 191). As highlighted earlier, if the name of the destination appears in a communications strategy, it does not necessarily mean that it is the branding strategy alone as all elements of the strategy need to be developed.

2.3.3 The development of the destination brand

Internationally, there are many possibilities with destination branding, which extend to NTOs looking to establish an identity for their country (Gibson and Nielson 2000: 223–224). As mentioned earlier, in the 1980s, there were several very successful marketing campaigns, which were based on a consistent communications plan. In New York, the *I♥NY* campaign was developed to counteract the image of the city as crime infested and tourist unfriendly. Indeed, the campaign's simple message led to the slogan being copied for many other products and destinations. In Glasgow, the city's campaign (*Glasgow's Miles Better)* was integrated into a wider regeneration and city marketing strategy (Morgan and Pritchard 2002: 22).

A destination brand can be built and promoted in a number of ways, most evidently in advertising through brochures, direct marketing, personal selling, public relations and in the incorporation of DMOs with event planners, film producers and the media. Destination promotion can be defined as the '*conscious use of publicity and marketing to communicate selective images of specific geographical localities or areas to a target audience*' (Gold and Ward 1994: 2). Ward (1998) suggests that destination promotion involves advertising, major developments and events in the arts, media, leisure, heritage, retailing and sports industries (Morgan and Pritchard 2004: 59).

2.3.4 Tourism event branding

Events are strongly related to destinations and are used to promote a destination's image, like the Oktoberfest (Munich, Germany), the Rio Carnival (Rio de Janeiro, Brazil) and the Wimbledon Tennis Tournament (London, UK). To enhance a destination's image, it would be easier to create a new positive association than try to improve old ones. When many people hear the word 'Chicago', *Chicago Bulls* and *Michael Jordan* comes to mind more often than *Al Capone* (Kotler and Gertner 2002: 254–255).

Morse (2001) describes the success of the Sydney Olympic Games in 2000 and the public relations work of the Australian Tourism Commission[4] (ATC). It was claimed that the Games altered forever the way the world perceives Australia, advancing its brand by a decade (Brown *et al.* 2002: 175). Brown *et al.* (2002: 173–174) also found in their research that such events can enhance a destination's image, particularly those events that possess the following characteristics:

- Longevity – time that is needed to allow the event to become associated with the destination in the minds of potential tourists;
- Community support – events, which have strong support in their host communities, are more successful as image-makers;
- Professionalism of an organization – where an event has a reputation for professional management, this is seen to rub off on the image of the destination;
- Compatibility with the destination – an event needs to fit with the destination with the intention of becoming victorious in its imaging;
- Media coverage – this is necessary for an event to play a key role in destination branding (Brown *et al.* 2002: 173–174).

2.4   Emotional Branding

Successful image positioning establishes destination competitiveness in potential travellers' minds (Ahmed 1991; Echtner and Ritchie 1991, 1993). The best way competitively to position one destination over another is to produce and broadcast positive images to prospective tourists (Baloglu and McCleary 1999a; Gartner 1993; Milman and Pizam 1995). As a destination image is the only differentiable factor among competing destinations (Baloglu and McCleary 1999b), many DMOs have tried to influence potential tourist behaviour by using conventional marketing tools such as personal selling and sales promotion (Dore and Crouch 2002; King 2002).

A destination brand with emotional roots can persuade local drinks, crafts and food suppliers, to use their product brand values and emotions as part of their advertising campaign. Nevertheless, on a positioning map, brand frontrunners are those destinations that are plentiful in emotional roots, have great conversation value and holiday anticipation for prospective tourists. By comparison, brand

---

4 The ATC is Australia's international marketing authority and is responsible for promoting Australia overseas to attract visitors for business and leisure travel (ATC 2008).

losers have little meaning, even less status, practically no conversation and zero anticipation for tourists. Problematic destinations are those that are mentioned for all the wrong reasons and far from holding an emotional appeal, they actively repel potential tourists. Destinations that presently have a 'small emotional pull' like the Ukraine **(see Figure 2.1)** face an uphill battle if they intend to become successful destinations. Other destinations which do indeed have an emotional pull but currently have limited (although growing) celebrity value and an untapped potential, can become successful tourist destinations, namely India and South Africa **(see Figure 2.1)** (Morgan and Pritchard 2002: 23–24).

Figure 2.1

Destination Brand Positioning Map

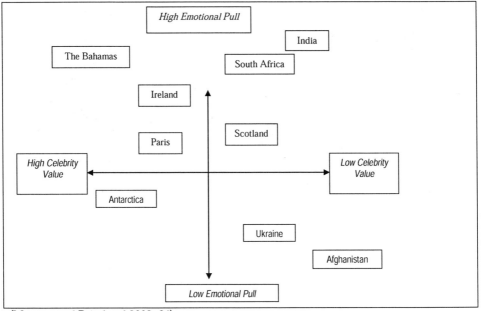

(Morgan and Pritchard 2002: 24)

This supports the WTO's findings in that the emerging tourist destinations are India and South Africa and their development as prime tourism destinations has grown significantly in recent years (WTO 2006). Most of this can be attributed to the fact that they have a strong emotional pull factor. On the opposite end of the scale Afghanistan, Antarctica and the Ukraine have low emotional factors. This has been due to many reasons, for instance, the current unstable Afghan economy (terrorism linkages) and the Chernobyl (Ukraine) nuclear power station disaster in 1986 (Morgan and Pritchard 2002: 23–24).

Ireland is in a key position of having quite a high emotional pull with its heritage and culture, which makes it easier to brand as a tourism destination. The appearance of Ireland as a fashionable destination for example, is the result of over twenty years of economic growth and also a breakthrough of Irish culture onto the world stage. Such instant stardom challenges long-term marketing activity and any investment that is built on detailed marketing planning, research and consistent positioning. Ireland's core values **(see Figure 2.2)** can be used as an important selling tool to the international market, illustrating how brand values and emotions can be used by tourism planners as part of their marketing strategy to maximize on their destination's tourist appeal (Morgan and Pritchard 2002: 37).

Figure 2.2

Core Values of Ireland Translated to Brands

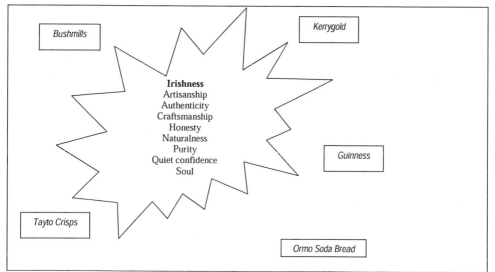

(Adapted from Springpoint 1999)

Ireland has invested a great deal in product development and in its marketing activities. Today, it constantly outspends all of the British destinations in the main markets. Scotland, which is one of Ireland's main competitors has a high emotional pull, which is demonstrated in **Figure 2.3** (Gilmore 2002a: 61–62). The challenge for the marketers in these destinations is to shape identities that strengthen their emotional appeal and that will (re)turn them into a destination with high celebrity value (Morgan and Pritchard 2002: 23–24).

Figure 2.3

Core Values of Scotland Translated to Brands

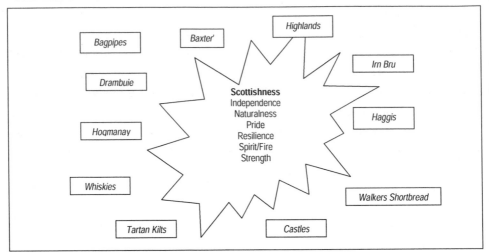

(Adapted from Springpoint 1999)

The creation of a strong image for destination requires a meticulously planned brand strategy based on:

- A clear and distinct brand personality;
- A range of the right positioning strategies;
- Dependable and appropriate marketing;
- Observant brand guardianship;
- Themed product development (Davies 2003).

These must be built on a thorough understanding of tourist needs. The success of brand image development will depend on how the perceptions of the tourists can be encouraged to believe that one destination is different and better than its competitors (Davies 2003). If these brand strategies are well planned and carefully introduced in Afghanistan, the Antarctic and the Ukraine, they could strengthen their emotional ties with tourists. This has already been seen to be the case of both Ireland and Scotland who have already proven themselves as successful tourism destinations.

Other destination branding strategies include guidebooks. By providing the opportunity to either support or reduce the effect of some of the other imaging efforts, guidebooks can have a significant influence on the image of a destination. In general, they are produced independently of the tourism stakeholders. Thus, it is essential that a close relationship between the tourism stakeholders, the guidebook authors and the publishers is developed (Beeton 2005: 91).

Recognizing that the medium of films can improve awareness of a destination and affect decision-making processes, marketers are working more than ever with film stakeholders to market their destinations as promising film locations (Seaton and Hay 1998; *Economist* 1998). Despite this, the process by which films influence destination images and related decision-making has not been widely investigated (Morgan and Pritchard 1998: 72). To appreciate the importance of destination branding in such locations, it is necessary that the destination's image is assessed to identify whether it will aid the *development of a model to be used as a best practice framework for the successful integration of film induced tourism in a destination marketing strategy*, which is this researcher's main objective.

2.5   Brand Image

Imagery is one of the most researched aspects of tourism marketing and there is a general consensus (see Ashworth and Goodall 1998; Fakeye and Crompton 1991; Hunt 1975; Mansfeld 1992) that tourism image is *an individual's overall perception of a place*. Pearce (1988: 162) points out that '*image is one of those terms that will not go away, a term with vague and shifting meanings*'. More recently, Echtner and Ritchie (1991: 4) have proposed that '*image is not only the individual traits or qualities but also the total impression an entity makes on the minds of others*'. The terms *image* and *imagery* can refer to movement, pictures, words and other sensory inputs symbolized in a message (Stern 1988). There are many other definitions for tourism destination image as seen in **Table 2.1.**

Table 2.1

Definitions of a tourism destination image

Authors	Definitions
Assael (1984)	*... is an overall perception of a product that is created by processing data from a range of sources over time.*
Dichter (1985)	*... can be applied to a political candidate, a product and a destination.*
Embacher and Buttle (1989)	*... is comprised of the ideas held independently or communally of the destination under investigation.*
Fakeye and Crompton (1991)	*... is the psychological concept developed by a potential tourist on the basis of a few chosen impressions.*
Gartner (1993)	*... is made up of the attitudes, beliefs, emotional feelings, impressions, information an individual has regarding a particular destination.*
Lawson and Baud-Bovy (1977)	*... is the expression of all objective knowledge, imaginations, impressions, prejudice and emotional thoughts an individual or group might have of a particular place.*

(Adopted from Gallarza et al. 2002)

Murphy (2006: 148) asserts that many image studies have found differences in image perceptions between pre-visitors and post-visitors (Chon 1990); before and after trips (Andreu et al. 2000); before and after advertising campaigns (Perry et al. 1976); between first-time and repeat visitors (Fakeye and Crompton 1991); between visitors and non-visitors (Hu and Ritchie 1993); before and after internationally significant political events (Gartner and Shen 1992); and between ideal and actual images (Botha et al. 1999). Irrespective of such research offerings, Baloglu and McCleary (1999a) and McKay and Fesenmaier (1997) suggest that there have been very few empirical studies aimed at examining which factors influence a tourist's image of a given destination (Murphy 2006: 148).

2.5.1 Overview of destination image studies

Since the early 1970s, many studies on destination imaging have investigated the effect of image on tourist behaviour. Some of the most popular published research areas focus on affect-related images, image differences between different segmentation groups and the effect of visitation itself which seems to be the most widely studied. This suggests that the travel experience is deemed to be a crucial factor in shaping a destination image (Pike 2002).

Image plays an important part in how tourist destinations (Bolan and Davidson 2005: 5) are viewed, as it has been largely recognized as a primary decision-making and motivational factor in holiday travel. It has also been a research interest for tourism academics such as Chon (1990), Crompton (1979), Echtner and Ritchie (1993), Pearce (1989) and Reilly (1990). Creating and sustaining a dependable image throughout individual promotions has become an issue. This is due to the uptake of destination marketing by individuals, which requires DMOs to effectively liaise with the relevant tourism stakeholders to create a destination image that is maximized upon by everyone (Beeton 2005). Brand managers can use numerous tools to publicize the destination's image. One such tool is a captivating slogan such as Spain – *Everything under the Sun*, Flanders (Belgium) – *Europe's Best Business Location*, Miami (USA) – *Financial Capital of South America*, and Scotland – *Silicon Glen* (Kotler and Gertner 2002: 254).

One of the most important roles of brand image is its impact on the tourism decision-making process. Many researchers (Mayo 1973; Mayo and Jarvis 1981) have clearly shown that the perceptions of destinations and the purchase decisions are positively linked, indicating that the image of a destination is a key selection factor (Woodside and Lysonski 1989). Lawson and Baud-Bovy (1977) suggest that the destination image should be cost effective, new and sincere (Kim and Richardson 2003: 218). More often than not tourism destinations are only vaguely positioned and as a result most tourists, primarily first-time visitors, will have restricted knowledge of the destination. These tourists can neither check what they are purchasing nor can they try a sample of it. For this reason, many will rely on their perceptions of the destination and as such, choosing a holiday will generally be considered as a high risk decision. Hunt (1975) believes that what potential tourists assume about a destination may well shape perceptions or images, which take away from the successful development of a destination (McGuckin and Demick 2000: 396).

The destination image is a decisive factor in positioning and differentiating destinations from each other (Ahmed 1991). It performs a vital function as destinations with biased, familiar, positive and strong images have a greater likelihood of being selected by tourists (Pearce 1982; Ross 1993). The main purpose of destination marketing is to sustain and improve destinations' images to prospective tourists (Awaritefe 2004). A destination image can influence the destination choice process of a tourist before, throughout and after a holiday (Cai 2002; Fakeye and Crompton 1991; MacInnis and Price 1987). It provides tourists with a vivid experience before their actual trip (Chen and Kerstetter 1999; Coshall 2000), increases fulfilment during the trip (Chon 1990; Jenkins 1999) and plays a reconstructive role via recollections or souvenirs (Jenkins 1999; MacInnis and Price 1987).

McGuckin and Demick (2000: 396–397) suggest that many tourism destinations employ marketers in the job of corrective marketing, changing a negative image into a more positive one. Examples of such tourism destinations which have lost their magnetism include particular regions of Spain, or those destinations which have encountered a natural disaster such as extensive flooding, or those where bloodshed has occurred like in the Lebanon. The role of overcoming a negative image of a destination is the main concern of the stakeholders involved in destination marketing. Their focus on creating a positive image for a destination is imperative in this time of intense rivalry among destinations (McGuckin and Demick 2000: 396–397). There are three types of images (visual, vocal, personal/literary) of concern to a destination. These will now be reviewed in more detail.

2.5.1.1 *Visual imagery*

Regardless of the undeniable power of visual tourism images (film and television) (Morgan and Pritchard 1998: 77), symbols also play a role in endorsing a destination's image, for instance; *Big Ben* (London/UK), the *Eiffel Tower* (Paris/France), *Red Square* (Moscow/Russia), *the Statue of Liberty* (New York/USA), and the *Corcovado-Christ Statue* (Rio de Janeiro/Brazil) (Kotler and Gertner 2002: 254–255). Images often use trendy culture, consisting of visual images connected with destinations. Like this, early commercials for Irish beers in Europe contributed to the configuration of the Irish image. These advertisements used highly visible typecasts such as *smiling, red-headed girls running through green fields and farmers drinking stout.* A similar process is in place in Scotland (*Whiskey*), France (*Cointreau*) and the American south (*Southern Comfort*) (Morgan and Pritchard 1998: 78).

2.5.1.2 *Vocal imagery*

Songs are very significant channels for tourism images, since music has the ability to arouse wonderful feelings. Songs such as *I Left My Heart in San Francisco, I Love Paris* and *Viva Las Vegas* carry wonderful images **(see Table 2.2)**. In the same way, *The Beach Boys* characterize the 'Californian Surf Beat' culture and *The Beatles* the 'Merseybeat' of Liverpool. Tourism marketers, also intentionally take advantage of the power of music. For instance, traditional Irish music is used when Ireland is the destination, rock and roll and Elvis Presley music are used to sell the whole of USA, blues music markets the southern USA states and country music the USA Corn Belt States in particular (Morgan and Pritchard 1998: 81).

Table 2.2

The tourism image in song

City	Song
Barcelona	*Barcelona*
California	*California Girls*
Dublin	*Molly Malone*
Ireland	*Danny Boy*
Japan	*Madame Butterfly*
Las Vegas	*Viva Las Vegas*
London	*A Nightingale Sang In Berkeley Square*
New York	*New York, New York*
Paris	*I Love Paris*
Rio de Janeiro	*The Girl From Ipanema*
San Francisco	*I Left my Heart In San Francisco*
Spain	*Carmen*

(Morgan and Pritchard 1998: 81)

2.5.1.3 *Personal and literary imagery*

As referred to previously, visual and vocal imagery can be very productive in branding tourism destinations. Tourism Ireland Limited[5] (TIL) now markets not only Ireland's built heritage and natural environment but also its literary giants including Samuel Beckett, James Joyce, Oscar Wilde, George Bernard Shaw and W.B. Yeats. In the UK, Dorset is *Hardy County* (Thomas Hardy), Yorkshire is *Brontë Country* (the Brontë sisters), Wordsworth is deeply associated with The Lake District, Stratford is linked with William Shakespeare and Swansea in South Wales with the poet Dylan Thomas.

Media containing 3D-visual and acoustic effects, for example film, DVD and television can help create organic images of a destination by presenting a vivid experience which appears less biased or is less recognizable as promotional (Schofield 1996). Such data clearly increases destination awareness, which can lead to a tangible visit to the destination depicted in the film (Riley *et al.* 1998; Riley and Van Doren 1992a; Stewart 1997). For that reason, understanding the building of vivid mental images is very important in understanding the impact of images on tourist attitudes and behaviours (MacInnis and Price 1987; Schlosser *et al.* 2003).

---

5 TIL is the government agency responsible for marketing the island of Ireland both north and south, as a holiday destination abroad.

Film-associated promotion can be one of the most successful tools for enhancing tourist awareness, as it presents product features and builds a visual image of a destination (Belch and Belch 2001). Its advantages over other means of communication include its emotional appeal and visual images, which provide potential tourists with a pre-taste of a destination (Hanefors and Mossberg 2002). Furthermore, distinctive visual components are crucial for effectively forming and communicating images (Smith and MacKay 2001).

Famous people and films associated with destinations can all enhance the destination such as Catherine Zeta Jones – Wales and *Crocodile Dundee* (1986) – Australia (Nielson 2001; Frisby 2002). The location of celebrities' homes and birthplaces now provide the incentive to visit some destinations (Morgan and Pritchard 2004: 209). Winterset, Iowa, USA currently attracts over 30,000 tourists annually, simply because it is birthplace of the actor John Wayne. Similar locations connected with films and their stars, such as the Hollywood Street of Stars in Los Angeles (USA), have become the very tourist attraction itself (Morgan and Pritchard 1998: 82).

In particular, films play a key role in influencing people's images and perceptions of a destination prior to their arrival at the destination. As Butler (1990) argues, films as visual media are more important to tourists than printed sources of information because they tend to be more reliable. This is supported by Schofield (1996), who maintains that media images do not have the same perceived bias of printed marketing material. It is well documented that film can positively enhance the awareness of destinations and affect the tourist decision-making process (Macionis 2004a: 4).

The international film market is growing, with popular films reaching a vast audience in important tourism markets. Films that replicate the authenticity of a destination, be it scenery, the culture, key landmarks or even universal themes, are influencing tourists to visit the scenes that they have seen on the big screen. Tourism stakeholders can endorse destinations, leveraging off carefully chosen films, which emulate the image of the destination in partnership with their own (Beeton 2005).

Macionis (2004a: 4) suggested that films can provide a destination with an international advertisement seen by millions of potential tourists, who are tempted by these images and as a consequence might be classed as film induced tourists. A film may undoubtedly create and prolong more interest **(See Table 2.3)** in a destination in a way that DMOs cannot financially afford to do (Tooke and Baker 1996: 87–94). Tourists can also learn about destinations in a passive way without the aggressive impressions intrinsic in paid advertising (Riley and Van Doren 1992a: 270).

Table 2.3

Film induced increases in tourism at selected destinations

Title	Location	Increase in tourism	Source
Brideshead Revisited (1979–1981)	Castle Howard, Yorkshire, England	30%: 1984	Tooke and Baker (1996)
Close Encounters of the Third Kind (1977)	Devils Tower National Monument, Wyoming, USA	75%: 1977–1978 (Film release), 39%: 1980 (TV release)	Riley and Van Doren (1992a)
Dances With Wolves (1990)	Fort Hays, Kansas and Badlands National Park, USA	25%: 1991	Riley and Van Doren (1992a)
Deliverance (1972)	Raeburn County, Georgia, USA	20,000: 1973	Riley et al., (1998)
Field of Dreams (1989)	Dyersville, Iowa, USA	35,000: 1991	Riley and Van Doren (1992a)
Heartbeat (1992–)	Goathland, North York Moors National Park, UK	41%: 1991–1993	Tooke and Baker (1996)
JFK (1992)	Book Depository, Dallas, Texas, USA	45%: 1992	Riley et al. (1998)
Little Women (1994)	Orchard House, USA	65%: 1995	Riley and Van Doren (1992a)
Steel Magnolias (1989)	Natchitoches, Louisiana, USA	48.1%: 1989	Riley and Van Doren (1992a)
The Fugitive (1993)	Great Smoky Mountain Railroad, North Carolina, USA	11%: 1993	Riley et al. (1998)
The Last of the Mohicans (1992)	Chimney Rock Park, North Carolina, USA	25%: 1992	Riley et al. (1998)
Thelma and Louise (1991)	Arches National Monument, Utah, USA	19.1%: 1991	Riley and Van Doren (1992a)
To The Manor Born (1979–1991)	Cricket St Thomas, Somerset, UK	37%: 1978–1980	Tooke and Baker (1996)

Even if the case for film induced tourism is difficult to corroborate, the economic benefits of film production on various destinations show a considerable rise in tourist numbers following a film's release. This is reflected by many researchers (Bolan and Davidson 2005; O'Connor *et al.* 2005; Stewart 1997; Tooke and Baker 1996).

Beeton (2002: 2) argues that there are three basic types of film induced images which can be deemed undesirable, the first being created by a negative storyline, such as criminal activities. There are times where pressure from the destination has succeeded in prohibiting filming access to a location due to such perceived negative storylines, but it is disputable as to whether the negative images actually deter or attract tourists **(see Chapter 3).** Secondly, a negative tourism image can result from the formation of idealistic tourist expectations and aspects of authenticity. For instance, tourists to some destinations have been disappointed when the community does not behave or dress in the way shown in a film or television series. A third negative image can arise when a destination is too successful in attracting tourists, giving rise to negative community impacts such as loss of privacy and overcrowding. For example, 'Amish country' in Lancaster County Pennsylvania, USA received a great deal of tourist interest following the popular film, *Witness* (1985). This was not greeted enthusiastically by the community (Beeton 2002: 2) **(see Chapter 3).**

As branding has become a fundamental element of tourism destinations with image being one of the most significant parts of a brand, it is vital that these images presented by the popular media are reviewed and one must bear in mind how they transcend to tourism (Beeton 2004a: 126). These images can be closely linked with film induced tourism which will be considered next.

2.6   Film Induced Destination Branding

Falling loosely into the area of cultural tourism, film induced tourism is becoming a growing international subject of academic research. The benefits of film induced tourism are constantly becoming more noticeable. Appealing to wide and diverse markets, destination marketers can use a film as a catalyst for marketing campaigns if the film is seen as a suitable fit for the destination. Marketing opportunities are created when the film is being internationally premiered and distibuted. Auxiliary businesses and services can be developed through film induced tourism, which in turn can assist in reducing the seasonality problem (Hudson and Ritchie 2006a: 256).

Quite a new occurrence in destination related branding is the growth of tourism in destinations where film or television series have been recorded. Attention has been given to how destinations capitalize on their film images in destination marketing campaigns by researchers such as Riley

(1994) and Stewart (1997). Substantiations from around the world confirm the power of film and television in inspiring tourism demand in showcase destinations, hence, many destinations have to deal with a dramatic invasion of tourists as a result of film induced tourism (Connell 2005a: 763).

Consequently, it is apparent that a range of industries can benefit from the affiliation between tourism and films. The obvious increase in holiday programmes now being transmitted would seem to advocate that media has come to see that closer cooperation between the film and television stakeholders is imminent, serving both industries. Many see watching films and television series as a distraction from reality and going to see a film destination supports this sentiment. Couldry (1998: 128) talks about the aura linked with the media world, as such people picture themselves *in situ* participating in scenes and the storyline. The attraction of holidaying at these destinations as opposed to traditional tourist destinations is enjoying the ambience and being affected knowingly by the event one is experiencing (Corlett 1998: 130).

Mishra *et al.* (2006: 90) propose that destinations around the world have a new means of enticing tourists to their destination. The tourist industry has realized that tourists are stimulated by films they have seen when deciding where to go on holiday. One destination that is certain of the effect of films on tourism is Australia. The Tourist Office of Queensland state that the film *Crocodile Dundee* made Australia the well-liked destination it is today. In the three years after the film's release, tourist numbers doubled, many of these came from the USA. VisitScotland[6] maintains that the two Scottish depicted films *Rob Roy* (1995) and *Braveheart* (1995) facilitated the increase in the number of tourists to Scotland. In research undertaken the year following their release, it was found that 20% of all tourists to Scotland felt that one of these films had encouraged them to visit. The underlying principle is that the film makes potential tourists aware of the existence of the destination (Mishra *et al.* 2006: 90).

2.6.1   The integration of film induced tourism and destination branding

According to Uysal, Chen and Williams (2000) there is a universal belief that images and perceptions of a destination do not change quickly, which supports the use of a particular imagery for a few years. If there are reruns of a television series or a further series is filmed, the image will remain longer, as has happened with *Ballykissangel* (1996–2001) (O'Connor and Flanagan 2000) and *All Creatures Great and Small* (1978–1990) (O'Connor *et al.* 2006). Tooke and Baker (1996) argue that there is evidence which suggests that resilient cinematic images linger for some time,

6 VisitScotland supports the development of the tourism industry in Scotland and markets Scotland as a quality destination (VisitScotland 2008).

which ensures maximum international exposure. This can be seen in relation to the comprehensive identification of Devil's Tower Monument from *Close Encounters of the Third Kind* (1977), many years after the films initial release (Beeton 2005: 74).

Films and television series play a variety of major roles in influencing tourists' travel behaviour in terms of their choice of the UK as a tourist destination. Film and television series can:

- Create images of the UK, conductive to travel, such as the character of the different regions;
- Support travel to specific media related British destinations, by simulating potential tourist appreciation and interest;
- Facilitate tourists in retaining their interest in the UK by providing supplementary information;
- Finally, act as a form of travel guidebook, which supplies information about images and associations of the UK (Iwashita 2006: 194).

2.6.2 Destination name change

A further rather dramatic destination marketing tool that has been recommended is changing the actual names of the towns for example from Barwon Heads to *Pearly Bay* (*SeaChange*), Goathland to *Aidensfield* (*Heartbeat*) and Avoca to *Ballykissangel*.[7] While such ideas have met with substantial conflict from many in the local communities, New Zealand renamed the area around Wellington as *Middle Earth*, for the duration of the world premiere of *The Lord of the Rings*[8] (2001–2003), with little conflict from the local community. *Welcome to Middle Earth* signage on the main access points to Wellington, in addition to verbal announcements from Air New Zealand pilots, when landing at Wellington airport, created a sense of actually being there. A way to harness the imaging power of film without in fact changing the place name is to develop a regional title such as *Heartbeat Country* which has been done in Yorkshire (UK). In spite of this, such changes must be supported by product and other marketing activities or else it will not be a success (Beeton 2005: 92). O'Connor, Flanagan and Russell (2005) and Swan (2003) also reinforced the idea that film and/or television can effectively market a destination.

---

7 The three television series referred to include *SeaChange* (1998–2001) which was set in Barwons Head, Australia, *Heartbeat* (1992–) in Yorkshire, UK and *Ballykissangel* (1996–2001) in Avoca, Co. Wicklow, Ireland.

8 The researcher acknowledges that she regularly refers to research on *The Lord of the Rings* as it is one of the few well researched examples of how film induced tourism and destination branding can be successfully integrated. *The Lord of the Rings* trilogy was also universally popular across all market segments.

2.6.3 Successful film induced branding

Corlett (1998: 127) has established that with the transformed interest in the British film industry, the recent triumphs of many British films (mentioned previously), the sizeable subsidy by the National Lottery and the increased use of the UK as a filming destination, the British film industry is embarking upon a period of growth and film induced tourism is a likely consequence. Recognizing that film induced tourism is still in its formative years, it remains to be seen whether such destinations will lose their desirability or if they will increase in attractiveness as a successful form of tourism (Corlett 1998: 127).

Film can also be used to direct attention towards geographical areas or draw attention to lesser known destinations. France, for instance, uses the film *Chocolat* (2000) to draw attention to Burgundy and *Charlotte Gray* (2001) to the Aveyron and Lot Valley. Films can make destinations popular, that might otherwise struggle to find any other viable reason to develop a tourist industry. When the film has been chosen, the marketing campaign should to be centred on the film cycle (Mintel 2003: 8). It is vital that destinations use successful film induced branding examples to initiate their own strategies **(See Table 2.4).** This can be supported by using the best practice framework that New Zealand developed in its partnership with *The Lord of the Rings* (Piggott *et al.* 2004).

Table 2.4

Film Tourism Guidelines

Film Production Cycle Post Production	Tourism Business Role / Opportunity
Film distribution	Marketing and promotion
Premiere	Brochure / leaflets
Cinema release	Signage / interpretation
Video sales / rental	New business opportunities
Television broadcast	Trails
Cinema and television re-release	Local business formation and survival

(Mintel 2003: 8)

2.6.4   Best practice: Film induced tourism and destination branding

The global media coverage of *The Lord of the Rings* trilogy has been enormous. Entirely filmed in New Zealand, the trilogy has linked the country with stimulating activities and splendid scenery over a three-year period. Tourism New Zealand's[9] (TNZ) International Media Programme team worked hard to bring media visits to New Zealand throughout 2001, in the lead up to the release of the first part in the trilogy, *The Fellowship of the Ring*. *The Lord of the Rings* exposure has been firmly focused on the USA and the UK. TNZ's aim was to ensure that wherever possible, a component of destinational coverage of New Zealand was incorporated in the newspaper and magazine supplements and any features dedicated to the films. In the UK, major editorial features on *The Lord of the Rings* (run with TNZ images) have materialized in the *Guardian*, the *Independent*, the *Sunday Times*, the *Telegraph*, the *London Evening Standard* and the *Observer* newspapers. In the USA, New Zealand has attained a similarly strong print presence with a feature appearing in the upmarket magazine, *Conde Nast Traveler*. This feature emphasized the links between New Zealand, the film and the spectacular locations (Morgan and Pritchard 2004: 216).

The scope for leverage that *The Lord of the Rings* offered to New Zealand is in many ways unprecedented. The New Zealand government launched funding packages to encourage and measure positive spin-offs from the trilogy and they (Clark 2001a) acknowledged tourism promotion as a vital opportunity created by the films, increasing the profile and perception of New Zealand as a tourism destination. Tourism is vitally important to New Zealand's economy, both directly and indirectly, contributing nearly 10% of national Gross Domestic Product (GDP) (Ministry of Tourism 2003). Films are re-occurring events, with DVD/video launches, television airing and other spin-offs providing opportunities for frequent viewing, that strengthen the association between a film and its location (Tooke and Baker 1996). The task of internationally creating and exploiting *The Lord of the Rings* connection has been driven by TNZ and complemented by the media and individual tourism stakeholders (Jones and Smith 2005: 923–945).

Swan (2003) demonstrates that the marketing strategy developed in conjunction with the Scottish television series *The Monarch of the Glen* (1998–2005) has not been a success. This is in contrast to the marketing campaign that Tourism New Zealand put in place with *The Lord of the Rings* trilogy, which proved to be enormously successful (Piggott *et al.* 2004). Swan (2003) initially thought that regardless of the considerable marketing possibilities presented by film induced tourism, not all stakeholders may support this form of tourism. Even though it is not exactly evident why, some stakeholders in Badenoch and Speysicie have not taken up marketing opportunities presented by

---

9 TNZ is the marketing agency responsible for marketing New Zealand internationally (TNZ 2008).

46

Monarch of the Glen. They have not supported the formation of the marketing partnership *Monarch Country* (Connell 2005b: 233).

Table 2.5 illustrates Beeton's (2005: 158-159) summary of the actual marketing responses to a number of examples of film induced tourism in the UK and the USA.

Table 2.5

Summary of marketing responses to film induced tourism in the UK and the USA

Site	Strategy: Reduce Promotion
Holmfirth, UK – *Last of the Summer Wine* (1973–)	No
Goathland, UK – *Heartbeat* (1992–)	Promotion was always limited; Some marketing by individual businesses; Main source – media articles.
Luss, UK – *Take the High Road* (1980–2003)	No, low key anyway Primarily advertised by independent tour operators
Intercourse, USA – *Witness* (1985)	State Film Commission agreed not to promote films on the Amish; Some of the costumes used in the Amish Experience Theatre.

(Adapted from Beeton 2005: 158–159)

The filming of *The Lord of the Rings* in New Zealand provided universal interest and a platform for promotional campaigns. Perhaps *The Lord of the Rings* presented an exceptional opportunity, which was the envy of other destination marketers. At the same time, not all destinations have had such an opportunity, too few manage to capitalize on such opportunities, perhaps because of a lack of flexibility in their strategic planning, a lack of resources or because of poor direction from senior management (Piggott *et al.* 2004: 222).

Croy and Walker (2001) instigated research into the importance and use of films in imaging destinations in New Zealand. After surveying New Zealand's local government offices and Regional Tourism Authorities[10] (RTA), it was found that 71% of respondents thought that films

---

10 The RTA has three key areas of responsibility, namely organization development and staff management, product and market development and enterprise development with their allocated region (Fáilte Ireland 2008).

produced in their region could be used for destination image promotion, while 58% considered the use of films produced in the region to be important in tourist promotions. Internationally, this has led to the development of movie maps, indicating the location of film and television series and has become a key destination promotional tool in the UK and the USA. Movie maps are a unique marketing opportunity, for such film induced destinations to entice tourists (Beeton 2005: 27–28).

2.6.5 Movie maps

Film can reach markets where premeditated traditional marketing cannot as a '*movie may generate and sustain interest in a destination in a way which destination marketers cannot afford to do*' (Tooke and Baker 1996: 88). Big screen film presentations can give a destination something most tourism promotion organizations could not pay for, nor have the ability to produce (Bolan and Davidson 2005: 6).

VisitBritain's Movie Map is perhaps the most successful long-running campaign (Urry 1990) featuring some 200 film and television locations around the UK that tourists could visit. Recently, a new series of movie maps have been created in connection with the film *King Arthur* (2004), and newer additions have included trails in connection with the hugely successful British films; *Bridget Jones – The Edge of Reason* (2001) and *Closer* (2004) (Bolan and Davidson 2005: 6). VisitScotland has also been very supportive of the film tourism concept (predominantly since the 1995 film, *Braveheart*) (Beeton 2005) whereas smaller districts such as Wicklow County Tourism, Ireland have not been as much to the fore due to their financial limitations (O'Connor and Flanagan 2000).

About eight Bollywood hits are filmed in the UK annually and this is increasing. The UK is following a trend set by Switzerland, which was once a Bollywood favourite, where filming has now ceased but the tourism remains. With more than 200,000 Indian tourists spending €212 million in the UK in 2002 and the influx growing by 13% a year, VisitBritain published a *Bollywood Movie Map* to support the growth of this market. The *Bollywood Movie Map* highlights 22 films shot in the UK since 1990 and 17 classics from the 1960s, 1970s and 1980s. Some 55,000 copies of this movie map were disseminated through offices in India and the Middle East (Mintel 2003: 9).

The Santa Barbara Conference and Visitors Bureau produced *Sideways* (2004) – *The Map* in 2004, a guide to the film locations of *Sideways,* even before the film was released. Shortly after its premiere, tourists keen to see the diners, hotels and wineries used in the film, purchased 10,000 copies of the guide (Hudson and Ritchie 2006a: 259). Beeton (2005: 62) discusses the creation of the highly successful Australian Movie Map, which includes films such as *Babe* (2002) and the world's first feature film *The Story of the Kelly Gang* (1906). New Zealand also published movie maps identifying the country as the home of *Lord of the Rings*, promoting road trips to the film locations and incorporating a pictorial journey of the key film locations on its tourism websites. In Ireland, the Wicklow Film Commission has produced the *Film Action in County Wicklow Guide*, which illustrates the film trails that the county has to offer such as the *Braveheart Drive*, the *Excalibur Drive* and the *Michael Collins Drive*, however, due to a lack of promotion and financial support, these have not been as successful as the American, Australian and British examples (O'Connor *et al.* 2005). The growth of the movie map is an integral element of film induced tourism, which can have a very positive impact on the development of a tourist destination. The 31 marketing activities outlined in **Figure 2.4** suggest that DMOs can take on a variety of marketing activities both before and after release of a film. These will be discussed in more detail in the following section.

Figure 2.4

Film Tourism: A Model for exploiting film tourism marketing opportunities

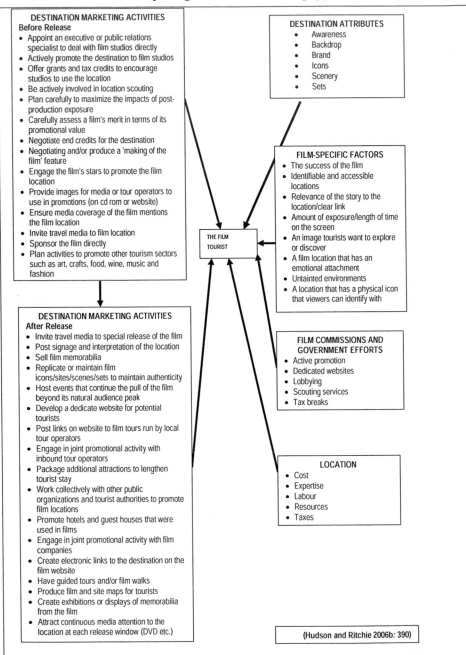

DESTINATION MARKETING ACTIVITIES
Before Release
- Appoint an executive or public relations specialist to deal with film studios directly
- Actively promote the destination to film studios
- Offer grants and tax credits to encourage studios to use the location
- Be actively involved in location scouting
- Plan carefully to maximize the impacts of post-production exposure
- Carefully assess a film's merit in terms of its promotional value
- Negotiate end credits for the destination
- Negotiating and/or produce a 'making of the film' feature
- Engage the film's stars to promote the film location
- Provide images for media or tour operators to use in promotions (on cd rom or website)
- Ensure media coverage of the film mentions the film location
- Invite travel media to film location
- Sponsor the film directly
- Plan activities to promote other tourism sectors such as art, crafts, food, wine, music and fashion

DESTINATION ATTRIBUTES
- Awareness
- Backdrop
- Brand
- Icons
- Scenery
- Sets

FILM-SPECIFIC FACTORS
- The success of the film
- Identifiable and accessible locations
- Relevance of the story to the location/clear link
- Amount of exposure/length of time on the screen
- An image tourists want to explore or discover
- A film location that has an emotional attachment
- Untainted environments
- A location that has a physical icon that viewers can identify with

THE FILM TOURIST

DESTINATION MARKETING ACTIVITIES
After Release
- Invite travel media to special release of the film
- Post signage and interpretation of the location
- Sell film memorabilia
- Replicate or maintain film icons/sites/scenes/sets to maintain authenticity
- Host events that continue the pull of the film beyond its natural audience peak
- Develop a dedicate website for potential tourists
- Post links on website to film tours run by local tour operators
- Engage in joint promotional activity with inbound tour operators
- Package additional attractions to lengthen tourist stay
- Work collectively with other public organizations and tourist authorities to promote film locations
- Promote hotels and guest houses that were used in films
- Engage in joint promotional activity with film companies
- Create electronic links to the destination on the film website
- Have guided tours and/or film walks
- Produce film and site maps for tourists
- Create exhibitions or displays of memorabilia from the film
- Attract continuous media attention to the location at each release window (DVD etc.)

FILM COMMISSIONS AND GOVERNMENT EFFORTS
- Active promotion
- Dedicated websites
- Lobbying
- Scouting services
- Tax breaks

LOCATION
- Cost
- Expertise
- Labour
- Resources
- Taxes

(Hudson and Ritchie 2006b: 390)

2.6.6   Before release – marketing activities

Regardless of the fact that DMOs frequently cannot influence the films being made, they can be proactive in marketing their own destinations to film stakeholders. Many destinations have a short-term focus that facilitates film production and focuses on the related economic impacts (Croy and Walker 2003). Others are becoming active in supporting producers to shoot films in their destination to profit from the associated long-term tourism impacts. For a time, VisitBritain[11] has targeted Indian film producers, as the organization feels that they can be convinced to use its locations for Bollywood films, thus creating important economic benefits for the British tourist industry (Woodward 2000). In the USA, Kansas's Travel and Tourism Development Division[12] allocates US$1.2 million per annum on tourism and film promotion. In 2004, the Singapore Tourism Board[13] launched a three year US$7 million scheme to entice the chief international filmmakers to produce their work there (Jeffery 2004). Another successful example previously mentioned (see also Chapter 3) is New Zealand, which included a destination guide with *The Lord of the Rings* DVD that highlights where different scenes were filmed (Hudson and Ritchie 2006b: 389–390).

Hudson and Ritchie (2006b: 391) assert that during production of a film there are many occasions which can create worldwide exposure for a destination. Liaising with media throughout the film production process is one way to guarantee coherent promoting of the destination. For instance, during filming of *The Lord of the Rings*, media clippings cited that the film was being shot in New Zealand, offering important early linkages between the film and the destination. The film's stars also endorsed New Zealand (Zukowski 2003). VisitBritain works very hard with Bollywood actors to gain similar support for British destinations, in the knowledge that they can add a positive feel to the destination, hence making it a must see destination for many Indians and Asians (Woodward 2000).

Publicity can also be created around the activities of the actors while on location. While making *Captain Corelli's Mandolin*, media releases featuring the two main actors (Nicolas Cage and

---

11 VisitBritain, the national tourism agency, promotes the UK internationally in 36 markets and England in the UK, France, Germany, Ireland and the Netherlands (VisitBritain 2008).
12 The mission of the Kansas Travel and Tourism Division is to promote and encourage the travelling public to visit and travel within Kansas and to generate and facilitate tourism and travel-related spending throughout the state by promoting recreational, historic, cultural and natural attractions (Kansas Travel and Tourism Division 2008).
13 The Singapore Tourism Board is an economic development agency for one of Singapore's key service sectors - tourism. The mission of the Board is to develop and champion tourism, so as to build the sector into a key driver of economic growth for Singapore (Singapore Tourist Board 2008).

Penélope Cruz) were shown around the world, significantly raising the profile of Cephalonia, the location of the film (Ward 2001). Actors are also used after production of a film to market a destination. The ATC used the actor Paul Hogan in its marketing campaign for many years subsequent to the success of *Crocodile Dundee* (as did Jersey, Channel Islands, with *Bergerac's* (1981–1991) John Nettles) (Hudson and Ritchie 2006b: 391).

Marketing partnerships are occasionally developed by DMOs and they can also organize prepared marketing material in advance of a film's release. In recent times, VisitBritain has joined forces with both Sony Pictures and Columbia Pictures ahead of the release of *Closer* (2004), a film shot in London. On VisitBritain's website, tourists could download a *Closer* movie map **(see Chapter 3)** that illustrated the '*many iconic London locations used in filming*' (VisitBritain 2005). Destinations and attractions used in the film also worked together in the marketing initiative. For example, the London Aquarium had a printable discount voucher on the map. VisitBritain's website also had a direct link to Sony Pictures, which was advertising the *Closer* movie map on its home page (Hudson and Ritchie 2006b: 391).

2.6.7   After release – marketing activities

Hudson and Ritchie (2006b: 391) argue that before, during and after the release of a film, media attention can be attracted to the film location. The Tourism Authority of Thailand (TAT)[14] for instance, advertised the country's attractions during the release of the film *The Beach* (2000) (Grihault 2003). The marketing campaign incorporated a considerable amount of joint activity with 20th Century Fox and tried to take advantage of the expected further popularity of Thai beaches, when the film was released. Besides heavy advertising in cinemas, TAT brought the British media and travel stakeholders on familiarization trips. Such marketing of a destination during the screening of a film is another way to promote a destination.

VisitScotland disseminated direct-response postcard adverts in cinemas that were screening *Braveheart* **(see Chapter 3)** tempting viewers to send for information on *Braveheart Country* (Grihault 2003). Branding a destination around a film like this is very common, such as the district of Hambleton in North Yorkshire which branded itself *Herriot Country* and developed The World of James Herriot Museum after the success of *All Creatures Great and Small* **(see Chapter 3)**. *Brontë Country* still hosts trade and press familiarization visits exclusively based on any related film and television series (Brontë Country 2005; Hudson and Ritchie 2006b: 391).

---

14 TAT supplies information and data on tourist areas to the public, publicizes Thailand to both Thai and international tourists, conducts studies for tourist destination development plans and co-operates and supports the production and development of personnel in the field of tourism. (TAT 2008)

Hudson and Ritchie (2006b: 391) suggest that following a film's release is when many DMOs undertake marketing activities connected to film induced tourism. This is when the challenge for DMOs is to translate a viewer's interest in a film into a future visit. Marketing opportunities are created at every release window (cinema, pay-per-view television, free television, video/DVD rental and purchase). Usually, this lasts for many years, even though it may get shorter as Hollywood maximizes on the success of DVD sales, by releasing them earlier (Buckley 2004). On the other hand, it is not unusual for a successful film to have a shelf life in excess of 25 years (Lazarus 1994). The little town of Clayton, Georgia, USA continues to thrive in the attention from the film *Deliverance* (1972). Tourism was so successful following the film's release, that the state of Georgia created its own film commission, Georgia Department of Economic Development – Film, Video and Music Division[15], which has continually attracted film stakeholders, notably for *Driving Miss Daisy* (1989) and *Fried Green Tomatoes* (1991). Finally, in New Zealand, there are a number of *The Lord of the Rings* related tours, such as *The Lord of the Rings* flight with Nelson Helicopters, a drive around *Lord of the Rings* country with Nomad Safaris, and tours to Hobbiton in Waikato. The growth of such destinations is also evident in Ireland, due to the popular film *The Quiet Man* (1952) which was filmed in Cong, Co. Mayo, and *Ryan's Daughter* (1970) in Dingle, Co. Kerry.

Accommodation outlets and attractions used in films are often marketed to the public to lure tourists. In Greece, a local woman continues to advertise her apartment as the site for the alleged affair between Nicolas Cage and Penélope Cruz during the filming of *Captain Corelli's Mandolin* (2001) in Cephalonia. On the Greek island of Mykonos, tourists can rent a room at the Manoulas Beach Hotel, scene of the film *Shirley Valentine* (1989), and in Tunisia tourists can sleep at the hotel used as the location of Luke Skywalker's childhood home in *Star Wars* (1977–2005) (Jeffery 2004). Lastly, having a devoted film website that links the film to a destination and location tours is also considered vital (Croy and Walker 2003). Using the internet to relate film to a destination was emphasized in New Zealand, where TNZ designed part of its website exclusively marketing *The Lord of the Rings* and its film sites throughout New Zealand. Since the Academy Awards in 2002, a series of advertisements publicizing New Zealand as 'Best Supporting Country', has been used by TNZ, and their website had more than 1 billion hits in 2003 (**see Chapter 3**) (Zukowski 2003; Hudson and Ritchie 2006b: 392).

2.6.8   Film induced tourism and destination branding: the key issues

The results from an assortment of studies such as Busby and Klug (2001) and Gartner (1993) seem to be incomplete descriptive understandings of the functions of film induced tourism and do not

---

15 The mission of Georgia's Department of Economic Development (Film, Video and Music Division) is to attract, support and grow the entertainment content creation industries in Georgia. The focus is on feature and independent films, television series, video game development and the music industry.

offer a theoretical insight into why this phenomenon is happening. Some of the results explain that increased tourism induced by films suggests that a film could be a helpful tool to change a destination's image, and therefore affect audience interest in visiting the destination. It is clear from these studies that further research is required to better understand the relationships between films and tourism (Kim and Richardson 2003: 232) and these should consider the following points.

2.6.8.1 *Destination management team responsibilities*

For the most part, many destinations have superb five star resorts and attractions and every destination maintains that it has a unique culture, landscape and heritage. Each and every destination describes itself as having the friendliest people, the highest standards of customer services and the best of facilities which are now expected. Subsequently, the need for destinations to create a unique image and brand so as to distinguish themselves from their competitors is crucial. Undeniably, it has become the basis for survival within an internationally competitive marketplace dominated by a few leading destinations which Morgan, Pritchard and Pride (2002: 11) maintain exert a strong pull on the global tourism market.

Only those destinations that have a transparent market position and enticing attractions will continue to be best placed in tourist minds when they reserve their holidays in the current market. Even though travel agents continue to supply booking and support services, the selection of destination clearly lies with the tourist. In an aggressive and vibrant international tourism environment, there is a need to develop a truly distinctive identity or brand, while also reflecting the fundamental strengths and personality of the product on offer. In a congested marketplace, creating and preserving brand value is the key to business success and as a result brand management is fast becoming a core business strategy. This is very true of destinations and according to the WTO (Jones 1998) there is a clear trend towards well-branded destinations. It is worth considering Ahmed's (1991) statement: '*The holidaymakers of the 21st century will be looking for destinations with a trendy image*' (cited in Crockett and Wood 2002: 124–125).

2.6.8.2 *The importance of a strong image*

There is a consensus that image is a key part of marketing strategy for a destination, and various researchers (Chon 1990; Heath and Wall 1991) have examined the use of image in brand formation for destinations. Regardless of a large quantity of products and services under the one brand umbrella, the formation of a brand identity can be reached to give the destination a common marketing goal (Palmer 2004: 129). Despite the fact that many destinations have acknowledged the potential of film induced tourism and how it can create a powerful destination image, few

54

destinations have retained control over how and to whom the destination is presented through films and television series. Film stakeholders are primarily interested in creating the film they want and not necessarily the type of image that the tourism stakeholders may desire. A DMO, however, may want to encourage high spending tourists, look to establish images of a good quality tourist destination and the community may see their town as a welcoming area; such images can be incorporated into a destination marketing strategy (Beeton 2005: 154). Nevertheless, a film studio that wants to use the destination to create a film about a small-minded, racist community, presents an image that is unable to coexist with the DMO's desired image (Beeton 2005: 154). Morgan and Pritchard, (1998: 8) claim that the challenge for destination marketers is to find the best way to use images, stories and emotions to capture the tourist's attention and create the destination's brand.

2.6.8.3 *Understanding destination branding*

As the viewing of films and television continues to expand through the development of new media outlets e.g. the Internet, DVDs, so too will their influence on destination images. Even if images developed through these media may be untrue, they have the ability to influence both tourism marketers and tourists. Improved theoretical understanding of the impacts which films have on destination perceptions, will enhance knowledge about the image formation process as it relates to popular culture and closes the gap between spontaneous belief and empirical evidence as films familiarize potential tourists with destinations and the attractions featured in them (Morgan and Pritchard 1999: 102–119). Aaker (1996) highlighted the importance of the tourism destination brand, as it should reflect the true nature of the destination and also the way in which a national brand is perceived internationally should be often reviewed (Morgan and Pritchard 1998). The creation of a good image – whether personal, visual, vocal, film or television related – is the key to success, but the brand must reflect the destination such as Tourism Ireland's marketing of Ireland's built and natural environment (*Observer* 1996).

2.6.8.4 *The influence of real life films and television*

Television can unequivocally influence the tourism image through the transmission of tourism advertisements. It is the most efficient medium for promoting the look and the sound of a destination whether in the form of a short commercial or a thirty minute travel documentary such as BBC's *Holiday* (1992–), CNN's *Travel Show* (1982–) and RTE's *No Frontiers* (2001–). These are the key tourism image vehicles, which are often developed in close collaboration with the destination's tourism stakeholders: however, there is a shortage of research gauging the impact of such programmes on image formulation (Morgan and Pritchard 1998: 70–71). Hence, tourists tend to be influenced by real life films and television series more rather than by direct marketing activities seen on these shows.

2.6.8.5 *Best practice example*

As mentioned earlier, New Zealand has been very proactive in terms of supporting film induced tourism particularly in relation to *The Lord of the Rings* trilogy. The ensuing economic benefit from the high level of tax breaks available to film makers in New Zealand, pooled with these promotional overheads was queried by the Organisation for Economic Co-operation and Development (OECD)[16] in 2003. This is not to say that the organization thinks such investment is not practical, but that the public investment in tourism promotion and private enterprises needs to be observed (Beeton 2005: 230–231). *The Lord of the Rings* example also serves as one of the first major cases of strategic alliances between an NTO (TNZ) and a film stakeholder (Film New Zealand – FNZ) 17 on a synchronized strategy (Bolan and Davidson 2005: 6). This level of support is unique and needs to be reflected upon: could this best practice example be re-produced elsewhere? The stakeholders involved should weigh up the cost and benefits of being a film induced destination and brand it as such. However, they need to consider Mordue's (2001) study of Goathland which showed that an approach like this can in fact bring many negative downsides specifically congestion, pollution, and local resistance (**see Chapter 3**).

2.7   Final Thoughts on the Integration of Film Induced Tourism and Destination Branding

2.7.1   *The importance of tourism research*

Destination marketers need well-founded and dependable research from which to make branding decisions (Harrill 2004). Harrill also claims that this research should form the hub of a new area of destination branding, one that concentrates not only on the demand side of the industry and how it can attract tourists to the destination but also the supply side, in the steps that should be undertaken to provide an attractive and pleasurable tourism product (Harrill 2004).

---

16 The OECD supports sustainable economic growth, boosts employment, raises living standards, maintains financial stability, assists other countries' economic development and contributes to growth in world trade.
17 FNZ is New Zealand's film locations office providing information, introductions and support to filmmakers, both internationally and nationally (FNZ 2008).

2.7.2 Film re-imaging rural destinations

The impact of film in re-imaging rural destinations has proven to be extremely important, as exemplified by *Heartbeat* in Goathland, *Hamish MacBeth* (1995–1997) in Plockton, *SeaChange* in Barwon Heads and *The Lord of the Rings* in New Zealand (Beeton 2005: 236). The use of film images and storylines in destination marketing is one of the most recognizable uses of film induced tourism. Emotionally based images from films and television series can provide some competitive advantages for a destination and help it to compete in what can be a crowded marketplace (Beeton 2005: 237), a claim which is supported by Busby and Klug (2001) and O'Connor *et al.*, (2006). If Beeton's (2005: 74) research findings are accepted, in that *SeaChange*, the Australian television series, is a fitting destination marketing image for the town of Barwon Heads, the question that should be addressed is how long this image will be important for tourists visiting the town.

2.7.3 The power of the media

Morgan and Pritchard (1988: 68–71) maintain that media has the ability to modify, create and strengthen the destination image and without doubt, film has become a prevailing source of information. Film also has the power to influence tourist actions by generating interest within individuals which can tempt them to act in certain ways. Having said this, it is also assumed that tourists can actively make their own sense and explanation of films, newspapers, novels, magazines and television series (Morgan and Pritchard 1988: 68–71).

More attention in understanding how film viewing changes destination images is required, as it is expected that the film induced tourism phenomenon will continue to grow while participation in leisure pursuits by prevailing international markets increases in tandem with films being globally circulated and viewed (Kim and Richardson 2003: 233). As more potential tourists are exposed to increasing amounts of visual media, it may be assumed that popular images represented in films play an imperative role in determining destination images and influencing tourists' expectations of a specific location.

Tourist agencies should also be aware of the possible gain for having positive images of a destination in a film (Bordelon and Dimanche 2003: 9). Then again, the promotional potential of each film is not the same and some films and television series have little impact while others may be both powerful and memorable, helping to create a long lasting film encounter. Beeton (2004: 135) insists that films, reports and stories available in the mass media market are far more significant to tourism than has been accredited in the past, but this is not to say that film images intrinsically support tourism. Tourism, however, by its very nature of recording the participant's 'gaze' in photographs and video is closely coupled with the image making media such as imaginary films (Beeton 2004: 135).

2.7.4   The development of an image management strategy

Films have been, without a doubt, a tourism inducing ingredient, turning destinations of little or no importance to tourists, into much visited tourist attractions, for instance Dubuque County and Dyersville, Iowa, USA, which were the locations for the film *Field of Dreams* (1989). These have become significant tourist destinations in their own right. For that reason, it is important for a well-planned image management plan to be produced for destinations. This is fundamental in ensuring the sustainable and successful development of the destination. In the advancement of the image management strategy, a long-term view is also necessary. The outcomes of research in New Zealand suggest a focus which smoothes the progress of film production, concentrating on the short-term economic impacts. In addition to this an understanding of film as a positive image enhancer is also necessary. Planning needs to consider a long-term deliberation of image and the impact of film on such an image (Croy and Walker 2003: 128).

2.7.5   Destination management planning

The portrayed image for destination management and how it is perceived by potential tourists is vital and for that reason should be given particular attention in destination management planning. The elements of the destination image as portrayed in the media are vital for destination marketing, primarily as it has been acknowledged that films can act as promotion for the destination, to possible tourists and production companies. The potential impacts of image enrichment in film induced tourism have been recognized as potentially harmonizing with the objectives of economic growth (Croy and Walker 2003: 127).

Turning film locations into economically viable tourism attractions comes back to the community as they form the foundation of all tourism experiences, even if it is merely providing a cup of tea, taking a photo or giving directions to a specific destination. Beeton (2006: 14) asserts that many of the smaller communities used in films are in a state of degeneration and are looking for ways to boost their economic and social existence. While tourism and film can help, without proactive guidelines, planning and backing, overall development will not happen. To accomplish this, purely marketing a destination to film-makers and then to tourists is not adequate and the image will not progress without the host community's encouragement. The partnership between these three stakeholders is potentially strong and should not be ignored. The support of these relationships can and should be promoted by the film corporations themselves, who also need support if they and also the DMO wish to return (Beeton 2006: 14).

2.7.6 The challenges facing destination marketers

There are definite challenges facing destination marketers pursuing their strategies. It should be noted that successful branding brings many rewards as seen with the branding initiatives in Glasgow and New York already considered earlier in this research. Destinations cannot afford to ignore film induced branding as it proposes a pioneering and valuable tool with which managers can create emotional links with the tourist (Morgan *et al.* 2002; 351). As we progress further into the 21st century, advances in multi-media technology, coupled with the growing leisure time available for tourism, will undoubtedly reveal a number of new and interesting ideas for investigation on the relationship between tourism and film. In light of this, there is no explanation why the two cannot continue to draw shared benefit from each other (Corlett 1998: 131).

Kulshreshtha and Akoijam (2006: 7) suggest that regardless of where destinations are in the lifecycle, they all face a number of marketing challenges. Most NTOs have inadequate budgets and yet they have to market worldwide, competing not just with other destinations but also with international brands. Successful destination branding is about developing a winning public relations approach to a marketing problem. Another challenge for destination marketers is the real diplomacy of overseeing local, regional and national politics. Public sector destination marketers are also constrained by a multiplicity of political pressures as they have to bring together a range of local and regional interests while promoting an identity within the acceptable limits of the destination (Kulshreshtha and Akoijam 2006: 7).

2.8   Conclusion

Chapter 2 has presented the academic foundation for this research study's main objectives (**See Table 1.2**). It also has highlighted the importance of determining the results of promotional activities pertaining to film induced tourism. Measuring the impacts of such tourism needs to be a major development in the move towards accepting the opportunity film induced tourism presents, a proposal made by earlier researchers (Cohen 1986; Tooke and Baker 1996). The results of this chapter show that only a small number of DMOs are critically evaluating the impacts of film induced tourism. Increasingly, the measurement of film induced tourism should be incorporated into current tourist research on brand awareness and tourist motivation (Hudson and Ritchie 2006b: 395).

CHAPTER 3

LITERATURE REVIEW II
FILM INDUCED TOURISM

3.1 Introduction

Film as a medium can have a powerful effect on its audience. It can bring about all types of motivation, including the wish to travel to where the film is set (whether actual or fictional) (Bolan and Davidson 2005: 1). This power to truly induce tourism is a key focus of this chapter. Chapter 3 will study this evolving research area by investigating the background and theoretical context of the film induced tourism phenomenon. This concept and its emergence as a research discipline within the tourism area will also be examined. Furthermore, this chapter will look at both the negative and positive impacts that film induced tourism can have on a destination. Conclusions, which can be put forward in light of the findings from this literature review, are presented at the end of this chapter.

3.2 Background

Ever since the introduction of film, many viewers had been inspired by the scenery and local culture of film locations, which have motivated them to holiday at these destinations. It is only since the 1980s however that this phenomenon has been recognized in the academic literature. The recognition of impacts experienced with the film *Field of Dreams* (1989), which continues to entice viewers to visit the film's location in Iowa, (USA), marks a considerable milestone in this new travelling trend (Riley *et al.* 1998). As it is becoming increasingly fashionable to visit these film induced tourism sites, more such destinations are materializing and a new tourism product is continually being created (Lam and Ap 2006: 166).

Macionis (2004a), quoted in Pilling's (2004) article, states that tourists in search of film destinations as their desired travel location might be stimulated by escape, fantasy, nostalgia or a sense of a vicarious experience (Lam and Ap 2006: 167). Katz and Foulkes as far back as 1962 claimed that many types of mass media are used by potential tourists to escapes realism. Nevertheless, film induced tourism research on themes such as its characteristics and its effects on community resident and tourist behaviour were not carried out until the mid 1990s (Lam and Ap 2006: 167).

3.3   The Film induced tourism phenomenon

Film induced tourism is tourist visits to a destination or attraction as a result of the destination being featured on cinema screens, television or video.

(Evans 1997: D35)

Film induced tourism can be referred to as an experience that is very much personalized and distinctive to each individual based on their own understanding and use of media images (Macionis 2005). Riley *et al.* (1998: 920) argue that when tourists seek the destinations they have seen on screen, this is when they really become film induced tourists. Many useful definitions have been presented in earlier studies and there also appear to be numerous terms for this phenomenon, such as; *Media Induced Tourism; Movie Induced Tourism; Film Induced Tourism;* the *Cinematographic, Tourist;* and *the Media Pilgrim on a Media Pilgrimage.* Nevertheless, one general theme indicates that this newly defined tourism niche refers to a post-modern experience of a place that has been depicted in some form of media representation, namely, an experience that is very much personalized and exclusive to each individual based on their own understanding and consumption of media images (Macionis 2004a).

Macionis (2004a) maintains that there are several contexts or perspectives from which to characterize the term *film induced tourism.* In its most simple and logical context, it has been defined as '*tourist visits to a destination or attraction as a result of the destination featured on the cinema screen, video or television*' (Busby and Klug 2001: 316). Iwashita (2003) adds to this by stating that film, television and literature can shape the travel preferences and destination choices of individuals by exposing them to the attributes and attractions of destinations. Following this type of supply or production driven approach, film induced tourism has also been examined in a cultural, heritage and historical framework (see Busby and Klug 2001). Films are often made at famous historic or heritage sites such as castles and gain greater than before popularity as tourism destinations after the film has been released. In actual fact, it has been mentioned that some of these locations only become popular tourist attractions because of the film produced there. Crucially, it should be noted that film induced tourism does not simply occur at identifiable film locations; that is, the sites where films have been made, but it also exists in purpose built, commercialized sites (with entry fees) such as *Universal Studios,* Los Angeles, USA or *Granada Studio Tours,* Manchester, UK (Macionis 2004a).

Film symbolizes a one-off opportunity, whilst television generates and encourages interest in the television series and destination over the duration of its run, especially where a television series is on at peak time, it has the possibility to act as an advertisement for such a destination. Loyal viewers will look for exact film locations, frequently assisted by websites or destination images that induce travel (Kim and Richardson 2003). The destination must be prepared to develop a strategy to manage this influx in a sustainable, yet profitable way. Such an option is likely to very much affect rural communities more so than urban ones (Connell 2005b: 230–231).

Kim and Richardson (2003: 218) discover that to date particular films have improved the awareness of the destinations they portray and have tourist inducing effects (Riley et al. 1998; Riley and Van Doren 1992a; Tooke and Baker 1996). In recent years the Scottish Tourist Board (now VisitScotland) carried out a survey in the Stirling area depicted in the film Braveheart (1995). The end result revealed that seeing the film on the big screen had a substantial effect on tourists' decisions to visit Stirling and to see specific attractions and destinations shown in the film (Stewart 1997). In other research linked with Braveheart (Seaton and Hay 1998), the film was not the objective reality of the destination (much of Braveheart was actually filmed in Ireland, despite the fact that tourists indicated that they came to Scotland to visit destinations shown in the film), but instead the meaning it represents which transforms these film destinations, into symbolically meaningful tourist attractions in their own right (Beeton 2005: 31).

Hudson and Ritchie (2006a: 257) suggest that the growth in film induced tourism is related to both the increase in international travel and the history of film making. This began in earnest in the 1970s/1980s due to the increase in on-location filming as opposed to on-set studio filming which took place during Hollywood's golden era. It is particularly coupled with the development of the big budget USA film, beginning with Jaws in 1975. There has been an impressive growth in cinema attendance in recent times, which was highlighted by the release of The Lord of the Rings, which was launched in 10,000 screens internationally, while almost 30 years earlier, Jaws opened in only 465 cinemas in the USA. A typical film with global distribution can now reach over one hundred million viewers as it moves from box office to DVD and television. Likewise, television series have become noticeably successful in influencing the attractiveness of destinations. Hawaii 5-0 (1968–1980) and Magnum PI (1980–1988) enhanced Hawaii as a tourist destination in the 1980s and lately, 20th Century Fox's North Shore (2004–2005) and ABC's Lost (2003 to present) are drawing even more tourists to the islands. Regrettably, many tourism stakeholders have been slow to tap into the potential benefits of such film induced tourism, possibly due to a lack of focused research, which would demonstrate the capability of film induced tourism (Hudson and Ritchie 2006a: 257).

There is a small amount of academic research, which looks at the impacts of film and television on the attractiveness of media related sites as tourist destinations. Some material exists on the effects of film induced tourism and how this can in actual fact support the development of the tourism product in a destination (Tooke and Baker 1996: 87). The study of such tourism is difficult and needs to incorporate aspects of other academic disciplines, for example sociology, in addition to industry based sectors like destination marketing, film making and strategic planning. Despite the fact that previous tentative studies contemplated the nature of film induced tourism, the suggested further research has been slow. Riley, Tooke, Baker and Van Doren took up the challenge in the 1990s but after distributing their interesting results, they appear to have moved on to other research areas (Beeton 2005: 17–18).

Several researchers have investigated how films have played a key part in developing a destination's image (Beeton 2001b, 2002, 2004a, 2004b and 2005; Busby and Klug 2001; Croy and Walker 2003; Frost 2004, 2005; Kim and Richardson 2003; Macionis 2004a; Riley *et al.* 1998; Sargent 1998; Singh and Best 2004; Tooke and Baker 1996). Some of these concentrated on the impact of film on developing tourism in rural destinations and towns (Beeton 2001a, 2004a, 2004b and 2005; Croy and Walker 2003; Sargent 1998). These investigations found that many films and television series seem to be based on small rural communities, as in *All Creatures Great and Small, Heartbeat* and the *Last of the Summer Wine*, frequently with likeable characters in an ideal setting. Many such productions have become very popular, predominantly among city based viewers which has resulted in strong tourism flows to the filming locations (Frost 2005: 3–4).

While the effect of films on tourism has been seen for many years, with cinema attendance growing (as well as further familiarity through video/DVD, television and the internet), film induced tourism is a growing occurrence worldwide (Mintel 2003: 1). What has been absent in the debate on film induced tourism to date, is a bigger bank of data to support the suggestion that film encourages tourists to holiday at locations (Riley *et al.* 1998). As referred to beforehand, the focus of this research is *to develop a model to be used as a best practice framework for the successful integration of film induced tourism in a destination marketing strategy.* With this in mind, recent literature in this evolving research area will be reviewed in more detail.

3.4 Theoretical Context

In the midst of some notable exceptions (Beeton 2005; Busby and Klug 2001; Connell 2005a, 2005b; Riley *et al.* 1998; Tooke and Baker 1996), tourism orientated literature on film induced tourism tends to consist of unsubstantiated statements on the economic impacts of such tourism (Fernandez-Young and Young 2006: 126–127). The influence of media on the travel decision-making process has been scrutinized by many researchers (Butler 1990; Echtner and Ritchie 1991; Hunt 1975; Schofield 1996), who propose that tourists can obtain tourism destination data in many ways. This allows them to build their own explanation which shapes the basis of their destination choice.

Films, play a very important role in manipulating potential viewer's images and perceptions of a destination (Beeton 2000, 2001a, 2001b, 2002, 2005). Connell (2005b: 228) revealed that films and television series are broadly accepted as a stimulus that can attract people to visit destinations. Tourists in search of filmed destinations, display what Reeves (2003) terms an 'irresistible drive' to find sites to which an emotional connection has been made due to a film or television series. Individual destinations can become fundamentally linked with a specific film: for instance, Thailand and *The Beach* (2000), Ireland and *The Quiet Man* (1952). This can occur (as in these examples) on the scale of a complete country as the pulling factor for tourists. On the other hand, the possible effect of film on the tourist can link films in a more definite way to actual cities or resorts within a destination such as Vienna and *The Third Man* (1949), Florence and *A Room with a View* (1986), Salzburg and *The Sound of Music* (1965) (Bolan and Davidson 2005: 7).

Butler (1990) argues that films as visual media are more significant to tourists than printed sources of data like advertising brochures, as they appear to have higher levels of reliability and do not carry the same perceived prejudice as promotional material. Therefore, it is recognized that film can increase awareness of destinations and influence the decision-making process of potential tourists (Schofield 1996: 34). Also, Butler (1990) discusses the power of the media and the ways in which people obtain images, information and awareness of destinations. He also highlights that as people read less, what is shown in film, videos/DVDs and television will become all the more important (Tooke and Baker 1996: 88). Several films are based on books (i.e. Haworth and the Brontë sisters), as are a high percentage of television series. Many anecdotal studies are cited in Tooke and Baker's (1996) work, which considers four case studies from British television: *To the Manor Born* (1979–1991), *By the Sword Divided* (1983–1985), *Middlemarch* (1984) and *Heartbeat* (1992 to present). They also refer to *Cadfael* (1994–1998), a historical detective television series, filmed in

Hungary, which still attracts large numbers of tourists to Shrewsbury, where the originating novels were set (Fernandez-Young and Young 2006: 126–127).

Within the community of Regional Screen Agencies[18] (RSA), tourism promoters and media writers, the concept of film induced tourism has been accepted, even though little has been done to use this information until recently. Taking advantage of it has only happened when videos and film maps (**see Chapter 2**) have been produced by tourism stakeholders looking to hold the attention of prospective. These marketing efforts have been embarked on with the aim of taking full advantage of the film induced tourism phenomenon (Riley *et al.* 1998: 920).

3.5   Understanding Film Tourism

Though there are exceptions, the success of a film can by and large be used as a predictor of film induced tourism (Grihault 2003). It is worth noting that most film induced tourism research addresses relatively small tourism destinations where actual variation in numbers can easily be measure. For films outside of the USA, success in the box office does offer wonderful opportunities for destinations to exert a pull on the lucrative US market in addition to other overseas nationals. For instance, *Out of Africa* (1985), set in Kenya and Tanzania, has been recognized in bringing American tourists to the African continent. In 1993, in excess of one in six visitors to Ireland mentioned a film as grounds for visiting the country. Similarly before the war started, the film *Gorilla in the Mist* (1988), improved Rwanda's tourism by 20%. The new millennium has seen the strongest plan for film and television inspired tourism up until now with the serial films *Harry Potter* (2001 to date) filmed in the UK and *The Lord of the Rings* recorded in New Zealand (Hudson and Ritchie 2006a: 257).

Other decisive factors influencing such tourism are the amount of exposure or length of time the destination is on the screen and more importantly the profitable link needs to be made between the film and the destination, for example *The Lord of the Rings* and New Zealand, *Braveheart* and Scotland, *Crocodile Dundee* and Australia. In terms of coverage, *The Lord of the Rings* unquestionably had a powerful effect on tourism because of its scope (over 100 million people have seen the films to date) and the fact that it was a trilogy thereby reinforcing the images (Hudson and Ritchie 2006a: 257–258).

---

18 The UK Film Council invests STG£7.5 million a year into regional film activities through the Regional Investment Fund for England (RIFE), which supports the nine RSAs in England providing a variety of resources aimed at developing public access to, and education about, film and the moving image (UK Film Council 2008a).

Hudson and Ritchie (2006a: 257–258) maintain that there is no doubt that film viewing has some influence on travel decisions. A relatively recent survey in the UK found that eight out of ten Britons get their holiday destination ideas from films and one in five will in fact visit the destination of their favourite film (Anon 2004). Nevertheless, researchers do not have a clear insight into why and very few have investigated the phenomenon in much detail. **Figure 3.1** is based on a conceptual framework for understanding film tourism. At the core of **Figure 3.1** is the film tourist, who is inspired to go to see a destination due to various push or pull factors. In turn, these factors are stimulated by one or more of three factors – destination marketing activities, film specific factors and the destination attributes. Film induced tourism can generate both positive (**see 3.8**) and negative impacts (**see 3.7**) and in the model a feedback loop shows that these impacts will in turn impact on the destination attributes (Hudson and Ritchie 2006a: 257–258). The elements of the model – destination marketing activities, film specific factors, destination attributes, film tourist motivations, film tourist typologies and impacts are now discussed in more detail.

Figure 3.1

Conceptual Framework for Understanding Film Tourism

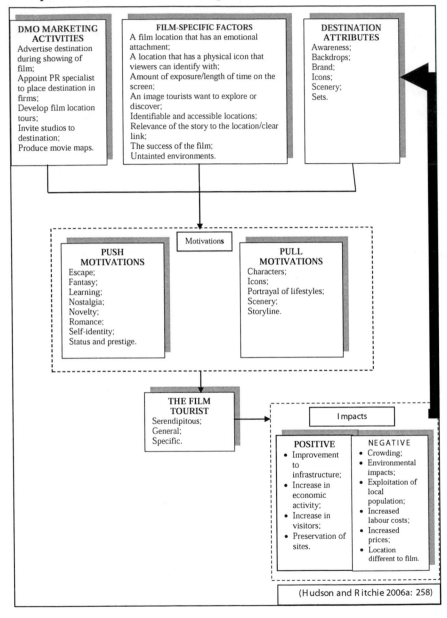

DMO MARKETING ACTIVITIES
Advertise destination during showing of film;
Appoint PR specialist to place destination in firms;
Develop film location tours;
Invite studios to destination;
Produce movie maps.

FILM-SPECIFIC FACTORS
A film location that has an emotional attachment;
A location that has a physical icon that viewers can identify with;
Amount of exposure/length of time on the screen;
An image tourists want to explore or discover;
Identifiable and accessible locations;
Relevance of the story to the location/clear link;
The success of the film;
Untainted environments.

DESTINATION ATTRIBUTES
Awareness;
Backdrops;
Brand;
Icons;
Scenery;
Sets.

Motivations

PUSH MOTIVATIONS
Escape;
Fantasy;
Learning;
Nostalgia;
Novelty;
Romance;
Self-identity;
Status and prestige.

PULL MOTIVATIONS
Characters;
Icons;
Portrayal of lifestyles;
Scenery;
Storyline.

THE FILM TOURIST
Serendipitous;
General;
Specific.

Impacts

POSITIVE
• Improvement to infrastructure;
• Increase in economic activity;
• Increase in visitors;
• Preservation of sites.

NEGATIVE
• Crowding;
• Environmental impacts;
• Exploitation of local population;
• Increased labour costs;
• Increased prices;
• Location different to film.

(Hudson and Ritchie 2006a: 258)

3.5.1 DMO marketing activities

According to Morgan and Pritchard (1998), placing a destination in a film is the ultimate in tourism product placement. Film images live on for decades, provide publicity and create identities. The coverage that a film gives a destination is like a television commercial viewed by millions of potential tourists, an audience that could not be targeted by specifically using tourism promotions (Hudson and Ritchie 2006a: 258–259).

A DMO can engage in various marketing activities both before and after the release of a film (**see Chapter 2**) with the aim of leveraging film tourism. For the most part, however, destinations have a short-term concentration that assists with film production, focusing on the related short-term economic impacts (Croy and Walker 2003). Some destinations are becoming dynamic in encouraging producers to make films in their locations with the intention of profiting from the long-term tourism impacts. VisitBritain has been targeting Indian film producers for some time in the belief that they can be convinced to use British locations for Bollywood films, thus creating significant economic benefits for the British tourism industry (Woodward 2000). Often, British locations are used as backdrops for Bollywood destinations like India. VisitBritain works in tandem with the film stakeholders on strategic promotions to ensure that such attention is drawn to their film locations (Hudson and Ritchie 2006a: 258–259).

Some employ destinations public relations specialists to position their regions in films. Canada and the Bahamas, for instance, have acknowledged film tourism as a marketing opportunity and employ Weber Shandwic[k19] to obtain good publicity for their destinations in film and television (Weber Shandwick 2005). Chicago's Film Office[20] has also positively increased the number of films made there by making use of a product placement specialist. Then again, these appear to be the exceptions. Croy and Walker (2003) in a recent survey conducted in New Zealand established that most destinations, including New Zealand, conduct little planning to make best use of the impacts of film production and that the post-production exposure impacts on image are not fully understood (Hudson and Ritchie 2006a: 259).

---

19 Weber Shandwick provide strategic counsel and programme execution services, that span the complete range of communications disciplines and industry sectors. Services range from marketing communications, media relations and issues management to public affairs, crisis communications, CEO and corporate reputation management (Weber Shandwick 2008).
20 The Chicago Film Office, a division of the Mayor's Office of Special Events, leads the city's effort to attract and facilitate feature films, television, commercials and all forms of film and video production (Chicago Film Office 2008).

3.5.2 Film-specific factors

Taking a different approach, Beeton (2005: 9–11) has developed a definition of film induced tourism which is quite broad as it incorporates the visits to destinations where film and television series were recorded as well as to film production studios and film theme parks. In this context the phrase 'film induced tourism', can be extended to include video/DVD and television. Significantly, Beeton's (2005: 9–11) research is based on the tourist perspective and the related activity of the film industry at such film induced tourism destinations.

3.5.3 Destination attributes

Gilbey (2004) states that some destinations are more likely to entice film tourists than others. It has been recommended that in order for the ideal film destination to inspire film tourists it should be made up of wonderful landscape qualities, distinct social and cultural attributes and/or an image that tourists can relate to. The superb scenery in *The Lord of the Rings* films was one of the prime reasons people visited New Zealand after the film, according to an International Visitor Survey in 2003. For similar reasons, Romania was picked as the destination to shoot, *Cold Mountain* (2003). It was felt that nowhere in the USA, had the unblemished beauty needed to re-create the image of North Carolina in the 19th century (Hudson and Ritchie 2006a: 260).

Iwashita (2006: 183) claims that nowadays popular media induced tourism thrives in many urban destinations. Hollywood films such as *Roman Holiday* (1953) set in Rome, Italy and *The Sound of Music* (1965) shot in Salzburg, Austria continue to encourage foreign tourists to visit the screened destinations. Other examples of this urban phenomenon include *Notting Hill* (1999) – London and *The Full Monty* (1997) – Sheffield, UK. In the case of *Notting Hill*, in which Kenwood House was featured, this heritage site experienced a 10% increase in tourists in August 1999 alone, after the preliminary screening of the film (Busby and Klug 2001). On a broader scale, this film turned the Notting Hill area of London into a celebrated attraction once more, although it has also featured prominently in other films such as *A Hard Day's Night* (1964) (Bolan and Davidson 2005: 12).

In the USA, New Orleans enthusiastically connects itself with the Vampire Chronicle novels of Anne Rice (*Observer* 1996) and Salem with Arthur Miller's film *The Crucible*. Interestingly, on occasion, the same piece of literature can be associated with different destinations. Bram Stoker's *Dracula* (1992) provides Transylvania in Romania with a tourism and cultural icon. At the same time, Whitby in Yorkshire on the north east coast of England, which also features a great deal in the novel, hosts an annual Dracula festival and has a Dracula experience attraction (Morgan and Pritchard 1998: 69). The popular *Manhattan TV Tour* offers its tourists an opportunity to see television locations like the *Friends* (1994-2004) apartment building, the Huxtable house on *The Cosby Show* (1984-1992) or Carrie's apartment in *Sex and the City* (1998-2004) (Torchin 2002: 247).

3.5.4 Motivations

Butler (1990) accepts that destination based research has been of great importance in the improvement of tourist locations. He predicted that as tourists place reduced importance on reading as a form of getting information about destinations and depend more on the visual forms, films and television would become even more significant (Butler 1990). Butler (1990) also suggests that the importance of visual media in influencing images and visitation is in all probability very much under-researched. A number of researchers have used the push and pull factor theory of motivation to develop a framework to inspect film tourism from a tourist perspective. Push factors are internal drivers like the need for socialization or the need for escape. Other than that, film tourists may be stimulated by including the externally driven pull factors derived from the screen. Macionis (2004a) divides these factors into three categories – place (destination attributes, landscapes and scenery), personality (cast, characters, celebrity) and performance (genre, plot and theme) (Hudson and Ritchie 2006a: 260).

Major films have also been referred to as 'hallmark events' in terms of the potential impact they might have on a destination, special tourism events or as tourism promotion (Croy and Walker 2004; Riley and Van Doren 1992a). Actually, it was Riley and Van Doren (1992a) who characterized films as a non-marketer controlled category of hallmark event. Even though it is recognized that films are not produced with the purpose of inducing tourism visitation, it is generally accepted that films, seen by mass audiences, can indeed enhance the awareness of the destination in the film, in addition to the appeal of these tourist destinations (Riley and Van Doren 1992a).

A film induced destination can be an attraction in its own right or film induced tourism may materialize where the filming is only supposed to have taken place. Recently, Macionis (2004a) developed a continuum of film induced tourism motivation, which extends from the serendipitous film tourist to the specific film tourist (Hudson and Ritchie 2006a: 261) **(see Figure 3.2).**

Figure 3.2

Continuum of Film Induced Motivation

	Increasing interest in film →	
Serendipitous Film tourist	General Film tourist	Specific Film tourist
Those who just happen to be in a destination portrayed in a film.	Those who are not specifically drawn to a film location but who participate in film tourism activities while at a destination.	Those who actively seek out places that they have seen in film.
Motivations include: • Novelty • Social interaction	Motivations include: • Education • Escape • Nostalgia • Novelty	Motivations include: • Ego-enhancement • Fantasy • Nostalgia • Pilgrimage • Romance • Self-actualization • Self-identity • Status/prestige • Vicarious experience
	Increasing self-actualization motivations →	
	Decreasing importance of authenticity →	
	Increasing importance of push factors →	

(Macionis 2004a: 22)

Macionis (2004a: 11) suggests that this could prove a practical classification for examining film induced tourism motivations as it emphasizes the specific media representations and attributes that are imperative for film tourists, namely *what is the tourist experience as it relates to a motivation to visit a site-specific destination? What do these tourists want to do when they arrive at a film location? What is important to tourists in fulfilling a given motivation?* For instance, is it the stunning destination attributes of *Place* that instigates travel to a well-known location seen on film or is it the amorous plot attributes of *Performance* that induces travel to fulfill a drive for escape and romance through a vicarious experience? On the other hand, it may be the pilgrimage motivating factor to visit a destination that has showcased their much-loved film star or *Personality*. Consequently, this *3 P* classification will set a framework for exploring the definite attributes of film tourism motivation (Macionis 2004a: 11).

The framework in **Figure 3.2** suggests that the push and pull framework does not offer a sufficient approach for explaining the motivations triggering film tourist behaviour. Even though the two factors have been seen as relating to two separate decisions, it has been recommended that they should not be viewed as functioning wholly autonomously (Klenosky 2002), as people may travel because they are pushed by their own motivations and at the same time pulled by the external forces of the destination attributes (Macionis 2004a: 10).

3.5.5   The film tourist

Macionis (2004a: 5) suggests that through the proposed classification of media portrayal of *Place, Personality and Performance*, it might be possible to bring to the literature a film tourist based on integrating push and pull motivation factors. By doing this, a continuum of film created motivation will present an examination and breakdown of specific film tourists compared to general film tourists, based on specifically recognized motivations (Macionis 2004a: 5).

Much research has defined this tourism niche from the consumer perspective highlighting the behavioural aspects of the film tourist which is usually set within Urry's (1990) framework of the 'tourist gaze' in terms of film constructing a gaze for an individual to observe. In this instance, people may be induced to visit the places they have gazed upon on the cinema screen. Riley *et al.* (1998: 320) argue that it is when 'people seek the sights/sites they have seen on the silver screen; it is then that they, indeed, become movie induced tourists'.

3.5.6 Impacts

Particular films are likely to have more of a pull for tourists than others. Research has revealed that film is a viable medium for tourism, if the storyline and destination are closely interconnected and the film includes the viewers in the story, providing them with an emotional experience, which they can relate to the destination (Tooke and Baker 1996). Repeat viewing gives supplementary exposure ensuing greater awareness, affection and recognition, all of which may result in a desire to visit the destination, meet the residents and share in the local experiences and fantasies depicted in the film. Films that imitate a genuine image of the destination and acquire the essence of it, whether it is the countryside or cultural subject matter, tend to be more successful in being a magnet for film tourists (Grihault 2003). Examples of this include *Shirley Valentine* (1989) and Greece, *Sleepless in Seattle* and New York (1993) and *Crocodile Dundee* (1986) and Australia. The latter was used to cultivate more international interest by showing both ancient and modern culture. Historical films can also have a huge impact internationally (Hudson and Ritchie 2006a: 257–258) such as *Braveheart* as highlighted earlier.

Cohen (1986) has recommended a number of variables that can have an effect on the impact of films on tourism. At the outset, the location of the film will affect the tourists' perception of a destination as a possible tour location. Cohen (1986) also suggests that the more the destination is in the forefront of the story, the more it will leave an imprint on the potential tourist's mind. *Out of Africa* (1985) promoted the beauty and mystique of Kenya and Tanzania and for that reason was a powerful incentive for potential tourists to visit Africa. An additional variable is for how long and when the destination setting appears in the film. For example, in the film *10* (1979), Mexico is presented as an idyllic and romantic getaway where dreams can come true. This contributed towards Cancun becoming a major tourist destination (Hudson and Ritchie 2006a: 258). This illustrates the idea that the length of time a destination appears on screen may not be the only factor which draws the viewing public to it but at what stage of the film and in what context the destination is actually shown.

Various researchers have made attempts at considering the impact of certain films on tourist visitation. However many of their studies were quite basic. Riley and Van Doren (1992a) cite many cases in the USA where films have had a major impact on tourism. Riley *et al.* (1998) collected visitation facts at twelve film locations in the USA, for example Gettysburg – *Dances with Wolves* (1990) – to measure the escalation in visitation, subsequent to the release of the film. They estimated that the impacts of using a location in a film can last for four years. From the perspective of visitation motivation, they highlight the importance of an 'icon', or focal point for visitation, which can be the film's symbolic content, an isolated event, a favourite actor, the destination's physical features or even a theme (Fernandez-Young and Young 2006: 127).

The impacts of film induced tourism have been observed in various international destinations – *Heartbeat* in Goathland, *Hamish Macbeth* (1995–1997) in Plockton, *SeaChange* in Barwon Heads and *The Lord of the Rings* in New Zealand – generating a series of positive and negative impacts for host communities (Connell 2005b). The literature on film induced tourism reveals that films and television series have the strength to influence and even pull visitors to a destination (Riley and Van Doren 1992). Alternatively, less attractive impacts are often generated by spontaneous increases in tourist demand within a short timeframe (Connell 2005b: 228). Despite the fact that the effect of film and television on certain destinations has been studied by quite a few academics (Beeton 2001a; Mordue 2001; Tooke and Baker 1996), the subject matter is not yet theoretically advanced, nor have implications for sustainable tourism development been sufficiently investigated (Connell 2005a: 228).

Tooke and Baker (1996) and Grihault (2003) both present four cases, for which the results plainly demonstrate that the films reviewed instigated an influx in tourist numbers at the film destinations. Croy and Walker (2003) demonstrate how the effects of films on tourist numbers in mainly rural and natural areas have in some cases been immense. Cousins and Andereck (1993) supply evidence from two regions in North Carolina illustrating that film can have considerable effects on destinations used as film locations. Busby, Brunt and Lund (2003) provide a variety of examples of destinations that have seen an influx of tourist numbers subsequent to the release of films made in their locality. Even though it should be recognized that the capacity of film tourism presents many issues, it is evident from the literature, that film and television can have very optimistic impacts on tourism visits (**see 3.8**) (Hudson and Ritchie 2006a: 261).

There are also a range of probable negativities to film induced tourism. Riley *et al.*, (1992) state that even before the release of a film, prices may have increased by the arrival of the production crews. When the tourists actually arrive, Beeton (2001a) indicates that by forming a new invasive style of tourism, the customary holiday-maker is disenfranchised. Tooke and Baker (1996) propose that very often the film destinations will not have the carrying capacity to cope with large increases in tourists. This could result in a number of possible undesirable impacts, like the loss of privacy and local facilities, increased vehicle traffic and pedestrian congestion. The damage to the natural environment is also an issue, for example with the beach on the Thai island utilized in the film *The Beach* (2000) which was flattened, extended and had much of the native plant life removed (Beeton

2001a). As highlighted earlier, a further problem that can arise is when the destination appears dissimilar to how it is depicted in the film, ensuing in a loss of tourist contentment (Hudson and Ritchie 2006a: 261).

Whereas some attention has been given to how destinations take advantage of film images in destination marketing campaigns (by researchers such as Riley *et al.* 1998), Tooke and Baker (1996) have investigated the impact of image and film induced tourism on both destinations and its residents. An influx of tourists is not always appreciated or advantageous with many destinations unable to support the associated tourism development because of inadequate infrastructure, facilities and services. For the most part, the community does not usually seek to be the destination for filming, yet they are left to deal with the consequences of increased traffic, overcrowding and pollution (Beeton 2000: 129).

3.6   The Emergence of film induced tourism

The current British series *Last of the Summer Wine* has been screened on British television since 1973 (Mordue 2001). As a result the audience relationship with the story and setting has developed over time. This keeps the destination where the series is filmed in the public mind, supporting the motivation to visit. Television series usually have more long-term impacts than film; *Dallas* (1979–1981) and *Heartbeat* (1992 to present) are prime examples, unless the film is extremely popular such as was the case with *Crocodile Dundee* (1986). According to Beeton this film shot in Australia provided immediate destination recognition in the USA (Beeton 2005: 11).

The film induced tourism phenomenon has formed new types of cultural tourism (Riley *et al.* 1998), film induced tourism (Beeton 2005), and media related tourism (Busby and Klug 2001: 316). These new forms of tourism can be clustered together as fashionable media induced tourism involving tourist visits to a destination, which has strong links with films and television series. In other words, popular media induced tourism comprises of destinations or film locations (both real and story bound), which have been popularized as tourist destinations by the media (Iwashita 2006: 183). The emerging forms and characteristics of film induced tourism are outlined in **Table 3.1**.

Table 3.1

Forms and characteristics of film induced tourism

Form	Characteristic	Example
On location		
Film tourism as primary motivator	The film destination is an attraction in its own right – strong enough to motivate visitation.	Isle of Mull (*Balamory:* 2003 to present); Avoca (*Ballykissangel:* 1996–2001);
Film tourism as part of a holiday	Visiting film destinations (or studios) as an activity within a bigger holiday.	Yorkshire, UK; Hollywood, USA;
Film tourism pilgrimage	Visiting destinations of films so as to pay respect to the films likely re-enactments.	Doune Castle (*Monty, Python* 1969–1974); *The Lord of the Rings* (2001–2003) sites;
Superstar film tourism	Superstar homes, destinations that have taken on celebrity status.	Hollywood (USA) homes;
Nostalgic film tourism	Visiting film destinations that characterize another era.	*The Andy Griffith Show* (1960–1968) – (1950s);
Commercial		
Constructed film attraction	An attraction created after the filming simply to attract tourists.	The *Heartbeat* Experience (Whitby, Yorkshire);
Film tours	Tours developed to a range of film destinations.	On location tours;
Guided tours (Specific sites)	Tours of particular locations, frequently on private property.	Hobbiton, Middle Earth, New Zealand;
Mistaken Identities		
Film tourism to places where the filming is only believed to have taken place	Films and television series that are recorded in one destination and made to give the impression of being another for financial reasons.	*Deliverance* (1972) Clayburn County (film shot there but set in Appalachia, USA);
Film tourism to places where the film is set but not filmed	The film has increased curiosity in a specific destination where the story is based not where it was in really filmed (Authenticity and displacement).	*Braveheart* (1995) Scotland (film shot in Ireland);
Off location		
Film studio tours	Industrial tours of functioning film studios where the authentic filming process can be seen.	Paramount Studios (USA);
Film studio theme park	Commonly adjacent to a studio purposely built for tourism with filming or production happening.	Universal Studios (USA);
One-off Events		
Film premieres	Mainly those outside the normal setting (Hollywood).	*Mission Impossible II* (2000) (Sydney);
Film festivals	Several cities host film festivals that attract film fans.	Cannes (France), Venice (Italy);
Armchair Travel		
Television travel series	The successor to travel guidebooks.	Getaway Pilot Guides;
Gastronomy television series	Some cooking series take the viewer to many destinations.	*French Leave – France* (2003); *Jamie's Great Escape* – Italy (2005).

(Adapted from Beeton 2005: 10–11)

The very successful and long-running television series, *Dallas*, which was shown in many countries, influences international audiences to visit the USA. Southfork Ranch, the family home depicted in the series, still exerts a pull of 500,000 tourists annually, in spite of the restricted on-site inspections opportunities (Riley and Van Doren 1992a). Riley and Van Doren (1992a) imply that Southfork is not a place that American tourists put on their must-see list but international tourists, primarily tourists from western Europe, often want to visit the house where they can apparently experience '*open and democratic American society and authentic American culture*' (Iwashita 2006: 183).

For generations, the UK has been the filming location for international films and television series, comprising some very successful recent productions like *Four Weddings and a Funeral* (1994), *Braveheart* (1995), *The Full Monty* (1997), *Notting Hill* (1999), *Pride and Prejudice* (2003) and *The Da Vinci Code* (2006), which have attracted international tourists to the screened locations. Australia also considerably expanded their recognition worldwide as a tourist destination after successful films such as *Mad Max* (1980), *The Man from Snowy River* (1982), *Crocodile Dundee* (1986) and *Crocodile Dundee II* (1988). The natural environment represented in the films is a factor which provoked many Americans, who have a special attachment to the wilderness, to travel to the destinations (Riley and Van Doren 1992a). More recently, films and television series set in different regions of South Korea have motivated a number of new international tourist flows, especially Japanese female tourists to South Korea (Iwashita 2006: 183–184) as television series (especially tele-soaps) viewership tends to be predominately female.

It can be argued that the types of film and television that provoke people to travel are varied (Riley *et al.* 1998). Riley and Van Doren (1992a) indicate that when films and television series are filmed on location, they can create specific images of these destinations for the viewer. In addition, the destinations linked with exciting story-lines, symbolic contents and celebrated actors become special locations for potential tourists (Iwashita 2006: 184).

Schama (1996) states that a whole world of associations is encapsulated in viewers' minds as memories, which give meaning to the scenes and backdrop. Tourists can be encouraged to visit those destinations with meanings for them. Conversely, destinations have been transformed by films and television series into something full of symbolic meaning. When tourists visit the actual film destination, the scenery that has specific associations becomes blended with figments of their imagination. Being in the actual place of filming brings out the special moment of being at this particular destination, and tourists can find contentment in their emotional investment (Iwashita 2006: 184).

3.6.1 Authenticity and displacement

Bolan and Davidson (2005: 7) advocate that authenticity (also referred to in the film indced tourism literature as displacement) in the film induced tourism context refers to '*the aspect of a film or television series being shot in one place but in reality representing somewhere else entirely, which means that the location where the film or television series was recorded, may not positively gain from its international release*'. Butler (1990) also highlights this as an issue and points out that films are often not shot at the destinations they profess to be. A case in point being the film, *The Last Samurai* (2003) which showcases Japan's landscape and culture, except that it was filmed in New Zealand.

Films and television series can motivate tourists to visit a destination but they often do not give an authentic view of the destination compared with the realism of what the visitor will find there. Tourists visiting a destination may wish to recapture in what they saw or felt while viewing a film. Films and television series, by their nature, can offer something that distorts the authenticity of the 'actual' place. Consequently, it may prove difficult for the tourist to find exactly what they seek. This can be further compounded with the growing trend for films and television series to be shot in a different place from that which they portray on screen (Bolan and Williams, 2008: 387)

For example, the Philippines were used to portray Vietnam in *Platoon* (1986) and Canada is often used as an alternative to the USA, as occurred with the film, *The Blues Brothers II* (1998) (Beeton 2005: 31). As mentioned earlier, another recent film, which showcases some great landscape cinematography, was the Oscar winning film *Cold Mountain*. The film is set in South Carolina (USA), but was filmed in the Carpathian Mountains (Romania) (Bolan and Davidson 2005: 7).

Beeton (2001a: 18) highlights that a significant aspect to be considered when trying to take advantage of the benefits of film induced tourism is that of the actual versus the image (created by the film). In this context, the term 'displacement' is used to reflect this. A situation can easily arise where tourists are basing their knowledge on fabricated expectations, thereby developing false expectations of destinations they choose to visit, resulting in dissatisfaction with the experience. Hall (1995) claims that the appeal of tourist attractions clearly relates to the image that the tourist brings with them (Beeton 2001a: 18). An example of how this can be rectified can be seen with the bar from the television series *Cheers* (1982–1993), which provides a setting similar to the set as well as special menus and memorabilia (Beeton 2005: 33). This is illustrated even further in **Table 3.2.**

Table 3.2

On location tours scripted on location information

Current New York Site	Historical / Cultural reference from tour	New York Film Tour background
Jacqueline Kennedy Onassis High School	High School of the Performing Arts.	High School of the Performing Arts in *Fame* (1982–1987), interiors filmed in Hollywood.
Flatiron Building	Most photographed building in New York City.	Houses the imaginary offices of *Veronicas Closet* (1997–2000), a television series set in New York but shot in Hollywood.
West Village apartment block	Apartment renting for $US3000–5000 monthly	Apartment block where the characters from *Friends* (1994–2004) reside.
West Village brownstone terrace style house	Four apartments renting for $US2000 per month.	Residence of the Huxstable family on *The Cosby Show* (1984–1992*)*, recorded in studios in Brooklyn and Queens.
Al's Soup Kitchen International	Lunch setting of the writers of *Seinfeld* (1989–1998).	Real life centre for the fictional Soup Nazi on *Seinfeld.*

(Based on Torchin 2002: 259–260)

Bolan and Williams (2008: 387) suggest' that *films and television series play an increasing bigger role in creating people's image of a destination. This trend for highly in-authentic approaches such as using locations far removed from the actual place they are portraying sets a dangerous course as to what consumers' informed imagery and knowledge of places actually are'.* Butler (1990) argues that *we may be entering an era where people's geographical knowledge of the world is based on something inherently false that they have glean 'through various media forms such as movies and fictional literature.* This key issue correlates to both destination promotion and consumer image satisfaction and merits additional research (Bolan and Williams, 2008: 387).

3.7   Risks of film induced tourism Negative impacts

3.7.1   Negative impacts from too many tourists

Tooke and Baker (1996) recognize other problems associated with film induced tourism. They state that a film induced tourism destination may not have the carrying capacity to appropriately and sustainably facilitate the increased tourist numbers. This may result in a range of environmental and socio-cultural impacts that did not exist at the destination preceding the film screening, like parking restrictions (Macionis 2004b: 12).

The effects of film induced tourism are inspected exclusively in an Australian case study on the well-liked television series, *SeaChange* (Beeton 2005). This report researches the many impacts that the inhabitants of Barwon Heads experienced when surveyed about the benefits of *SeaChange* to their community. Although recognizing the economic benefits from increased tourism, it was felt that this media representation set off a change in the traditional nature of their tourist community (Macionis 2004b: 12). O'Connor and Flanagan (2001) testify this in their research of *Ballykissangel* which has had both a positive (tourist influx) and negative (residential resistance) impact on the village of Avoca, County Wicklow, Ireland. This is also evident with their research in Yorkshire (UK) (O'Connor *et al.* 2005) which is mirrored by Mordue's (1999: 2001) studies of *Heartbeat Country.*

Beeton (2005: 129) noted that the town of Goathland (the town described as Aidensfield in the English television series *Heartbeat*) has a population of 200 people and up to 1.1 million annual tourists. However, hoteliers experienced lower occupancy levels after the series became successful (Demetriadi 1996). The town which had been a quiet tourist sanctuary was now repositioned as a major day tourist attraction. There appears to have been an underlying change in the nature of the village and its affiliation with tourists resulting in overcrowding and the loss of opportunities for the local community to use its own amenities (Beeton 2001a: 129). Tooke and Baker (1996: 92) reinforce this as they stated that an influx in tourists is unavoidable and has an effect on the destination's economical, environmental and sociocultural balance. Their research highlighted the problems associated with the filming of *Last of the Summer Wine* in Holmfirth, (Yorkshire) which included traffic and pedestrian congestion instigated by tourists. Very often the destination will not have the carrying capacity to cope with a large increase in tourists, with many possible unwelcomed consequences (Tooke and Baker 1996: 92)

3.7.2   Negative impacts from negative portrayal in a film

Just as films and media can create positive destination images, there are cases, where films have formed an unfavourable imagery which may result in off-putting destination images and perceptions. Certainly, for a destination to take advantage of its film and media exposure, it is crucial that an appropriate and positive destination image is depicted in an attempt to put across a harmonious and legitimate destination image (Macionis 2004b: 13).

Tourism stakeholders do not design film images, however if an attractive landscape or alluring image were illustrated in a film, the result could be significant (Bordelon and Dimanche 2003). Beeton (2002: 2) implies that there are three basic forms of image that can be considered adverse to a destination: pessimistic storylines, films being too victorious in attracting tourists, ensuing in greater than before visitation, and harmful destination impacts and the unrealistic expectations of tourists (Macionis 2004b: 13).

In terms of uninteresting plot, misrepresentation of destinations may lead to misconception causing damage to tourist awareness and negatively impacting on prospective decisions of visitation (Macionis 2004b: 13). As lucrative as film induced tourism can be, unhelpful impacts may come about. Generally, a number of impacts are characteristic of tourism destinations but definite film induced tourism impacts can also be identified (Beeton 2000). Destinations also surrender control over how and to whom a destination is available through commercial film (Beeton 2000: Kim and Richardson 2003). This brings up significant issues for the development of images and whether the image depicted in the film is in fitting with the image the film destination is endeavouring to endorse. Other film induced tourism impacts may consist of vandalism from souvenir seekers by way of stealing film icons such as street signs (Beeton 2005).

If more tourists are exposed to the ever-increasing amounts of visual media one might presume that popular images described in films play an important role in creating destination images and influence tourists expectations of a specific destination. Off-putting images of Los Angeles (USA) come to mind when watching *Boyz in the Hood* (1991) and *Colors* (1988). For many people, Los Angeles is perceived as a tough city, filled with racial tension, police brutality and gang warfare. It could be disputed that media, particularly visual medium such as film, can connect tourism and a destination image (Beeton 2001a).

Countless films have been produced on location in New Orleans (USA). Consequently, viewers have developed a sense of the people, places and attractions of the city. There are several portrayals of corruption, violence and poor weather in these films. New Orleans might also come across as a hazardous city that is not fitting for families. This is not essentially the case as portrayed in the film *Double Jeopardy* (1999). Bordelon and Dimanche's (2003) research supports Beeton (2001a) in that the unfavourable imagery issues linked with film induced tourism can have a harmful effect on the development of a destination. Riley *et al.* (1998) also recognize a number of repellent operational impacts due to the escalating tourist numbers at film related destinations in the USA (Riley *et al.* 1998).

3.7.3 Not recognizing the pulling power of a film

Residents do not always support film induced tourism as evidenced with the film *Mississippi Burning* (1988). The film attracted bad publicity for the small town of Philadelphia, Mississippi (USA), built on an unsavoury reputation in the 1960s when the Ku Klux Klan executed three civil rights employees (Riley and Van Doren 1992a). The film was shot on location there and in the resultant media hype the town gave the impression that it had altered little since the executions (Morgan and Pritchard 1998: 73). Philadelphia's unfavourable image suggests that branding on its own may not be effective enough to change image. Riley and Van Doren's (1992a) examination highlights the negative impacts of film induced tourism but investigations have shown that many impacts of such tourism can be positive (Beeton 2000; Bolan and Davidson 2005; Connell 2005a, 2005b; Tooke and Baker 1996).

3.7.4 A de-marketing strategy

De-marketing is defined as '*that aspect of marketing that deals with discouraging customers in general or a certain class of customers in particular on a temporary or permanent basis*' (Kotler and Levy 1971: 75) and as such the term 'de-marketing' is an fundamental characteristic of marketing management and an important element of the overall marketing mix (Beeton, 2002: 3).

Ever since the 1970s, de-marketing has been used extensively in an attempt to control extremely high demand and restrict disruptive behaviour (see Borkowski 1994; Kindra and Taylor 1990; Malhourta 1990; Reddy 1989). While it has not been widely applied to tourism, there are cases where de-marketing has been deliberately and even unconsciously used (see Beeton 2001b; Benfield 2001; Clements 1989). De-marketing in tourism is an influential tool. By broadening the variety of de-marketing instruments (Kotler and Levy 1971), a tourist management approach at the marketing stage of an operation (before tourists visit) can be taken. Several professed tourist management tools can be seen as extensions of Kotler and Levy's (1971) de-marketing tools, comprising of restricting access through pricing, making access more difficult and changing anti-social behaviour (Beeton 2001b; Benfield 2001). By viewing these as de-marketing tools, they can be introduced when expectations are formed and decisions on destinations to visit are made in the marketing mix (Beeton 2003: 4). Beeton (2001b) and Benfield (2001) propose many de-marketing strategies which could be applied to film induced tourism destinations for example by discouraging 'undesirable' markets and encouraging 'desirable' markets through the images used in promotional information (Beeton, 2002: 4).

3.8   Opportunities of film induced tourism Positive impacts

Film allows destinations to influence the products and services that they have on offer, which can also help them to enhance their tourism capabilities. While the existence of film induced tourism has been acknowledged for some time, little direct measurement of its influence has taken place and the phenomenon for the most part, remains unknown (Mintel 2003; Riley and Van Doren 1992a, 1992b; Riley *et al.* 1998; Tooke and Baker 1996). Regardless of some methodological complications in determining the effect of film induced tourism (Busby and Klug 2001), there have been few instances of films that seem to have boosted tourism in destinations (**see Table 2.3**).

3.8.1   *Increased visitation*

There is no doubt that film induced tourism is a fast growing sector of the tourism industry with rising economic significance. It not only presents short-term employment and publicity for the destination (Post Production Effect – PPE), but also long-term tourism openings (**see Table 2.3**) (Busby and Klug 2001). Though not sufficiently measurable, a range of benefits have been acknowledged by researchers exploring film induced tourism. Films can noticeably impact a destination, not just during the marketing campaign, but after the film has been released. Once seen in a major cinema, commonplace destinations can gain celebrity status, which has the potential to prompt visitation to that destination (Croy and Walker 2003; Riley *et al.* 1998; Tooke and Baker 1996). This phenomenon is referred to in the literature as Post Production Effects (PPE) (Macionis 2004b: 7).

Perhaps, the most noticeable and predictable PPE with regard to tourism, is a boost in tourist visitation. Busby and Klug (2001), Riley and Van Doren (1992a) and Tooke and Baker (1996) have all analysed how films generate improved tourist numbers at destinations seen in films. Riley and Van Doren (1992a, 1992b) present the argument that films have been enormously powerful in marketing tourist destinations. Their examination includes statistical case studies and anecdotal data of major films that have had a demonstrated impact on tourist visitation. A range of examples within the USA, where films have had a major impact on tourism, plus a discussion of the *Crocodile Dundee* (1986) effect witnessed in Australia in the 1980s was highlighted earlier (Macionis 2004b: 7–8).

Croy and Walker (2003: 123) evaluate the use of fictional media in rural areas to aid the development of a tourism destination's distinctiveness. They refer to examples of literary tourism, the use of television series for tourism promotion and the fictional media of feature films. Their research also demonstrates a growing appreciation and understanding by the RTAs in New Zealand for the role of the fictional media in branching out and developing their regional economic base. For instance, images of the Waitakere region of Auckland, where the film *The Piano* (1993) was recorded have been used for tourism promotional (TNZ's *100% Pure New Zealand* campaign), and according to the Auckland Regional Council[21], Karekare Beach still receives international tourists due to its featuring in the film (Macionis 2004b: 8).

3.8.2   Long-term impact of film induced tourism on a destination

Riley *et al.* (1992) established that although the peak of interest comes after a film is released, an increase in visitation can continue many years later (Bordelon and Dimanche 2003). These lasting effects would explain the achievement of some destinations that have redeveloped themselves to make film connections clearer and enhance tourism even when the film is not original (Grihault 2003). To illustrate this, they discuss the film *Deliverance* (1972), an action film shot in Raeburn County, Georgia (USA), which was the catalyst for the formation of its raft and adventure tourism industry. Historic Fort Hayes featured in *Dances with Wolves* noticed an increase of 25% in 1990–1991 **(see Table 2.3)**, in contrast with an average increase of 6.6% for the previous four years (Morgan and Pritchard 1998: 73). Ever since the release of the film, there has been an increase in British led package tours of 341% to the region.

Morgan and Prichard (1998: 73) determined that Devils Tower, Wyoming (USA) thanks to the film *Close Encounters of the Third Kind* (1977) grew to be a household name in USA in the 1970s. The Tower plays a key role in the film and due to its cinema release and television reruns, the region benefits from an incredible increase in tourists. The year after its release tourist numbers improved by 75% **(see Table 2.3)** and over a decade later 20% of tourists cite viewing the film as their most important source of destination information (Riley and Van Doren 1992: 270–271).

---

21 Auckland Regional Council manages the region's air and water quality, its growth and development, regional parks, public transport, the coastal and marine environment and natural and cultural heritage sites (Auckland Regional Council 2008).

JFK (1992), the film about the assassination of President John F. Kennedy was released in the early 1990s and, before long, tourists to the Book Depository Museum (the location from where the assassin supposedly shot the President) increased by 45% (**see Table 2.3**). Likewise the film, *Thelma and Louise* (1991) featured the Arches National Park, Utah (USA) which experienced initial tourist growth of 19.1% (**see Table 2.3**), with further increases in subsequent years (Safari Kinkead 2002: 32). These examples illustrate that film induced tourism can have an enduring effect on a destination as seen in destinations where an actual variation in tourist numbers can be easily measured.

3.8.3   Destination image alteration

In their investigation of the Las Vegas brand personality amongst British residents, Morgan and Pritchard's (1998: 75–77) research sample included respondents who had visited the city and some who had not. A variety of methods were used to construct a comprehensive study of the destination's general image. One of the most interesting results to come out was the intensity and consistency of the imagery. Respondents in particular talked about the films *The Godfather* (1972, 1974, 1990), *Honeymoon in Vegas* (1992) and *Casino* (1995). They had enchanting associations of champagne, dazzling nightlife and limousines (Morgan and Pritchard 1998: 75–77). The most fascinating result to materialize was the intensity and reliability of the imagery, most of which seemed to stem from film and television and the similarity of the image amongst those who had and those who had no familiarity with the destination (Iwashita 2006: 183).

Many researchers have made an attempt to summarize the process of image development as linked to tourism promotion and destination choice (see Echtner and Ritchie 1991; Hunt 1975). Without a doubt, destination image is more and more recognized as a fundamental element of the travel process in terms of its effects on normal tourist behaviour and the decision-making process in particular. The effects of the extremely successful trilogy, *The Lord of the Rings* in New Zealand have been reviewed earlier in this chapter. A major focus of Croy and Walker's (2004) research assesses the roles of organic images (film) versus induced images (advertising) in generating destination familiarity and motivation. In the case of *The Lord of the Rings*, the trilogy built on and improved New Zealand's tourism image. The improvement of the image, by way of organic and induced sources, was subsequently converted into travel behaviour with tourists saying that the films played a big part in their decision to visit (Macionis 2004b: 9).

Kotler, Haider and Rein (1993) insist that the Hawaiian location of the television detective series *Hawaii 5-0* (1968–1980) and *Magnum PI* (1980–1988) were both very successful showcases for the islands of Hawaii, as was the case with the location of the British detective series *Bergerac* (1981–

1991) in Jersey. The affiliation between television portrayal and the tourism image is complicated as it can alter the image of a place as in Dallas, Texas (USA) which was able to redefine its hostile image from the 1960s (JFK assassination and the Mafia links) as a result of the long-running television show, *Dallas* (Morgan and Prichard 1998: 71).

Chambers (1989) states that in some situations television portrayal may even change the reality of a destination and some television series have been the catalyst for this. Parts of the city of Miami, Florida were recreated for the American television show *Miami Vice* (1984–1989). In the 1980s, when *Miami Vice* initially emerged, the city was cautious of a negative impact, as the show was very much linked with crime and drugs. Nonetheless, the series, as well as providing a platform for Miami as a tourism destination, in reality became the catalyst for economic and environmental rejuvenation. The show's producers needed brightly coloured buildings and energetic Latin music to represent an indisputable image of Miami, so for filming purposes many of Miami's beaches and discoloured art deco buildings were redecorated in pinks and oranges. Due to this, Miami's residents began to take renewed gratification in its internationally celebrated art deco architecture. They repainted and restored their own buildings as seen in the show (Morgan and Prichard 1998: 71).

This has also occurred in Avoca, County Wicklow, Ireland, where locals took a positive interest in the tourism development of their village since the filming of the award-winning BBC television drama series *Ballykissangel* (O'Connor and Flanagan 2001), and the main positive impacts included the revitalization and upgrading of the village. The worldwide publicity that Avoca has received, has led to an increase in tourism numbers. The residents maintain that this brings extra money into the village, shows the village in a positive light, creates local employment and instils a feeling of pride in the community which is defended by Crandall (1994), Beeton (2000) and O'Connor and Flanagan (2001).

3.8.4 Government support

Yorkshire has featured in various media of the day incorporating the poetry of Wordsworth, books by James Herriot, television series such as *Heartbeat* and films like *Calendar Girls* (2003). Images of an English rural idyll is popularized in the Goathland case by television series such as *Heartbeat* and Herriot's *All Creatures Great and Small*. The public and private stakeholders, looking to take advantage of these productions are branding North Yorkshire as *Herriot Country* and the Goathland area particularly as *Heartbeat Country*. The place/product relationship is apparent and guidebooks, brochures, trails and maps are published to implant the televised myths in the tourist's minds. In this type of communication, the fictional and the actual are often blended together to form a packaged panoramic commodity offering the promise for tourists to re-experience the rural community life depicted in the series themselves (Mordue 1999: 5).

An example of how a lack of concern from the film industry can go wrong is demonstrated in *Baywatch* (1989–2000). The residents of the location chosen in Australia for filming objected strongly to the series being shot on their beach. There is limited research to support this occurring elsewhere. Such antipathy resulted in the producers filming the new series in Hawaii (USA). Coincidentally, the Hawaiian Tourism Authority identified that promoting filming in the state was one of their key tourism promotion policies (Hawaii Tourism Authority 1999) and the residents very much supported this (Beeton 2005: 7–8).

In an ever more celebrity-led universal society, the global opportunities offered through film induced tourism are vast but are only just starting to be realized. Although the success of film induced tourism can be linked to the success of a film, up until now there is no precise means to predict this. In spite of this, destinations hosting films seen by millions worldwide stand to benefit from film induced tourism: even if the plot is a failure, the landscape can be a winner. Some may think the film speaks for itself but the tourist stakeholders have become conscious that with well-targeted marketing and film industry support, they can further exploit the interest created. VisitBritain's movie maps (see **2.6.5**) and New Zealand's destination branding strategies in connection with *The Lord of the Rings* are prime examples of this (Mintel 2003: 21).

Collaborative campaigns with the film industry are a commanding way to induce film tourists (Grihault 2003). DMOs are beginning to form relationships with film stakeholders, with the intention of pursuing productions and film releases, so they are in a position to act as soon as they see the signs of film induced tourism. Executives at VisitBritain try to plan with studios at least one year in advance of a film release date. In the Bahamas, their film commission[22] is under the patronage of the Ministry of Tourism. When the Ministry of Tourism gets a film script, it becomes involved immediately. Some €21 million was spent on the film *After the Sunset* (2004), with the aim of guaranteeing maximum exposure for the island. The ATC is also very hands-on in forming partnerships with the film industry. In recent times, it has joined forces with Disney on *Finding Nemo* (2003) and became the first DMO to try endorsement through an animated film. Other marketing activities can involve guided tours and film walks. A recent travel magazine listed 25

---

22 The role of the Bahamas Film Commission is to promote the Bahamas as a film location in order to attract foreign productions, to support local film-makers and to assist the development of the local film industry.

film tourism destinations with information about tour packages developed just for film tourists (Anon 2004). After *Harry Potter*, quite a few tour operators emerged to show tourists around the locations featured in the film, and the James Bond films (1962–) have produced many innovative packages from tour operators (Hudson and Ritchie 2006a: 259–260).

3.8.5   Recognizing the pulling power of a film or television series to a destination

3.8.5.1 *Film induced tourism in Ireland*

The notion of films encouraging tourists to visit Ireland is not a recent occurrence (O'Connor *et al.* 2005). In fact, it goes back as far as the 1952 film, *The Quiet Man*, which still, over 50 years later, brings many American tourists to the small village of Cong in County Mayo, Ireland. If one film alone can still have such an impact five decades after its cinema release then there is great scope for film induced tourism in Ireland. Recently, the increased volume of high profile films being recorded in Ireland can only serve to invigorate this potential further. Such films include: *The General* (1998), *Angela's Ashes* (1999), *Agnes Browne* (1999), *Tailor of Panama* (2001), *Evelyn* (2002), *Reign of Fire* (2002), *King Arthur* (2004) and *Intermission* (2004) (Bolan and Davidson 2005: 17–18).

The picturesque scenery available in Ireland suits what many film directors seek in terms of the look they are after. Even if the film is not set in Ireland, the landscape it offers sits well with film viewers for specific locations. While a popular appeal for film makers, this does present a potential threat to the future of Ireland's film induced tourism industry (Bolan and Davidson 2005: 7–8). Bolan and Davidson (2005: 7–8), in their examination of film induced tourism in the UK and Ireland, surveyed a sample of 150 respondents to ascertain which films they identified with particular countries, the results for Ireland are shown in **Table 3.3**.

Table 3.3

Films that respondents associated with attracting them to Ireland

Film	Response %	Film	Response %
The Quiet Man (1952)	33	*The Commitments* (1991)	8
Ryan's Daughter (1970)	15	*Far and Away* (1992)	1
Braveheart (1995)	13	*Into the West* (1992)	4
The Field (1990)	11	*Circle of Friends* (1995)	2
Michael Collins (1996)	10	Other	3

(Bolan and Davison 2005: 12)

Interestingly, a substantial proportion stated that *Braveheart* (1995) influenced their selection of Ireland as a tourist destination. The films referred to most strongly are the less recent *The Quiet Man* (1952) and *Ryan's Daughter* (1970). In this study, 46% said they would rather visit the actual filming location, with 54% preferring to go to see where the film was set. Lastly, 77% of the respondents thought that film was an effective means of advertising destinations such as Ireland (Bolan and Davidson 2005: 12).

3.8.5.2 *Film induced tourism in the UK*

In relation to their study of the British film induced tourism industry, Bolan and Davidson (2005) discovered that the apparent frontrunners were *Notting Hill* (1999) and a number of *James Bond* (1962–) films for tempting tourists to visit Britain (see **Table 3.4**).

Table 3.4

Films that respondents associated with attracting them to the UK

Film	Response %	Film	Response %
Notting Hill (1999)	24	*Braveheart* (1995)	8
James Bond (1962–)	20	*Love Actually* (2003)	5
Four Weddings and a Funeral (1994)	13	*Chariots of Fire* (1981)	4
Harry Potter (2001–)	12	*Other*	2
Bridget Jones's Diary (2001)	11	*Rob Roy* (1995)	1

(Bolan and Davison 2005: 11)

As stated earlier, Tooke and Baker (1996) considered four British dramas and their ensuing impact on destination visitation. In all cases, the visitation to the destination improved considerably. With growing awareness of the British film industry since the recent successes of several British films, it seems the industry is embarking upon a period of growth. More UK destinations are being used as film induced destinations and in turn they are becoming more responsive to the remarkable prospects that filming can convey, and a swift growth in film induced tourism can be expected. Given that film induced tourism is still in its formative years, it remains to be seen whether the uniqueness of visiting destinations, will increase in popularity as a successful type of tourism in its own right (Corlett 1998: 127).

3.8.5.3 *Films and television series as a source of information*

Iwashita (2006: 186) noticed in her survey findings of Japanese tourists in the UK, that films and television series featuring the UK were the main source of information (70.1%) in increasing tourist travel to the country. This was followed by books and literature (64.2%), travel guide books (57.7%) and VisitBritain's promotional materials (47.5%). The results clearly show that popular types of cultural media like films, television series and literature, have more power to intensify interest to travel to the UK, than the tourism promotional materials themselves. Women seemed somewhat more likely to be influenced by literature (65.8% vs. 60.9%) and films and television series (71.9% vs. 66.3%) than men. Travel agents, including their advertisements, brochures, travel magazines and word-of-mouth did not exercise a great deal of influence in increasing interest to travel to the UK. Travel agents and advertisements were surpassed by the media such as newspapers, radio and television (Iwashita 2006: 186).

To facilitate the identification of which films and television series increased interest in visiting the UK, respondents whose interest was increased by the popular cultural forms of the media were asked to select all items from a pre-identified list of 36 films and nine television productions. The two most high-ranking films were *Harry Potter and the Philosopher's Stone* (2001) and *Notting Hill*, both of which were selected by about 37% of the respondents as the film which increased their interest in visiting the UK. The impact of *Harry Potter and the Philosopher's Stone* may reflect the fact that the film was released a month before the survey was undertaken and had become a cultural phenomenon in Japan attracting a massive audience at the box office. Alternatively, the memorable film *My Fair Lady* (1964) was the most seen film among the respondents (72.7 %), followed by *Notting Hill* (72.2%) (Iwashita 2006: 186).

Iwashita (2006: 188) also reviewed television series such as the *Sherlock Holmes* (1984–1985) series which was frequently (39.2%) referred to as a source of information, followed by the *Poirot* (1989–) series, Mr *Bean* (1990–1995) and the *Miss Marple* (1987–) series. These television series have been shown and repeated on the main television networks and are also available on video/DVD. Above all, BBC's *Pride and Prejudice* (1995) was an extremely popular television series, which captured many viewers' imaginations, particularly among the female audience and contributed to an increase in tourist numbers to destinations used in the series. It is worth noting that while the *Inspector Morse* (1986–1994) series, featuring Oxford (UK) was only shown on a satellite station in Japan, 25% of respondents had seen the series and it had influenced nearly half who saw it by increasing their curiosity to visit the UK (Iwashita 2006: 188).

3.8.5.4 *The impact of films and television on international tourism*

Films and television series appear to have an enormous capacity in helping tourists to develop a stronger interest in a destination by providing them with folklore, icons, imagery and sentiments, all of which stimulate tourist travel. Tourists have enthusiastically used them, not only as entertainment but also as a tool to become more knowledgeable about the UK and to maintain their interest in visiting the country. The sense of familiarity with the UK, plus an understanding about it, can very much play a part in conveying the UK as pleasurable and relaxing in tourists' minds. This can draw from earlier visits as well as from watching films and television series. The biggest impact of films and television series on global tourism rests in their capacity to create destination awareness, images and perceptions leading to a stronger interest in the destination and actual travel to the destination. They can also act as a verbal, visual and sensory motivation to encourage tourism, hence support tourists in their on-going decision-making (Iwashita 2006: 195).

Mishra *et al.* (2006: 90) claim that when the James Bond film *The Man with the Golden Gun* (1974) was shot in Phuket, Thailand, most Westerners had never heard of it. Nowadays, it is a key tourism destination. The film *The Beach* (2000) has enhanced tourism in a different part of Thailand. The film is about the discovery of the most idyllic beach in the world. Consequently, the Thai authorities have encountered a tourist surge in the film's location, Koh Phi Phi. Many tourists are influenced by a film's theme as much as its location, particularly if it is a romance. Romantic couples are seen at the top of the Empire State building, each time that *Sleepless in Seattle* (1993) is broadcast in the USA. *Four Weddings and a Funeral* (1994) has guaranteed that The Crown Hotel in Amersham, Buckinghamshire, UK, has been busy from the time when the film was originally screened. The inhabitants of a somewhat dilapidated part of London have seen property prices nearly double thanks to the astounding success of the film *Notting Hill* (Mishra *et al.* 2006: 90).

3.8.6   The use of imagery in media

Bolan and Davidson (2005) argue that various media do indeed have a strong influence on people's preference of tourist destinations and additionally, film above all, can be a powerful motivating factor to induce tourist visitation. In Ireland, the older and classic films tend to feature more strongly than those produced in recent times. The literature implies that films, which reflect the quintessence or authentic features of a destination, such as the landscape, the culture or the major landmarks, are enticing tourists to go to see the sites they have seen on the silver screen (Grihault 2003). In collaboration with Bolan and Davidson's (2005) research, Kennedy (1998) declared that abbeys, castles and stately homes are benefiting from a tourist growth due to the revitalization of the British film industry following films such as *Robin Hood – Prince of Thieves* (1992), *Sense and*

Sensibility (1995), *Hamlet* (1996), *101 Dalmatians* (1996) and *Mrs Brown* (1997) (Corlett 1998: 96).

Pendreigh (2002) stated that the Scottish countryside has been used as a setting in many films and television series and is vigorously marketed worldwide as a film destination. Primetime evening television shows, for instance BBC's *Hamish Macbeth* (1995–1997) and *Monarch of the Glen* (1998–2005) have increased familiarity and allure of the Scottish Highlands. The *Monarch of the Glen*, watched by more than 50 million viewers internationally, is one of the most successful BBC dramas on North American and Australian television. In a recent survey of tourists to Badenoch and Speyside, 83% of respondents were aware of the television series and 73% were conscious that it was filmed in the destination before their trip (Connell 2005b: 232–233).

Dumfries and Galloway Tourist Board[23] maximized on the filming of the BBC drama *Two Thousand Acres of Sky* (2001–2003) to gain marketing impetus for the southwest coast of Scotland. As a result, the show has had an immense effect on the local economy (Dumfries and Galloway Tourist Board 2003). The immediate popularity of the children's television programme *Balamory* (2003–), has encouraged the film induced tourism phenomenon on the Island of Mull in a manner not experienced elsewhere (Connell 2005b: 232–233) as it is based on a children's television series.

3.8.7   The economic impact of film induced tourism

Schofield (1996) suggests that on the whole, a rise in tourist numbers can only help a local economy. Owing to their connection with fame, buildings and streets that were formerly considered ordinary, all of a sudden acquire interest, status and ambience. One of the most important economic benefits and aspects of film induced tourism is that viewing past destinations can be an all-year, all-weather attraction, and therefore in tackling the unavoidable seasonality problem intrinsic in so many tourist attractions. Furthermore, both films and television series have an extensive socioeconomic appeal, potentially expanding the tourist market base (Beeton 2001a: 17).

In Scotland, Ross (2003) observed that the filming business is worth no less than €12 million annually to the Highlands and Islands economy. In the 1990s, many high profile productions were shot or set in Scotland, (*Braveheart* – 1995, *Rob Roy* – 1995, *Loch Ness* – 1996) with *Braveheart* alone inspiring over 500,000 Americans to visit Stirling, Scotland and creating in the region of €152 million in tourist spend. An economic impact review of the effect of the film *Rob Roy*

---

23 Dumfries and Galloway Tourist Board, as with the rest of the Scottish Tourist Boards merged to become one integrated VisitScotland in 2002.

acknowledged a €11 million injection, which created approximately €23 million in tourism revenue between 1996 and 2000 (Connell 2005b: 232).

The direct economic benefits of the long-running television series *Cheers* (1982–1993) involved attracting approximately 500,000 tourists annually to the pub, thus an annual food and beverage return of €4.7 million and related merchandising sales of about €5.4 million (Neale 1994). The English Tourist Board (now VisitBritain) claims that *All Creatures Great and Small* continues to produce a great deal of business in Yorkshire. James Herriot, the vet and author received a special award from the British Tourist Authority[24] (BTA) for bringing comedy and entertainment to millions and making even more potential tourists conscious of the pleasures of Yorkshire and the UK (Ruler 1984). In relation to the measurement of impacts, the National Trust[25] released tourist statistics for Basildon Park, a house featured in the latest *Pride and Prejudice* (2005) adaptation, which illustrated that weekly tourist numbers had grown by 3,000 in a matter of a few days.

In a *Times* Newspaper report, Dyrham Park, which was utilized for *The Remains of the Day* (1989) is cited as drawing tourists wishing to catch a glimpse of where the filming was carried out, even now many years later. The Giant's Causeway, County Antrim, Northern Ireland experienced a huge swell in tourist numbers given its use in the popular television series *Cold Feet* (1997–2003). These examples support the idea that the impacts of film tourism can be enduring and a more thorough analysis of the data is needed (Fernandez-Young and Young 2006: 128).

3.8.8   Closer collaboration between film and tourism stakeholders

The continuing effect of film and television series on destinations is crucial in the present international environment. Tooke and Baker (1996) recommend that encouraging media companies to film in destinations ought to be made part of destination policies and procedures, in light of the rising tourist numbers and inbound tourism statistics enticed by a film or a television series. For that reason, it is obvious that a wide range of industries should take advantage of the relationship between tourism and film/television (Corlett 1998: 128).

---

24 In 2003, VisitBritain was created by the merger of the BTA and the English Tourism Council and is legally constituted as the BTA under the Development of Tourism Act 1969 (VisitBritain 2008).
25 The National Trust is responsible for conserving and enhancing the natural beauty, wildlife, culture and heritage in the UK. The National Trust also promotes opportunities for understanding and enjoyment of the special qualities of National Parks by the public (The National Trust 2007).

3.9 Final thoughts on the film induced tourism phenomenon

3.9.1 On location tourism

Lam and Ap (2006: 178) assert that there has been a disparity in the number of research studies carried out between on-location and off-location film induced tourism, the latter being to some extent an abandoned subject matter of research. From the findings of this literature review, it is evident that with the exception of the studies carried out by Beeton (2005), Liu and Liu (2004) and Schofield (1996), the selected publications primarily focus on analysing on-location film induced tourism examples. Indeed, the impacts caused by on-location film induced tourism are more apparent and accessible than those of off-location film induced tourism (Lam and Ap 2006: 178). Therefore, the phenomenon of on-location film induced tourism can exert a pull on the attention of interested academic, researchers, and students. Yet, such a gap between the investigations of on-location tourism and off-location tourism should deal with the intention of developing a more thorough representation and appreciation of the film tourism phenomenon. Subsequently, researchers should concentrate even further on off-location film induced tourism (Lam and Ap 2006: 178).

3.9.2 Film induced tourism as a field of academic research

A film has the power to give a destination massive exposure, at little or no financial cost to the destination. Residents residing around film induced destinations are influenced by the business of films and tourism and are frequently convinced by the positive impacts of this phenomenon. However, research and evidence has been infrequent and often anecdotal. As a comparatively new tourism phenomenon, explicit literature relating to film tourism is fairly scarce. Riley (1994) remarked that there has been little empirical exploration of the phenomenon, whereby films might manipulate the travel inclination and destination choice of those who are cinema-goers or view DVD/video tapes at home, hence detecting an opening in the research and literature on film tourism. Couldry (1998) reports that the social importance of visits to film and television destinations has been poorly researched, whereas Busby and Klug (2001) stress the necessity for more behavioural and emotional film induced tourism related research (Macionis 2004b: 4–5).

The subject of film induced tourism has also been investigated from the viewpoint of tourism marketing (Beeton 2005). It is apparent from Beeton's work (2000, 2001a, 2001b, 2002, 2005) and the other research mentioned, that the importance of using media for promoting destinations is becoming apparent. To appreciate how the screening of a film or television series converts into a visit to a destination, the literature on media effects needs to be examined (Fernandez-Young and Young 2006: 128).

3.9.3 Emergent film induced tourism research

The existing research publications on film induced tourism are in short supply, in all probability due to its short history. Many destinations are presently putting efforts into developing such tourism. The changes taking place in the film induced tourism markets of many destinations will subsequently provide various themes for interested researchers to investigate.

Lam and Ap (2006: 177–178) perceive that the Western economy is presently the leading focal point for film tourism research. Subsequently, many destinations beyond the Western world, for example Asia and Africa, are frequently ignored by film induced tourism researchers. Then again, this does not mean that film induced tourism does not exist in these regions. Many Asian countries have unveiled a range of film-related tours and destinations to attract the attention of international tourists (Hsu *et al.* 2006: Tour2Korea 2006a, 2006b). These countries are acquiring a reputation for their work on the development of film induced tourism (Lam and Ap 2006: 177–178).

Studies on film induced tourism in different countries will increase the comprehensive understanding of this phenomenon. In light of the fact that there is little existing information and insight into film induced tourism development in the non-Western world, research on the film tourism market in Asia and other countries is needed. As a comparatively new and underdeveloped research area, there are still many unidentified areas and topics waiting to be studied in the film tourism discipline. As referred to by Riley (1994) and later, by Beeton (2005), more research on film induced tourism is very much needed (Lam and Ap 2006: 177–178). This is supported by Andereck who says (2006: 279) '*while film induced tourism is a fairly narrow area of interest and impact, it is a topic deserving more in-depth consideration than it has previously been given, because of its potential to dramatically influence specific communities*'.

3.9.4 Proposed future research

The growth in the amount of undergraduate and postgraduate students taking an interest in this subject area has increased, along with the media interest. This highlighted the unsuspecting community and also the research issues like an overabundance of invasive research procedures administered by frequently inexperienced and on occasion inadequately trained researchers (Beeton 2005: 243). On a practical level, literature review shows the significance of integrating film induced tourism into tourism and destination marketing planning, particularly in small communities which are most susceptible to tourism growth (Beeton 2005: 143)

Even though research conferences are an additional means for film tourism researchers to present and publish their results, it appears that such outlets have not been used to a large extent, as the amount of submissions on film induced tourism is still relatively small in contrast to other areas of research. There are many themes that reflect the phenomenon of film induced tourism which are waiting for interested academics, researchers and students to examine, even if the findings revealed by such subject matters may be immature. As a result, academics, researchers and students, who are interested in analysing the phenomenon of film tourism even further should make an active use of academic conferences with the intention of disclosing their preliminary research findings and to trade thoughts and ideas with other likeminded researchers (Lam and Ap 2006: 177).

Lam and Ap (2006: 177) suggest that nearly all of the selected publications chosen for their research study focus on a few broad objectives, like the benefits and impacts resulting from film induced tourism and the tensions between residents and such tourists. Surely, there are many potential topics on film tourism that can be contemplated by researchers and academics, such as the relationship between the film and tourism sectors, the diverse views between Eastern and Western film tourists, measuring the film induced tourism impacts on different film tourism products, investigating pilgrimages for televisions series or film stars and the psychology and behaviour of film induced tourists. The investigation of these issues could make an immense contribution to the film induced tourism literature. Thus, academics and researchers, who are passionate about this research area should broaden and vary their research (Lam and Ap 2006: 177).

Topics that only emerge in one publication of the literature, which uncovered some fascinating findings, are where more examination on such studies is required. Kim and Richardson (2003) recommend that the inter-relationship between the viewers' characteristics and perception alter during the film viewing process. This should be explored further, as they recognized that the viewers' characteristics were not taken into account during their experiment. More explorations extending from current studies may lead to the discovery of new insights and offer a better understanding into the study of film induced tourism. Thus, the review of subject matters that rarely appear in publications presents a starting place for additional research (Lam and Ap 2006: 177).

3.10   Conclusion

Chapter 3 has provided the academic foundation for this research study's main objectives (**See Table 1.1**). It has investigated the film induced tourism phenomenon which was previously introduced in Chapter 2. It has also examined the impact of film induced tourism and destination branding on locations featured in a popular television series, namely Yorkshire. Chapter 3 also investigated the characteristics of film induced tourism, as the need for a thorough and comprehensive investigation of this phenomenon was particularly evident. The results from this chapter provide an explanatory insight into the background of this phenomenon. Many of its findings describe how additional tourism induced by a film or a television series can impact a destination and suggest that they can be an invaluable instrument in changing a destination's image and positively influence an audience's desire to visit such a destination. It is apparent from these studies, that more research is imperative to better understand the relationship between films and tourism (Kim and Richardson 2003: 232).

CHAPTER 4

RESEARCH METHODOLOGY

4.1   Introduction

Chapter 4 provides the theoretical background for this research study's research objectives (**See Table 1.2**). It describes the methodology used for this research study. The main objective of this research is to *develop a model to be used as a best practice framework for the successful integration of film induced tourism in a destination marketing strategy.* The chapter commences with an introduction to the study and outlines the aim of this two-phase, sequential mixed methods study which is to acquire statistical quantitative results (tourist survey) from a sample, then follow up with individuals to investigate those results in more depth. In the first phase the quantitative research questions will investigate the relationship between film induced tourism and destination branding in Yorkshire. In the second phase, qualitative interviews (strategic conversations) will be utilized to explore the emergent themes and issues from the first phase with the key tourism and film stakeholders in Yorkshire. Chapter 4 concludes with an investigation into the data analysis used and the research limitations met during the course of the study.

4.2   Background

The UK in general and Yorkshire in particular were selected as the case study area owing to the many popular television series locations. Yorkshire has been the film destination for a number of popular English television series and as such is the focus of much destination research in the tourism discipline (Mordue 2001). In this research, the case studies being employed are *Last of the Summer Wine, Heartbeat* and *All Creatures Great and Small.*[26] They were chosen because of high levels of visitation due to their filming in the area (Beeton 2002: 3).

Much of the relevant secondary data has been summarized in **Chapters 2** and **3**. Additional secondary data is utilized to substantiate the primary research findings of this research as evident in **Chapter 5**. The emergent themes and assorted issues that arose from this secondary data (literature reviews), which form the basis for both the tourist survey and the strategic conversations are outlined in **Figure 4.1**.

)

---

26 The term 'film induced tourism' includes television which this research study examined.

Figure 4.1

Emergent themes and associated issues

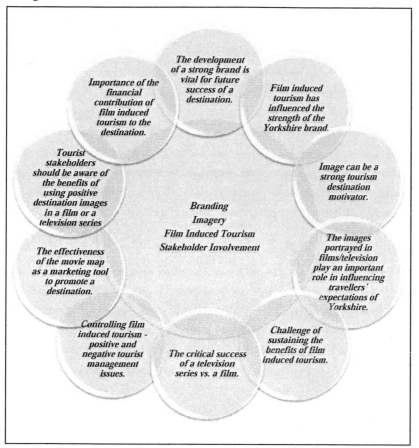

4.3 The Research Process

Pizam (1994: 91) argues that the aim of tourism research is to supply data that will help tourism managers when making decisions. Tourism research is an exploratory process that can be differentiated from other forms of exploration by three distinctive requirements: objectivity, reproductivity and systemization (Brown 1980). Objectivity necessitates an approach that is impartial of the researcher's personal views with reference to the answers to the problems under review. Reproductivity is a process that makes sure other researchers could replicate the research and acquire the same results. Finally, systemization is the most significant of the three research investigation requirements as each step needs to be planned so as to achieve the prerequisite for the next step. This requires the co-ordination of the research process into sequential steps which have to be specified and planned beforehand (Pizam 1994: 91).

The work of many academic researchers (Blaxter et al. 1996; Chrisnall 2001; Cooper and Emory 1995) was evaluated to select a model that best fits the research study being undertaken. Aaker, Kumar and Day (2004: 43) argue that the research process presents a logical and premeditated approach to a research study and guarantees that all features of such study are consistent (Aaker et al. 2004: 43). Brannick (1997: 28) proposes a statistical, planned approach to a research model and suggests that all phases of the model must be constant with one another. The literature, the researcher's ideas and data are entangled by the researcher through the process of reflection, which persists for the length of the research study. The research question is generally developed through the first key phase of the literature review, in relation to the early stages of the fieldwork. The theoretical perspective of the researcher is the most significant factor shaping the choice of methodology (Brannick 1997: 28).

Brannick's (1997: 28) model contrasts with the four stage approach portrayed by Jennings (2001: 23) that *is identify the research topic, develop the research design, implement the research design and report the findings.* It also compares with the seven stage process created by Neuman (2000a) which is *to choose a topic, focus on the research question, design the study, collect the data, analyse the data, interpret the data and inform others.* It also contrasts with Weaver and Oppermann's (2000) model, which includes seven phases *(problem recognition, question formulation, identification of data, data collection, data analysis, data presentation and data interpretation)* and Veal's (1992) four steps *(presentation and planning, investigation, analysis and writing up and presentation of the results).* Though, Veal (1997) increased the four phases into an eight phase model by splitting the four phases into smaller sub phases (Jennings 2001: 23).

4.4 Epistemology and Theoretical Perspective

Examination of theory facilitates the design of the approach to research. It should enlighten the researcher's definition of the research questions and objectives (Saunders et al. 2003: 25). Gill and Johnson (1997: 51) establishes that there is possibly no word that is more misused and misinterpreted in education than the word 'theory'. It is considered that material included in textbooks is theory, while what is occurring in the real world is practice (Saunders et al. 2003: 26).

4.4.1   Research paradigms

Sarantakos (1998: 30) differentiates between a paradigm, a methodology and the methods utilized in a study. A methodology is a model which involves theoretical principles, as well as a framework that gives guidelines about how research is carried out in the context of a specific paradigm (Sarantakos 1998: 32; see also Stanley and Wise 1990: 26). Guba (1990) views methodology as part of the structure that comprises a paradigm. Methods are tools used by researchers to collect practical evidence or to examine information (Sarantakos 1998: 32; see also Stanley and Wise 1990: 26). Consequently, a paradigm is the overlying view of the way the world works, the methodology is the corresponding group of guiding principles for carrying out research within the overlying paradigmatic view of the world, and the methods are the particular tools of data collection and analysis a researcher will put into place to collect data on the world, thereby creating theory about that world (Jennings 2001: 34).

Jennings (2001: 55) states that there are clear advantages and disadvantages connected with each of the key research paradigms, but the paradigm being implemented should take into account the *disposition of the tourism system that is being investigated. For instance, if a researcher wants to know what will happen when a user-pays system is put into operation in a tourism area, then a positivist paradigm could be applied with the intention of gaining an awareness of the ensuing drop off in visitation levels and the consequent lessening in income. Or if a researcher wants to appreciate the social impacts of a super event on the lifestyles of local inhabitants then an interpretative social sciences paradigm should be operated.* **Table 4.1** outlines each of the key paradigms considered in this research. At the outset, the ontology, epistemology and methodology of each paradigm are outlined. Subsequently a theoretical example is used to reveal the application of each paradigm corresponding to a single research focus. This permits the researcher to observe how a study can be measured using diverse paradigms to examine the same thing (Jennings 2001: 55).

Table 4.1   A summary of the paradigms of tourism research

Research Paradigms	Positivism	Interpretive Social Sciences	Critical Theory	Feminist Perspectives	Post-modernism	Chaos Theory
Ontology	Worldwide truths and laws	Multiple realities	Complex world organization by open and hidden power	World interceded by gendered interpretation	World is complex and ever changing; infinite explanation	World is volatile, non-linear and vibrant
Epistemology	Objective	Subjective	Objective / subjective	Subjective	Subjective	Objective
Methodology	Quantitative	Qualitative	Predominantly qualitative	Predominantly qualitative	Questioning and deconstruction, qualitative forms	Quantitative and qualitative, if used symbolically
Theoretical tourism example: New management taking over the operation of the RTA would like to create a database of visitation patterns.	The researcher might collect statistical data on tourist patterns from all accessible sources like transportation providers and assemble this into a database. The database would establish the factual (objective) arrangements of tourist patterns based on available statistics.	The researcher might opt to interview key people such as local residents to determine their perceptions of tourist patterns over the timeframe being examined. This would develop data of tourist patterns based on the subjective perspective of the interviewees.	The researcher might decide to study the tourist patterns of minority groups: the aged, the disabled or lower socioeconomic groups.	The researcher might wish to focus on the tourist patterns of single mothers, business / retired women, women with disabilities or the role of the women in decision making concerning visitation to the area.	The researcher might prefer to check tourist patterns by examining the types of packages offered via an analysis of promotional materials.	The researcher might concentrate on the development of descriptive algorithms to show what earlier changes in tourist patterns will mean for the future, by factoring them in and meeting the changes as soon as possible.

(Adapted from Jennings 2001: 56)

Generally speaking tourism research fits into the positivist paradigm and the interpretive social science paradigms which will be discussed in greater detail in this section. Other paradigms are starting to be practiced but the motivating force behind the paradigm that enlightens any research process is typically reliant on the background and training of the researcher. In the past, the importance for tourism has been on the quantitative methodology which is part of the positivist paradigm. It is only recently, in the search for knowledge as to why tourism phenomena are taking place that a qualitative methodological paradigm has been required to get at the deeper meanings, like the way in which people ascribe to tourism and tourism experience, events and phenomena (Jennings 2001: 55).

The researcher employs a quantitative methodology. Information is usually collected using a survey for instance, and then analysis is undertaken using mathematical formulae. Samples would be chosen to be representative of the population being investigated in addition to being randomly picked (Jennings 2001: 36).

Jennings (2001: 40) argues that there is much potential for embarking on a tourism research study using the interpretive social sciences paradigm. For example, a researcher might decide to carry out research into the study of hospitality, host / residents and travel experiences. The interpretive social sciences paradigm is set in the real world setting of social action. The paradigm necessitates that the researcher becomes part of the social group being examined, to be subjective and to employ a qualitative research methodology. Thus, knowledge of the world is thereby created inductively (Jennings 2001: 40).

Jennings (2001: 40) further suggests that the use of the interpretive social sciences paradigm in tourism research necessitates that the researcher has to turn into an insider, thus experiencing the phenomena. The insider's view is professed as giving the best view to appreciate the phenomenon's social actors and the researcher will need to be in the field setting for a time to facilitate the acquisition of an understanding and to be recognized. The interpretive social sciences researcher should be accustomed to qualitative methodology, so as to effectively acquire knowledge from the study setting. Additionally, the researcher should be aware that when applying an interpretative social sciences paradigm, they will get an in-depth knowledge of the tourism phenomena (Jennings 2001: 40).

4.4.2   Inductive and deductive theory

Brannick (1997: 4) argues that nowadays two main traditions exist, the empiricist and the hermeneutic. The empiricist tradition tries to explain human action while the hermeneutic tradition attempts to understand human realities. To clarify is to identify the applicable simplification, which involves the case to be described. The researcher working within the hermeneutic tradition should try to enter the culture of the phenomenon under review by learning to speak its language and by sharing its vision. 'This insider view permits the researcher to understand the phenomenon under study as it reveals itself' (Brannick 1997: 6). The hypothetico-deductive (explanatory) approach involves the development of a theoretical structure or framework preceding its testing through empirical data. Concepts that signify a central aspect of the theoretical structure can be seen directly and need to be defined, both nominally and operationally (Brannick 1997: 5). In the hermeneutic tradition (inductive theory) the researcher preferably enters the research site with few or no theoretical preconceptions. While this can be completely realized in reality, researchers are advised to avoid early conceptualization and alternatively are encouraged to let the key concepts upon which theory will be created, emerge from the empirical data (Brannick 1997: 5). What academic researchers understand as scientific knowledge depends on their philosophy of knowledge and their selected epistemology (Brannick 1997: 6). The major differences between the two approaches to research are summarized in **Table 4.2**.

Table 4.2

Major differences between approaches to Research

Deduction emphasizes	Induction emphasizes
The necessity to justify causal relationships between variables;	Gaining an understanding of the meanings humans attach to actions;
Shifting from theory to data;	An in-depth comprehension of the research context;
The gathering of quantitative data;	The collection of qualitative data;
A very structured approach;	A more flexible structure to allow changes of research emphasis as the research advances;
Researcher neutrality of what is being researched;	A recognition that the researcher is part of the research process;
The need to chose samples of ample size so as to generalize conclusions.	Less concern with the call for generalization.

(Adapted from Saunders et al. 2003: 89)

106

Creswell (2003) asserts that mixed methods researchers can apply theory both deductively (quantitative research) and inductively (qualitative research) as in this research study. Researchers are also starting to recognize the use of theoretical perspectives in their mixed methods studies. A significant initial issue that needs to be measured is the question of what is meant by scientific knowledge and how this varies from common-sense knowledge. These issues are eagerly deliberated in the philosophy of science where they are considered in the theory of knowledge or epistemology. The philosophy of science has created helpful values, which allow the science and forms of explanation including some basic assumptions that comprise the philosophy underpinnings of theory to be comprehended (Creswell 2003).

Jennings (2001: 22) suggests that inductive research begins in real world settings, that is in the empirical social world where information about the tourism phenomenon is collected, then analysed and theoretical constructions are either generated or modified (Jennings 2001: 21). Quantitative research is based on the positivist social science paradigm that mainly imitates the scientific method of natural sciences. Such a paradigm assumes a deductive approach to the research process. As such it starts with theories or hypotheses about a specific tourism phenomenon, collects data from the real world setting and then analyses the data to accept or reject hypotheses. Researchers who take on a deductive approach use theory to direct the design of an examination and the explanation of results. They contest, broaden or adapt the theory on the basis of results (Neuman 2000a: 61). **Table 4.3** illustrates the main differences between the qualitative approach and the quantitative approach (Jennings 2001: 132).

Table 4.3

Major Differences between Qualitative and Quantitative Methodologies

	Qualitative	Quantitative
Research approach	Inductive	Deductive
Ontological view	Multiple realities	Causal relationships
Nature of truth	Grounded in the real word	Hypothesis testing
Epistemological view	Subjective	Objective
Researcher situatedness	Emic (insider)	Etic (outsider)
Research design	Unstructured, emergent, specific	Structured, systematic, replicable
Research focus	Themes	Variables
Participant selection	Textual	Numeric
Analysis	Themes, motifs	Statistical analyses
Representation of data	Narrative	Statistical tables and graphs
Voice of the researcher	First person, active	Third person, passive
Reflection of the real world	Slice of life	Representative

(Jennings 2001: 132)

Researchers like Mintzberg favour close-in inductive approaches: *'[it] is the discovery that attracts me to this business about the checking out of what we think we know'* (Mintzberg 1973: 584). The researcher's epistemological perspective establishes what they deem as a valid and justifiable contribution to theory development or generation. These basic assumptions constitute the fundamentals upon which a research question is recognized and offers a basis for all research design decisions that evolve. The research question and the existing development of knowledge in the discipline may also manipulate the choice of method but method should never influence the research question (Brannick 1997: 28).

Creswell (1994) proposes realistic measures for selecting which research approach to adopt. Possibly, the most important of these is the nature of the research topic. A subject matter on which there is an abundance of literature from which a theoretical framework can be developed and a hypothesis emerges, lends itself more enthusiastically to the deductive approach. With research into a topic that is new and emerging and on which there is little existing literature, it may be more fitting to generate data, analyse and consider the theoretical themes the data is suggesting. Deductive research can be faster to complete although time must be dedicated to setting up the research prior to data collection and analysis. Typically, it is possible to predict accurate time schedules (Saunders et al. 2003: 90).

Alternatively, inductive research can be more long-drawn-out. Frequently the research is based on a much longer period of data collection, and analysis has to materialize steadily. This leads to another important thought – the extent to which the researcher is willing to indulge in risk. The deductive approach can be a lower risk strategy, notwithstanding the risks such as non-return of surveys. With induction the researcher continually has to live with the dread that no constructive patterns and theory will surface. Finally, there is the question of audience. Most managers know the deductive approach and are more likely to accept as true, the conclusions stemming from this approach and the findings of the person making the research report (Saunders et al. 2003: 90).

Saunders et al. (2003: 85) consider that theory should be made clear in the design of the research, even if it is typically made explicit in the presentation of the final research. The degree, to which the theory is clear at the start of the research, highlights a vital question regarding the design of the research study. This is whether the research should use the deductive approach in which a theory and hypothesis is developed and a research strategy is designed to test this, or the inductive approach, wherein the data is gathered and theory is developed consequent to the data analysis. Insofar as it is helpful to attach these approaches to the many research philosophies, the deductive approach owes more to positivism and the inductive approach to interpretivism. though such classification is potentially deceptive and of no realistic value (Saunders et al. 2003: 85).

4.5   Research Hypothesis and Objectives

A hypothesis 'is an unproven statement about a phenomenon that is of interest to the researcher' (Malhotra and Peterson 2006: 51). Pizam (1994: 96) ascertains that a hypothesis 'is a proposition that is stated in testable form and that predicts a particular relation between two or more variables. It is a tentative statement about things that the investigator wishes to support or to refute.' Even when hypotheses are not confirmed, they have power. Negative findings are sometimes as important as positive ones since they sometimes point out further hypotheses and lines of investigation (Kerlinger 1973: 26).

Hypotheses have two forms: null hypotheses and research hypotheses. The null hypothesis is the hypothesis of no relationship or no difference; essentially it is the one that is tested statistically. It is set up for a potential negative response and is a subjective gathering, hypothesizing that any relation or disparity in the findings is due to chance or sampling error (Isaac and Michael 1971:

142). The research hypothesis illustrates the expectations of the researcher in positive terms (Pizam 1994: 96). As Kumar (1996: 69) notes a hypothesis is an assumption about which the research process gathers data to prove whether it can be supported or not. Yet, Kumar (1996: 69) warns that the validity of a hypothesis may be incorrectly determined because of:

- A poorly developed research design;
- An insufficiently and imperfectly conducted sampling process;
- Imprecision in data collecting;
- Unacceptable diagnostic processes;
- Unsuitable statistical practices being used;
- Flawed findings or conclusions (Jennings 2001: 301).

Aaker et al. (2004: 50) define the research objective as '*a clear statement of what information is needed'*. They highlight three components: the first is the research question, which indicates the data that the researcher needs and the second component is the hypotheses which are fundamentally alternative answers to the research question. The research reveals which of these alternative answers are truthful. The third is the scope of the research such as 'Is the interest in current tourists or in all potential tourists?' (Aaker et al. 2004: 50). The main objective of this study is to add to the mass of film induced tourism research by presenting a case study **(See 4.6.2)** of a film induced destination and how it can be branded, so as to both validate theory and offer practical guidance to destination marketers through the development of the FMAP **(see Chapter 6)**.

The design of research questions requires conceptual organization, the consideration of the ideas, the connection of theory that is already known, the guidance of cognitive structures for data gathering and the presentation of this interpretation to others (Stake 1995: 15). Stake (1995: 15) advises that the hardest task of the researcher is to design high-quality research questions that will lead the researcher's train of thought. Each element may have to be broken down into research questions, which ask what exact information is required with regard to the problem components (Malhotra and Birks 2000: 47). Stake (1995) insists that researchers may differ on how much they want to have their research questions acknowledged in advance.

Mixed methods research **(see 4.7.1)** offers many challenges in writing research questions (or hypotheses) since only a small amount of the literature has dealt with this design step (Creswell 1999). Therefore, there appears to be a lack of models on which to establish guidelines for writing research questions in mixed methods studies. Nevertheless, by probing a number of these studies, it is possible to recognize some characteristics that may direct the design of the questions.

- Mixed methods studies should have both qualitative and quantitative research questions (or hypotheses) incorporated to narrow the research objectives.
- These should include the fundamentals of good questions and hypotheses previously discussed in the qualitative and quantitative approaches.
- In a two-phase, sequential study in which the second phase expands on the first phase, it is hard to spell out the second phase questions.
- Some consideration should be given to the order of the research questions and hypotheses. In a two-phase study, the order would consist of the first phase questions and after that the second phase questions, so that the researcher views them in the order in which they will be tackled in the research study.
- A variation often seen in sequential mixed methods studies is to present the questions at the start of each phase. For instance, assume that the study begins with a quantitative phase. The researcher might present the hypotheses. Afterwards the qualitative phase is focused on the qualitative research that emerges (Creswell 2003: 115).

To collect the views and perspectives, which allow for informed interpretations to be made, it is vital that the gathering of the information is undertaken in a well-thought-out manner. To establish if film induced tourism can bring significant benefits to the development of a destination, it was necessary to establish a framework for completion of this research study, which will be put into place through the data collection methods illustrated in **Table 1**.2. These will be elaborated upon throughout this chapter. In this study, the main objective is *to develop a model to be used as a best practice framework for the successful integration of film induced tourism in a destination marketing strategy.* This objective derived from the themes and issues **(See Figure 4.1)** which arose from the literature in **Chapters 2** and **3**.

4.6   Research Design

4.6.1   Types of research

A research design '*is the logic that links the data to be collected and conclusions to be drawn to the initial question of study'* (Yin 2003a: 19). Philliber, Schwab and Samsloss (1980) argue that the research design is an outline of research dealing with no less than four problems: what questions to study, what data is relevant, what data to collect and how to analyse the results. The main rationale of the design is to prevent a situation in which the evidence does not tackle the initial research question. The aim of the research design is to provide a plan to be followed to satisfy the research objectives. This plan is an effort to supply the best information possible subject to several limitations as described by McDaniel and Gates (1993: 4) which usually include access, costs and time.

Crotty's (1998) ideas form the foundation for the research framework. He recommended that in designing research, four questions need to be contemplated:

- What epistemology **(see 4.4)** enlightens the research?
- What theoretical perspective **(see 4.4)** lies behind the methodology being discussed?
- What methodology **(see 4.7)** oversees the choice and use of methods?
- What methods **(see 4.8)** are suggested for use? (Creswell 2003: 4–5).

Research design can be categorized in terms of its rationale, as well as by the research strategy used (Robson 2002: 59). The categorization most often used is the threefold one: exploratory, descriptive and explanatory. By the same token, more than one strategy may be used in the research study; therefore it may have more than one rationale which may change in during the course of the work (Saunders et al. 2003: 96). Pizam (1994: 97) insists that once the hypothesis has been devised, a researcher needs to think about their research design which is a meticulously developed and controlled plan to complete the research investigation. It shows what steps will be taken and when. The main aim of research design is to ensure that the study will be applicable to the problem (Churchill 1987: 48). Brannick (1997: 6) suggests that the nature of the research questions decides if the study can be categorized as an exploratory, a descriptive or an explanatory case study.

4.6.1.1 Exploratory research

Exploratory research is carried out when, normally, there is little preceding knowledge on which to build, and research hypotheses are either unclear or do not exist at all (Brannick 1997: 7–8). Its results can be used to develop a bigger research project (Jennings 2001: 6). Saunders et al. (2003: 96) argue that exploratory studies are an important means of finding out what is occurring, to look for new insights, to ask questions and to consider the phenomena in a new light (Robson 2002: 59). They serve above all to familiarize the researcher with the characteristics of the research problem. Typically exploratory studies are typically flexible enough to permit consideration of all aspects of the research problem (Pizam 1994: 97). As the research under review is very much exploratory, its aims are to explore the issues and problems, as very little is known about the situation. This is *supported by Domegan and Fleming (2003: 23) as they propose that a research study is 'exploratory when there is uncertainty about the dimensions of a problem '.*

4.6.1.2 Descriptive research

The purpose of descriptive research is to describe a precise chain of events, people, or situations (Robson 2002: 59). It may be an extension to a piece of exploratory research. It is essential to have a transparent picture of the phenomena on which data is to be gathered preceding the collection of the data (Saunders et al. 2003: 97). Descriptive designs are used when the aim is systematic descriptive and is accurate of the characteristics of a given population and/or destination. In such designs the researcher measures the subjects of interest as they exist naturally (Pizam 1994: 97).

Brannick (1997: 7–8) claims that descriptive research is used in a large amount of business research and is used when the questions who, where and when are to be answered. Its rationale is to give a precise picture of some characteristic of the business setting. With this type of research, hypotheses will frequently be present but they may be speculative in nature. It comprises all forms of research apart from experimental and historical and is not limited to any one method of data collection.

Neuman (2000a: 21–22) ascertains that exploratory research deals with 'what' and descriptive research encompasses 'who' and 'how'. Nonetheless, it is Jenning's (2001: 17) opinion that the how moves away from the descriptive research into explanation, thus is linked to the why of a phenomenon, the essence of explanatory research. Basically, descriptive research provides a picture (Neuman 2000a: 21) of the tourism phenomenon (Jennings 2001: 17), in this case film induced tourism.

Until recently, most tourism research originated from descriptive research. Conversely, there is a need to move away from the fundamentally descriptive nature of its research profile into more investigative research approaches so as to better understand the phenomenon of tourism and to develop and alter theoretical concepts with which to securely ground tourism as a discipline in its own right (Jennings 2001: 17).

4.6.1.3 Explanatory research

Brannick (1997: 8) asserts that studies which determine causal relationships between variables may be labelled explanatory studies. They answer both how and why questions and a well-prepared research problem usually contains some element of this. Research hypotheses which are planned to develop, lengthen or disprove a previously recognized body of knowledge, are integral to this approach. The emphasis here is on examining a situation or a problem with the aim of explaining the relations between variables (Saunders et al. 2003: 97–98). Pizam (1994: 98) argues that in tourism, this design is quiet often not used, in the belief that subjects do not behave naturally under examination. As Blalock and Blalock (1968: 333) indicate this as a serious mistake which is assumed by most social scientists as this design can be an indispensable and an important instrument in the study of social phenomena (Pizam 1994: 98).

4.6.1.4 Advantages of each research design

Further examination of the advantages of each of the above research designs can be seen in **Table 4.4**.

Table 4.4

Advantages of each research design

Exploratory	Descriptive	Explanatory
Frequently a first step to gain insights;	Usually developed from exploratory research findings;	Tries to spot cause-and-effect relationships;
Permits problems to be more loosely defined;	Gathers statistical data utilized in testing hypotheses, developed in exploratory research;	Links between variables should be carefully assessed – association is not automatically causation;
Quite fast;	Supplies data for comparative analyses;	Experiments and panel research are regularly implemented;
Inclined to use qualitative assessments first;	Appraises performance;	Tends to be involved and expensive;
Makes full use of published data;	Develops profiles.	Explanatory;
Valuable research filter before more extensive research.		Tries to spot cause-and-effect relationships;

(Chrisnall 2001: 35–38)

4.6.2   Case study research

Black and Champion (1976: 90) state that case studies are thorough examinations of specific social settings or particular aspects of social setting. According to Yin (1994: 13) a case study 'is an empirical enquiry that investigates a contemporary phenomenon within its real life context especially when the boundaries between phenomenon and context are not clearly evident'. Stake (1995: xi) on the other hand defines a case study as 'the study of the particularity and complexity of a single case coming to understand its activity within important circumstances'.

Robson (2002: 178) describes a case study as *'a strategy for doing research which involves an empirical investigation of a particular contemporary phenomenon within its real life context using multiple sources of evidence'.* This strategy is of particular benefit in an attempt to obtain a deep understanding of the context of the research and the methods being used (Morris and Wood 1991). The case study strategy also has substantial capability to produce answers to the questions; 'why?' 'what?' and 'how?'. The data collection methods used may be diverse. They may include documentary analysis, interviews, observation and surveys. A simple, well-constructed case study can allow the researcher to contest an existing theory and also supply a source of new hypotheses (Saunders et al. 2003: 93). Case studies integrate the use of participant observation as part of the range of methods that may be used to collect data on an individual case (Stake 1995: xi).

A case study methodology (Yin 1989) with a multi-method exploratory approach (Brewer and Hunter 1989) was used for this study. Case studies give depth and comprehensiveness for appreciating a particular topic, facilitating inductive and rich description. Case research is especially welcome in new circumstances, where not a lot is known about the phenomenon and in situations where existing theories seem lacking. It is a method of choice when the phenomenon under investigation is not quickly apparent from its context, as is the case in this research (Yin 2003b: 4). Cooper and Emory (1995: 116) recognize the role of the case study, as it conveys a full contextual examination of a smaller quantity event or conditions and their interrelations. They emphasize the constructive insight for problem solving appraisal provided in the detail of a case study, which is secured from several sources of information.

Case-based research is an experiential enquiry which examines a current phenomenon within its real life environment, when the limitations between phenomenon and context are not clearly understood (Brannick 1997: 13). Ethnography, action research and hypothetico-deductive case studies are all case-based research strategies. The hypothetico-deductive case study approach as summarized by Yin (1984, 1993) can be based on single or multiple case studies and can be used to perform exploratory, descriptive and explanatory investigations. This case-based approach starts by developing a model relating to the focus of the research and building on current knowledge and theory. This framework helps to identify and redefine the first broad research problem, which is process or context focused. This stage is followed by the selection of research sites and the design of the formal data collection techniques (Brannick 1997: 13–14).

Pizam (1994: 98) argues that while case studies have been portrayed as exploratory, unpredictable and too specific to be applied to the general, there is support in the wider social science discipline for the use of case studies. This can be extended to tourism, predominantly in situations where other research methods are not feasible possibly due to physical constraints (Hall and Jenkins 1995). Yin (1994) claims that through the study of a prominent case, the researcher is able to specify theoretical insights that may then be tested for wider applicability, on top of providing the prospect to test theoretical concepts against local and national experiences (Beeton 2001a: 19). Black and Champion (1976: 91) suggest that case studies have many advantages over the other types of research design: they can use flexible data collection methods, they can be used in almost any kind of social setting, they are economical, they can generate hypotheses and they can be valuable for acquiring background data for preparing large studies. On the other hand, they can have restricted generalizability, can be lengthy and can be susceptible to subjective bias (Pizam 1994: 98).

Yin (2003a: 10–11) found that case studies have been seen as a less attractive form of investigation than either experiments or surveys, perhaps due to the lack of rigor which case studies attain, they offer little basis for scientific generalization (Kennedy 1976) and they take too long and result in large badly written documents (Feagin et al. 1991). A major lesson is that good quality case studies are still complex and the problem is that there is little way of vetting the researcher's capability to do a first-class case study (Yin 2003a: 10–11). Somehow the skills for doing good case studies have not yet been defined and as a result (Yin 2003a: 10–11) 'most people, feel that they can prepare a case study and nearly all of you believe we can understand one. Since neither view is well founded, the case study receives a good deal of approbation that it does not deserve' (Hoaglin et al. 1982: 134).

Stake (1995) warns that case study fieldwork frequently takes the research in unforeseen directions, so too much advance commitment can be problematic. Nonetheless, logistics make it virtually impossible to get accustomed with the case prior to the design of the study. As a result, it is a style of research that becomes more manageable with experience (Stake 1995).

4.6.2.1   *Components of case study research design*

For case study research, such as being used in this study, five components of a research design exist – based on Yin's, (2003a: 21–26) research model:

- A study's questions – the case study method is almost certainly suitable for 'how' and 'why' questions so the initial task is to detect accurately the nature of the study question in this regard. In this study, many questions arose in relation to the nature of the research under investigation;
- Its propositions – each proposition leads the attention to something that should be scrutinized within the realms of the study. The case study being used brought many themes and issues to the surface, which will in turn be scrutinized;
- Its units of analysis – the problem here is defining what the 'case' is. In this instance the case study is simply the county of Yorkshire;
- The logic between the data and the propositions – these components indicate the data analysis steps in case study research and a research design should instigate a solid base for this *analysis*. In this study, a multi-method approach was used as it was felt that it would give the researcher a better insight into the film induced tourism concept as applied to Yorkshire;
- The criteria for explaining the findings – one promising approach for case studies is that of 'pattern matching' as created by Campbell (1975), whereby many pieces of information from the same case may be linked to some theoretical outlook (Yin 2003a: 21–26). The aim of this study is to compare and contrast its findings against the current thinking in the area (see Beeton 2000; Connell 2005a, 2005b; Hudson and Ritchie 2006a and Mordue 2001).

Yin (2003a: 33) proposes that a complete research design incorporating these five components in reality benefits from the development of a theoretical framework for the case study that is to be undertaken. Rather than resisting such a requirement, an efficient case study researcher should make efforts to develop this theoretical framework regardless of whether the study is to be exploratory, descriptive or explanatory. The use of theory in case studies not only helps characterize the appropriate research design and data collection but also becomes the most important vehicle for generalizing the results of the case studies (Yin 2003a: 33).

Five supplementary topics should also be a formal part of any case study preparation: the specific preparations for the case study, the development of code of behaviour documents for the research, the inspection of case study suggestions and the conducting of a pilot case study. Code of behaviour documents are a particularly good way of dealing with the overall problems of increasing the consistency of case studies. Then again, success with all five topics is necessary to guarantee that the case study data collection will proceed efficiently (Yin 2003a: 57–58). Yin (2003a: 57–58) concludes that good preparation for data collection starts with the skills of the case study researcher. These skills have rarely been the subject of their own consideration in the past. Nonetheless, some essential skills can be learned or practiced.

4.6.2.2 *Types of case studies*

The literature proposes many different types of case studies – exploratory, descriptive, explanatory, single, multiple (Yin 1994), intrinsic, instrumental and collective (Stake 1995). Jennings, (2001: 178–179) identifies the advantages of case study research as including the data being collected by means of quite a few data sources, comparisons can be made, case studies can be recurring and the findings are grounded in the tourism environment being considered. The disadvantages occur from the lack of impartiality of the researcher, the lack of generalizability of the findings and the lengthy nature of case studies (Jennings 2001: 178–179).

Pizam (1994) recognizes the need to be wary when using case studies, as singular instances can provide ambiguous results. Despite this, there has not been an adequate examination of the case study as a research tool in the tourism literature, apart from work carried out by Hall and Jenkins (1995). This raises questions as regards the methodology in tourism research up until now. Nevertheless, case studies are used widely in tourism research, with shifting degrees of success which depend on the scholarly rigor employed and their initial objective (Beeton 2000: 130).

It has been suggested that case studies are inclined to reflect the bias of a researcher, though bias can arise in the conduct of other research strategies, for instance the design of surveys (Yin 1994). Consequently, while the prospect of bias in any case study must be documented and dealt with, this issue is not restricted to this research type. Stake (1995) insists that the detection of researcher bias, by way of making the reader aware of personal experiences of those involved in the work, offers access to information that the reader may not otherwise acquire, emphasizing that the case study is in a positive sense, complicated, individual and situational. Adelman, Jenkins and Kemmis (1983) mention that case study research puts specific limitations on the researcher, for example confidentiality, discretion and secrecy. In view of that, the results that have been provided anonymously, where sensitive data was supplied, may badly impact on residents within the community. At the same time, such oversimplification of data can eventuate in some misrepresentation. However, if one is cognisant of these many limitations, this can endorse the validity of the results (Beeton 2001a: 20).

4.6.2.3 *Sources of evidence used in case studies*

The sources of evidence most commonly used in doing case studies are listed in **Table 4.5**. Yet, it should be taken into consideration that an entire list of sources can be vast including films, life histories, photographs and videotapes (Marshall and Rossman 1989). A constructive summary of the main sources reflecting on some of their comparative strengths and weaknesses can be seen in **Table 4.5**. It is evident that no single source has an absolute advantage over all the others. In actual fact, the many sources can be extremely harmonizing and a good case study, as a result, will want to use as many sources as possible (Yin 2003a: 85).

Table 4.5   Main Sources of evidence: Strengths and weaknesses

Sources of Evidence	Potential Strengths	Potential Weaknesses
Documentation	▪ Stable – re-examined frequently; ▪ Unassuming – not formed as a result of the case study; ▪ Precise – accurate names, reference and details; ▪ Wide exposure – long span of time; ▪ Exact and quantitative.	▪ Retrievability – can be low; ▪ Prejudiced selectively – unfinished collection; ▪ Biased coverage – replicates unknown bias; ▪ Right to use – purposely blocked; ▪ Accessibility – privacy motivations.
Interviews	▪ Targeted – directly on case study subject matter; ▪ Insightful – gives apparent informal suggestions.	▪ Bias – badly composed questions; ▪ Response bias; ▪ Inaccuracies -- weak recollections; ▪ Reflexivity – interviewee gives what researcher wants to hear.
Observations	▪ Realism – events in real time; ▪ Background – context of event; ▪ Perceptive – interpersonal behaviour and motives.	▪ Time consuming; ▪ Selectivity – bar wide coverage; ▪ Reflexivity – events may ensue in a different way as it is being observed; ▪ Expense – human observers; ▪ Bias – researcher directing events.
Physical Artefacts	▪ Insightful – cultural features and technological procedures.	▪ Selectivity availability.

(Adapted from Yin 2003a: 86)

Film induced tourism is a modern phenomenon, that has not at this stage been sufficiently contextualized within scholastic research. Therefore, taking a case study approach to this research will add to the body of knowledge in this discipline (Beeton 2001a: 19). The actual strengths of taking a case study approach lie in its authentic foundation and the attention to detail that is difficult to identify using tentative research methods (Adelman et al. 1983). To facilitate adequately dealing with the intricacy of this, a combination of theoretical methods has been used in this study, including the use of strategic conversations and on-location survey work. Such a mixed approach **(see 4.7.1)** based within a case study framework is defended by Hall and Jenkins (1995), who appreciate its ability to provide a wealth of detail and instructive power that is impossible within other research methods plus a contextual basis for tourism theory (Beeton 2001a: 19).

4.7   Methodology Strategy

Research methodology is fundamentally a decision-making process. Every decision made will have some bearing on every other decision. The decision to use a particular research design is restricted by the epistemological assumptions and beliefs of the researcher, the nature of the research problem and the prominence of scientific research and theory pertinent to the problem. Practical issues, such as time and economic resources, also play very important roles in the researcher's preference of a methodological strategy. As mentioned earlier, most business-related research studies implement one of the three methodological strategies – case based, experimental or surveys (Brannick 1997: 8)

4.7.1   The mixed methods approach

The notion of mixed methods refers to the mixing of both quantitative and qualitative methodologies in varying ways and degrees. Patton (1990: 195) offers a model that displays the potential ways of mixing methods based on such a dissection of paradigms **(see Figure 4.2)**.

Figure 4.2

Pure and mixed research approaches

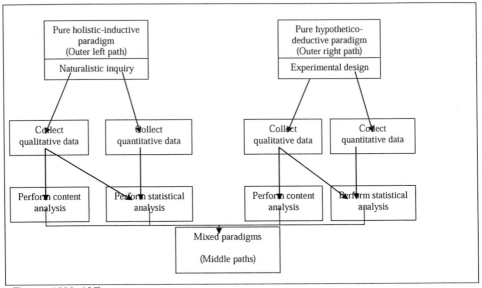

(Patton 1990: 195)

4.7.1.1 *Argument for the mixed method approach*

A mixed method design is helpful to encapsulate the best of both qualitative and quantitative approaches. For instance, a researcher may want to both simplify the findings to a population and develop a comprehensive examination of the meaning of a phenomenon for individuals. On the other hand, researchers may first survey a large quantity of individuals, then resume with a few of them to get their specific language and voices about the phenomenon. In these circumstances, the advantages of gathering both closed-ended quantitative data and open ended qualitative data prove beneficial to best understand a research problem (Creswell 2003: 22).

Morgan (1998: 362) suggests that practically every debate on the rationale for blending qualitative and quantitative methods starts with the acknowledgment that each method has its own particular strengths. It is tempting, therefore, to deem that research studies, which unite the strengths of two or more methods, will yield more than those same methods could offer independently. This prospect is even more attractive when amalgamating qualitative and quantitative methods, since this combination extends the capability to collectively bring separate strengths together in the same research study.

Sieber (1973) claims that studies that include gathering and examining both forms of data in a single study are not as well known as either the quantitative or qualitative strategies are. The thought of mixing different methods in all probability was initiated by Campbell and Fiske (1959). They inspired others to use their multi-method matrix to study multiple approaches to data collection in a research study. This encouraged others to use this approach and was quickly linked with field methods; for example interviews (qualitative) were blended with traditional surveys (quantitative) (Creswell 2003: 15).

Creswell (2003: 14–15) recognizes that all methods have boundaries and felt that biases intrinsic in any single method could counteract the biases of other methods. Consequently, the triangulating of data sources is a means for seeking unity across quantitative and qualitative methods (Jick 1979). From the initial concept of triangulation further reasons materialized for mixing different types of data. For instance, the results from one method can assist in developing or enlightening the other method (Greene et al. 1989).

Alternatively, one method can be nested within another method to afford insight into the different levels or units of analysis (Tashakkori and Teddlie 1998). Tashakkori and Teddlie (2003) suggest that the methods can carry out a bigger transformative function, to modify and encourage marginalized groups (Mertens 2003). These reasons for mixing methods have led researchers to develop measures for mixed method strategies of investigation and to take the many terms found in the literature and form research procedures (Creswell 2003: 14–15).

4.7.1.2 *Argument against the mixed method approach*

Presently, there are two simple reasons why it is difficult to mix qualitative and quantitative methods. The first stresses that blending methods is fundamentally a technological issue. According to some researchers (Brannen 1992; Brewer and Hunter 1989; Bryman 1984, 1988), it may not be straightforward to produce successful groupings of qualitative and quantitative methods, it is in essence a practical challenge that methodologists should instantly be able to sort out. As verification for the variability of research designs that use both qualitative and quantitative information, researchers in this practice mention a chain of studies that have done so (Morgan 1998: 363).

Morgan (1998: 363) states that the second argument contends that the fundamental obstruction in mixing comes from clashes between the various paradigms. According to some researchers (Creswell 1994; Guba and Lincoln 1994; Smith and Heshusius 1986), most applications of qualitative and quantitative methods rely on many diverse hypotheses about the nature of information and the suitable means of creating it; therefore the types of data that they manufacture are often inadequate. Researchers in this practice argue that most studies that declare to have pooled qualitative and quantitative research have normally ignored paradigm anxieties and as a result have not dealt with the bigger issues.

Integrating these two explanations necessitates vigilant consideration of the distinction between selecting methods and working within a paradigm. Above all, it is imperative to recognize that much debate of paradigm issues is not about the practicality of creating research designs that join qualitative and quantitative methods. Certainly, even an informal appraisal of those who support functioning within a solitary paradigm (Creswell 1994; Gilboe-Ford, Campbell and Berman 1995; Smith and Heshusius 1986) demonstrates that researchers willingly recognize the prospect of combining qualitative and quantitative methods. Their real apprehension lies with any failure to appreciate the larger disparities between qualitative and quantitative approaches to research that goes further than technical questions about how to use different methods in the same study. Equally, those who are mainly concerned with the technical features of combining various methods have also concluded that this can be done without infringing upon the fundamental paradigmatic hypotheses (see Reinhardt and Rallis 1994; Riggin 1997) (Morgan 1998: 363).

Morgan (1998: 363) maintains that the contemporary approach accepts the significance of paradigms, since there is much to be acquired from recognizing the profound epistemological disparities between qualitative and quantitative approaches in the search for information. Combining paradigms is certainly a hazardous business, however, this should not be confused with mixing methods with clear-headed consideration of paradigms. If a specific paradigmatic stance supplies the framework for a study, then choosing a fitting method or amalgamation of methods does very much become a practical task.

4.7.1.3 Mixed method groupings
Mixed methods are a form of triangulation, chiefly methodological triangulation. Sieber (1973) remarks that mixed methods can assist with data collection, data analysis and research design. Miles and Huberman (1994: 41) suggest that the questions researchers should centre on when taking into consideration the linking of methods, are: Should it be done? How will it be done? and For what reason?. Three types of mixed methods are recommended by Creswell (1994).

124

- In the first type, Creswell (1994) proposes a two stage research process of data collection using quantitative and qualitative methods detached from each other. The amalgamation of mixed methods happens at the analysis stage and is done again in the findings and discussion of the written research report.
- Jennings (2001: 135) suggests that the second type is planned using an assertive paradigm with the integration of another paradigm such as a positivist-based research study which includes the use of open ended questions to obtain a better insight of the phenomenon being examined.
- The third type described by Patton (1990) is a research study comparable to the first type in which both quantitative and qualitative methodologies are incorporated during all phases of the research study.

Nonetheless, Guba and Lincoln (1988) dispute that the internal reliability and justification behind each paradigm softens, against the methodological mixing of different inquiry modes and data collection strategies (Patton 1990: 193). How can a paradigm be at once deductive and inductive or hypothesis focus and open to emergent data? (Patton 1990). Trow (1970: 149 in Patton 1990: 196) proposes that the researcher should solve their problems with the widest collection of theoretical and methodological tools that they possess. This does not rule out discussion concerning the relative usefulness of different methods for the research of specific types of problems (Jennings 2001: 135).

Greene et al. (1989) advocate that the embracing of mixed methods in a research study should be based on contemplation of the distinctions between methods and the rationale for using each, the central point of the study, the key paradigm informing the study, and the research process itself. Punch (1998) defends this with a similar view, which claims that there is an array of mixes depending on whether the qualitative and quantitative methodologies will have the same weight and *if they will be used in a sequential manner.* Bryman (1988 and 1992 in Punch 1998: 247) for instance, upholds the notion of a range of mixes by highlighting eleven combinations outside of those suggested by Miles and Huberman (1994) and Creswell (1994) (Jennings 2001: 135–136).

Six main mixed strategies can be prepared around whether the data is gathered sequentially (explanatory and exploratory), concurrently (triangulation and nested) or with a transformative lens (sequential or concurrent). Each model has strengths and weaknesses, though the sequential approach is the easiest to apply (Creswell 2003: 225).

As the sequential explanatory strategy is the most uncomplicated of the six major mixed approaches, it is the one which is selected from this study. It is characterized by the collection and analysis of quantitative data and then the collection and analysis of qualitative data. Usually the priority is given to the quantitative data and the two methods are incorporated during the analysis phase of the study. As a result, this strategy may have a precise theoretical perspective. The rationale of the sequential explanatory design normally is to employ qualitative results to help in explaining and interpreting the findings of a primarily quantitative study (Morse 1991). In this case, the qualitative data collection that follows can be applied to investigate any unanticipated results in more detail. The clear-cut nature of this design is one of its main strengths. It is easy to put into practice because steps fall into clear separate stages. Additionally, this design makes it easy to explain and to report. The central weakness of this design is the length of time involved in its data collection due to the two separate phases. This is very much a disadvantage, if the two phases are given the same priority (Creswell 2003: 215). However, this study utilizes a blend of qualitative (strategic conversations) and quantitative approaches (tourist survey). This will permit the researcher to gain better insights into this tourism phenomenon, by extracting features from both methodologies. According to Dibb, Simkin, Pride and Ferrell (2001: 169) quantitative research is expected to produce data that can be statistically scrutinized and whose results can be articulated numerically. As qualitative research is more probing, it looks for a deeper understanding and deals with information too complex or costly to quantify. It can also add value, typically brought to light during interviews or discussion groups.

Creswell (2003: 32) indicates that in a mixed methods study design, the researcher employs either a qualitative or a quantitative approach to the research depending on the type of mixed methods design being implemented. In a sequential design, the literature is submitted in each phase, in a coherent way with the type of design being used. For instance, if a study commences with a quantitative phase, subsequently the researcher is likely to include a substantial literature review that helps determine a rationale for the research question or hypothesis. Eventually, the approach to literature in a mixed method study will depend on the type of strategy and the relative credence given to the qualitative and quantitative research in the study (Creswell 2003: 32).

By considering the framework for research completion in greater detail **(see Table 1.2)**, it is determined that the researcher is in a viable position to make an informed decision on the research objectives. To satisfy the research objectives, the research screens all the available sources of data to facilitate a review of the current perspective on the research discipline. The function of the various data collection techniques is to produce dependable verification that is relevant to the

126

research question being asked (Selltiz et al. 1976: 161). The choice of data collection methods (primary or secondary) is a decisive point in the research process.

This sequential mixed method approach was adapted for this research study **(see Figure 4.3)**. This allows the shortcomings of each method to be balanced by the opposing of the others (Mason 1996). The mixed method approach permits the use of diverse data collection methods within one study, to guarantee that the data is showing what the researcher thinks it is showing. Furthermore, different methods can be used for different purposes in a study. Before embarking on a survey, the researcher may wish to get a feel for the key issues. This would give the researcher the confidence *that they are focusing on the crucial issues (Saunders et al. 2003: 99).*

Figure 4.3

The multi-method approach

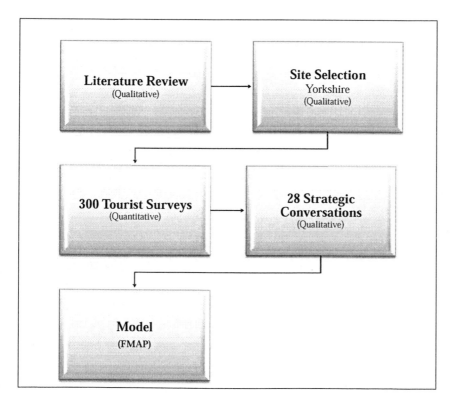

This research study applies both the positivist and the interpretive social science paradigms. The rationale for this is that the survey undertaken will allow the researcher to gain a statistical understanding of the tourist's interpretation of the film induced tourism phenomenon in Yorkshire (positivist paradigm). The strategic conversations with the stakeholders (insiders) involved in the development of Yorkshire as a tourist destination will identify their views in relation to this phenomenon (interpretive social sciences paradigm). As these paradigms use different approaches to research methodology (quantitative vs. qualitative), the data obtained will be richer in detail.

A challenge with multi-methods research is the need for extensive data collection, the time consuming nature of analysing both text and numeric data and the necessity for the researcher to be accustomed with both qualitative and quantitative forms of research (Creswell 2003: 210). The information needs of this study will help to establish the methodology upon which the research will function – that is qualitative, quantitative or mixed method, the type of sampling that will be used, and the design of the pilot study. Many models can be built to develop the research design and executing the research design is directed on two main activities: data collection and data analysis (Jennings 2001: 24).

4.8   Data Collection Approaches

The data collection process for case studies is more complicated than those used in other research strategies. The case study researcher must have a methodological flexibility not automatically required for using other strategies, and must pursue formal procedures to ensure quality control during the data collection process (Yin 2003a, 2003b). Beeton (2000: 129) argues that for a broad-ranging, emotionally complex field such as film induced tourism, there is no one suitable research method. Researchers in the social sciences operate a variety of research methods that can be applied to tourism depending on the type of research questions and the control that the researcher has over events and behaviour. To facilitate developing a comprehensive understanding of the phenomenon, various methods were used in conjunction with each other (Beeton 2000: 129).

Yin (2003a: 7) maintains that the initial and most important condition for distinguishing among the different research strategies is to recognize the type of research question being asked: how, what, when, where? **(see Table 4.6)**. This is possibly the most important step to be taken in a research study, and therefore sufficient time should be allowed for this task. For the case study, this is when a 'how' or 'why' question is being asked about a current set of events over which the researcher has very little control (Yin 2003a: 7).

Table 4.6

Relevant situations for different research strategies

Strategy	Form of Research Question	Requires Control of Behavioural Events	Focuses on Contemporary Events
Experiments	How, why	Yes	Yes
Survey	Who, what, where, how many, how much	No	Yes
Archival analysis	Who, what, where, how many, how much	No	Yes/No
History	How, why?	No	No
Case study	How, why?	No	Yes

(COSMOS Corporation 1983)

The form of the question can provide a vital clue concerning the appropriate research strategy to be used. A number of circumstances may arise where all research might be appropriate, such as with exploratory research, and other situations in which two strategies might be deemed to be equally suitable. Multiple strategies in any study can also be used like a survey within a case study. Numerous strategies are not mutually exclusive, although in some situations a specific strategy that has a distinct advantage should be identified. Therefore, it is worth being vigilant when using a multi-method approach, which can be logically integrated into any research study (Mason 1996: 79–80).

Yin (2003a: 9) claims that the identification of the questions that are most important for a topic and the formulation of these questions involves a lot of preparation. One way is to evaluate the literature on the topic (Cooper 1984). Sometimes novice researchers assume that the purpose of the literature review is to ascertain the answers about what is known on a subject matter. On the contrary, experienced researchers review earlier research to develop sharper and more perceptive questions about the subject matter under review (Yin 2003a: 9). The theoretical approach, the nature of the research question and the methodological strategy all impact the researcher's choice of data collection methods (Brannick 1997: 16). The data collection methods will now be examined in more detail.

4.8.1 Secondary data

Saunders et al. (2003: 489) indicate that 'secondary data is data that is used for a research project that was originally collected for some other purpose'. It is one of the cheapest and easiest means of retrieving information. Malhotra (1999: 113) advocates that the investigation of accessible secondary data is a prerequisite to the gathering of primary data which should only be carried out when the secondary data sources have been exhausted. Cooper and Emory (1995: 241) suggest that secondary data is suitable to use, as it serves a number of purposes: it gives a definite reference on some point to examine from other findings, it can supply information that can add to the current study and it can assist in identifying what further research is needed (Cooper and Emory 1995: 241). Two key reasons exist for assessing the secondary data (Sharp and Howard 1996), the initial investigation assists in creating and refining the research ideas and the second, frequently referred to as the critical review, is part of the research study (Saunders et al. 2003: 43).

4.8.1.1 *The critical review*

A critical review forms the basis on which research is constructed. Its primary function is to assist in developing an insight into appropriate preceding research and the trends that have surfaced. The exact purpose of the literature will depend on the approach used in this case. Such an approach cannot be taken without an in-depth knowledge of the chosen topic. The researcher's own ideas should not overshadow the ideas of the literature. If the analysis is effective, new findings and theories will come into view that no one else has contemplated (Strauss and Corbin 1998). Then again, when writing up the critical review, the findings should be revealed and the theories developed should relate to the work that has gone on before, thus indicating that the researcher is familiar with what was previously known about the research topic (Saunders et al. 2003: 45–46).

Within the framework of reviewing literature, the term critical refers to the researcher's judgement. It consequently merits the practice of presenting a comprehensive and warranted analysis of the intrinsic worth and shortcomings of key literature within the area under review. This indicates that for the review to be critical, judgement needs to be developed. Dees (2000) proposes that the following should be carried out:

- Refer to work by well-known specialists in the selected area;
- Reflect on the work that defends and the work that disagrees with the work under review;
- Formulate rational opinions concerning the value of other work;
- Differentiate initially, between fact and opinion (Saunders et al. 2003: 47).

Saunders et al. (2003: 47) ascertain that whilst preparing the review, the focus should be on the research questions and objectives. One way of facilitating this is to think of the literature review as thrashing out how far the literature goes in answering the research questions. The shortfall in the literature will be dealt with at least to a degree in the rest of the project report. An additional way of focusing is to ask how the review relates to the objectives. If this is not the case, there is a need for a clear focusing of the objectives.

In the critical review, the researcher will need to contrast the various academic ideas, and form views and assumptions based on these. A frequent error with critical literature is that it becomes uncritical listings of preceding research. Either way, the review must show that the researcher has evaluated the items found. The key to writing a critical review is to simultaneously join the diverse ideas uncovered in the literature, to form a rational and consistent case which sets in context and validates the research. Evidently, it should relate to the research questions and objectives. It ought to demonstrate a clear link for these, as well as a clear link to the practical work that will ensue (Jankowicz 2000: 161).

4.8.1.2 *Secondary literature analysis*

There are many objectives to be realized by gathering and analysing the literature. Primarily in this study, the researcher wants to provide a background to the study by putting film induced tourism in context, through investigating its contribution, by understanding destination branding and evaluating the relationship between these two concepts. Secondly, comparisons between the researcher's findings and existing research with regard to identifying similarities and/or differences needed to be made. Lastly, the comprehensive secondary research should help recognize where there is a shortage of information. This will enable the researcher to design and undertake primary research with the intention of closing the information gap. Secondary research will also influence the evolution of the primary research process.

Secondary literature analysis forms the basis of the literature review. The researcher conducted a seven year extensive review of the relevant literature which included academic books, journals, newspapers, online government and industry publications. This thorough review allowed the researcher to gain a comprehensive understanding of the topic and assist in the implementation of the primary research. Initially, secondary data was collected for this study in order to provide in-depth understanding which can be subdivided into two components: academic and industry specific information. This dual focus was necessary to give the study academic integrity, in addition to providing relevance to the tourist industry.

A recording system for secondary data was set up using Microsoft Word. References and notes were recorded which proved useful in maintaining accurate records and finding information quickly. Much of the relevant secondary data has been summarized in **Chapters 2** and **3**. The emergent themes and assorted issues that arose from the literature review which form the basis for both the tourist survey and the strategic conversations are outlined in **Figure 4**.1. Additional secondary data was utilized to substantiate the primary research findings of this research.

The secondary research provides a background to the film induced tourism phenomenon by exploring the linkages between film and tourism. It also assists in the research in making comparisons between this study's findings and that of existing international research with a view to identifying similarities and/or differences. Finally, the in-depth secondary research will help pinpoint, where there was a lack of information. This will allow that gap to be filled by designing and carrying out primary research. It is worth noting that secondary research also effects the progression of each stage of the primary research process.

The academic material focuses on destination branding, destination imagery and film induced tourism, while the industry material concentrates on the tourism trends worldwide and the future development plans proposed for Yorkshire. Preliminary secondary research carried out by the researcher established that the Yorkshire regional tourism organizations, the YTB, have tried to capitalize on film based tourism by producing a number of guides and trails such as the Yorkshire On Screen Film Trail (YTB 2001/2002). Furthermore, mention is made in the guidebooks relating to Yorkshire of its association with the many television series filmed in the county. However, it is unclear how effective such branding has been in terms of its impact on tourist numbers.

It should be taken into account that, while there is a wealth of information available on tourism destination marketing, tourism performance statistics at international and national level, the review of the existing literature in the film induced tourism discipline identified a gap **(see Figure 4.1)** in previous investigations in that there has been little research on the impacts of a film or a television series on a destination. In response, the tourist survey and the strategic conversations undertaken are an initial attempt to fill this gap.

4.8.2 Primary Research

4.8.2.1 Background

According to Jennings (2001: 26), research is an important tool for the tourism industry – locally, regionally, nationally and internationally. It provides information for planning and offers insight into the impacts, motivations, needs, expectations and levels of satisfaction of tourists. It highlights the educational needs of commercial operators and service providers and generates views of the past, present and future (Jennings 2001: 26). Saunders et al. (2003) assert that the choice of research tool employed will be influenced by a number of factors interconnected to the research questions and objectives, in particular the following:

- Characteristics of the respondents from whom you want to collect data;
- Significance of reaching a particular person as a respondent;
- Importance of respondent answers not being tainted;
- Size of sample you require, taking into account the probable response rate;
- Type and number of questions you need to ask to gather your data (Saunders et al. 2003).

McClinchey and Carmichael (2006: 25–26) advocate that merging both unstructured and structured methods to assess the impact of film induced tourism presents a viable way of measuring images by using a selection of question types (Selby and Morgan 1996). Reilly (1990) indicates that free elicitation of descriptive adjectives can be useful with greater ease of data collection, uncomplicated analysis and can also permit the measurement of inter-segment differences. Echtner and Ritchie (1991) ascertain that there is a recent trend in destination branding research to include qualitative analysis (McClinchey and Carmichael 2006: 25–26).

In this study primary data was obtained at regional level. This allowed the researcher to establish industry observations related to the research topic, attempt to substantiate the findings of secondary data, support or dispute the research objectives and finally suggest appropriate recommendations and conclusions in response to the research objectives undertaken. The research was divided into two phases, the first being a survey of the tourist population and the second, strategic conversations with key stakeholders from the local authorities, tourism planners and the RSAs involved in the development of the Yorkshire brand.

4.8.2.2 *Tourist survey*

A survey approach can be used to conduct exploratory, descriptive and analytic investigation. 'Survey research is the systematic gathering of specific information about particular persons or entities' (Brannick 1997: 11). As previously mentioned, surveys and strategic conversations were used as the primary collecting techniques in this study, as this is a balanced way of measuring the impact of film induced tourism. The initial phase of the primary research was a survey conducted through face to face interviews with a sample of tourists to Yorkshire. Cooper and Emory (1995) advocate that to survey is to question the population and document their answers for further examination. The survey itself has three particular objectives which should convert the information required into a set of specific questions that the respondents can answer, encourage the respondent to cooperate in the interview, and reduce response error (Malhotra 1999: 293).

Brannick (1997: 17) considers that a structured survey is a competent data collection instrument when the researcher knows exactly what data is required. It is typically administered to a large sample of respondents (over 50). The aspects of survey design, question content, question phrasing and survey response format necessitate special attention when putting together a structured interview (Brannick 1997: 17). Domegan and Fleming (2003: 272–296) state the general guidelines for survey development in a progression of steps. These steps were used by the researcher to guide the survey design. The two part questionnaire comprised 33 questions and classified the respondents by age, first visit to Yorkshire, gender, length of stay, origin, occupation, party size, travelling party, whether they travelled independently or as part of a package.

Several researchers have evaluated the various data collection strategies (Cannell et al. 1987; Groves and Kahn 1979; Hochstim 1967; Mangione et al. 1982), and creditable analyses of results have been completed by academics such as de Leeuw and van der Zouwen (1988) and Dillman (2000). For most survey studies, the results achieved by personal interview, telephone interview and self administered procedures have been comparable (Fowler 2002: 63). Pizam (1994: 100) claims that surveys have many advantages over other data collection techniques including their relatively low cost, they require virtually no skills to carry out and they can be dispensed to a large number of respondents at the same time. In contrast, surveys have some disadvantages including their lack of control over the research setting (Bailey 1978: 156; Selltiz et al. 1976: 296).

a) Question content

When investigating the content of the questions, the researcher reflected on Proctor's (2005: 193–195) key elements of an effective question:

- *Is* the question required? If the answer provided by a question does not help meet the research objectives, it should to be omitted.

- Does the respondent understand the question? The language of the question is at the level of the respondents being interviewed.

- Does the question extract the required data? Questions which are poorly expressed or too vague to generate detailed information should not be included (Proctor 2005: 193–195).

Brannick (1997: 18) claims that the wording of question can also generate problems, which should be considered before designing the survey questions:

- Can the question be misinterpreted (complex phrasing)?
- Is the question twofold (more than one question)?
- Is it a leading question?
- Is it an overloaded question?
- Would a more personalized or less personalized wording of the question yield better results?
- Would the question be better asked in a more direct or indirect form? (Brannick 1997: 18).

b) Question types

In general survey questions can be classified into two groups; those for which a list of suitable responses (closed questions) is presented to the respondent and those for which responses are not provided (open questions) to the respondents. When open and closed questions have been outlined, a series of open ended questions and structured attribute statements on destination branding, destination imagery and film induced tourism were included in the tourist survey for this research study. The rating scale was a 5-point Likert scale based on the level of agreement with each statement.

- Open ended questions

Due to the conceptual difficulty of destination branding, Echtner and Ritchie (1993) propose a mixture of structured and unstructured methodologies, to calculate the success of the destination brand. They propose open ended surveys to summarize holistic components and more distinguishing features of the destination image. Subsequently, a series of open ended questions and structured attribute statements on destination branding, destination imagery and film induced tourism were included in the surveys.

With open ended questions, the researcher does not restrict the response choices. The respondents are allowed to answer in their own words and the researcher may get answers that were unexpected. By their nature, they may also demonstrate more closely the legitimate views of the respondents. Saunders *et al.* (2003: 293) advise that open ended questions are useful if one is uncertain of the response; for example, in exploratory research when a comprehensive answer is needed or to find out what is utmost in the respondent's minds (Saunders *et al.* 2003: 293). In a personal interview, the respondent reports the answer to the researcher, who then records it on the survey. Domegan and Fleming (2003: 281–282) argue that open ended questions are simple to devise and elicit a broad range of answers from which to draw conclusions. Respondents are less likely to be persuaded towards a response that does not indicate their genuine opinion, as regards the area under discussion. This makes them extremely suitable for exploratory research. The major weakness however, is the interview bias they may represent (Domegan and Fleming 2003: 281–282). An example of an open ended question included in this tourist survey is:

What would you say was the highlight of your visit to Yorkshire?

- *Multiple choice questions*

Fowler (2002: 91) suggests that in spite of the advantages of using open ended questions, closed question (dichotomous, Likert scale, multiple choice) are by and large a more satisfactory way of producing data because:

- The respondents can perform more consistently when answering the question as other substitutes are given.
- The researcher can translate the meaning of answers, when the alternatives are successfully given to the respondents (Schuman and Presser 1981).
- When an open question is posed, many respondents give uncommon answers that are not methodically constructive (Fowler 2002: 91).

Domegan and Fleming (2003: 283) indicate that in multiple choice questions the researcher gives a choice of answers and respondents are asked to pick the answer that most clearly expresses their opinion. They rise above many of the disadvantages linked with open ended questions stated earlier, such as interviewer bias. Multiple choice questions are usually easier for both the

136

researcher and the respondent as they guarantee greater ease of data recording and tabulation, thus eradicating researcher bias and control of subjectivity. Nevertheless, there are limitations to the multiple choice question format. Firstly, designing good multiple choice questions necessitates time and effort. Exploratory research may be compulsory to ensure that all potential answers are built-in. An additional problem with multiple choice questions is the respondent's inclination to opt for an alternative merely because of position bias (Domegan and Fleming 2003: 283).

An example of a multiple choice question included in this tourist survey is:

Was any of the following television series actually filmed in Yorkshire?

All Creatures Great and Small		Heartbeat	
Brookside		Hollyoaks	
Coronation Street		The Royal	
Eastenders		Peak Practice	
Emmerdale		Last Of The Summer Wine	

- Dichotomous questions

Malhotra and Peterson (2006: 298) found that dichotomous questions are primarily used to gather demographic and behavioural information when only two answers logically exist. In addition, dichotomous questions have a lot of the strengths and weakness of multiple choice questions. However, the main weakness of the dichotomous question technique is that the question's wording can have a major effect on the answer given (Malhotra and Peterson 2006: 298). They are the easiest type of question to code and examine (Malhotra and Peterson 2006: 298).

An example of a dichotomous question incorporated into this tourist survey is:

Is this your first time in Yorkshire?

| Yes | | No | |

- Likert style rating scale

Proctor (2005: 178) states that the Likert style rating scale measures attitudes and comprises statements with which the respondent has to agree or disagree, while McDaniel and Gates (1993: 396) describe it as a scale, which permits the response to indicate a level of agreement or disagreement with statements that articulate a favourable or unfavourable attitude toward the topic under consideration. The Likert style rating scale has many advantages. It is straightforward for the researcher to create and dispense and it is easy for the respondent to comprehend. This is the main reason that this question style was adapted for this research study. As a result, it is suitable for electronic interviews or administration via mail, personal (which was used in this study) or telephone methods. The main disadvantage of the Likert style rating scale is that it takes longer to complete than other itemized rating scales as respondents have to read the whole statement rather than a short phrase (Malhotra and Peterson 2006: 265).

An example of a Likert style rating scale question integrated into this tourist survey is:

How important was the television association of Yorkshire a factor in your decision to visit the area?

Very important		Important		Neither important or unimportant		Unimportant		Very unimportant	

c) Aim of the survey questions

A descriptive survey was chosen to investigate tourist attitudes towards film induced tourism in Yorkshire. In planning the survey, the research questions and target tourist population were both considered. For the most part, the items used in the survey were derived from previous studies (Akama and Kieti 2003; Hu and Ritchie 1993). Fowler (2002: 105) asserts that a perquisite to conceiving a good quality survey instrument is settling on what is to be measured. This may seem straightforward and patently obvious but it is a step that is regularly ignored to the detriment of results (Fowler 2002: 105). The aim of this survey was to ascertain from the general tourist population, the extent to which television series and the image they portrayed of the area had influenced the tourist's pre-visit perception of Yorkshire. It also investigated the extent to which their 'formed image of the area' lived up to expectation. Finally, it explored what key aspects of each television series had stayed in people's minds. This latter question hoped to identify to what extent Yorkshire as portrayed on television (culture, scenery and way of life) had stayed in the tourists' minds.

Questions were structured so as to achieve the main objective of this research study which is *to develop a model to be used as a best practice framework for the successful integration of film induced tourism in a destination marketing strategy.* The ensuing questions (emergent issues) were designed to meet **Research Objective 1** – the tourist survey: to identify the film induced images that tourists presently have of Yorkshire.

- The level of imagery that Yorkshire has in the mind of the tourist

The aim of this question was to identify if the respondents had any image of Yorkshire before they arrived at their destination and more specifically, if the image that they had was related in any way to a television series filmed in the county. The tourists were simply asked if they had an image of Yorkshire before they arrived and what that image consisted of. This was an open ended question and it identified if branding based on the television series was strong, i.e. if the images associated with television series would be mentioned.

- The awareness of the Yorkshire based television series

This question aimed to identify whether or not the respondent's image of the destination prior to arrival corresponded to what they found on arrival at their destination. This would evaluate how effective the marketing and branding of the county had been. This question also sought to measure the influence of television and its aim was to identify if the respondents associated any of the previously mentioned television series with Yorkshire. A number of further questions were more direct in their exploration of the effects of film induced tourism.

This question outlined in this section tried to establish what imagery if any the respondents associated with the television series which are based in Yorkshire. The second question explored how effective the direct marketing of the television brand had been, by asking respondents directly if they had received any information regarding the association of the county with film and television. The final question exploring this theme was included towards the end of the survey and sought to ascertain the extent to which tourists were actually aware that certain television series were filmed in Yorkshire.

- Images tourists associate with key Yorkshire based television series

The aim of this question was to identify the images associated with the highlighted Yorkshire based series. This was an open ended question where respondents were asked to comment on the imagery that the following Yorkshire based television series portrayed: *All Creatures Great and Small, Emmerdale, Heartbeat, The Royal* (2003 to present) and *Last of The Summer Wine.*

- Recognition of the television associated marketing brands used by the YTB

The main aim of this question was to ascertain whether any of the tourism information that respondents had received mentioned the county's association with film and/or television. The respondents were asked to state which newspapers, tourism information magazines, tourist brochures or television advertisements they had seen before their arrival and if this tourism information had mentioned Yorkshire's many television locations.

- The key success factors of Yorkshire tourism product

This question was included to establish the highlights of respondents' visit to Yorkshire. It was included to again evaluate the extent to which television series/locations had influenced respondents' visit to Yorkshire.

d) Pilot study

Yin (2003) believes that the ultimate preparation for data collection is performing of a pilot study which allows the researcher to refine their data collection plans with regards to both the content and the procedures to be followed (Yin 2003). A pilot survey is simply a trial run, carried out to test the survey, the response of prospective respondents and the process for carrying out the actual survey (Jennings 2001). Jennings (2001: 152) states that pilot studies are part of both qualitative and quantitative research. In both types of research, tools for collecting data are developed (Jennings 2001: 152).

Prior to going into the field to collect the data, the researcher must ensure that these tools work. The pilot study allows the researcher to test the categories of questions, if data will be worthy and dependable, the terms are logically comprehensible, the question order flows and the length the tool takes as well as the appropriateness of the measures for examination. If the researcher has developed a survey, subsequently this has to be tested to make sure that the questions are fittingly framed to obtain the required data (Jennings 2001: 253). As soon as a survey instrument has been designed and the researcher feels it is nearly ready to be used, a field pre-test (pilot study) of the instrument and procedures should be carried out. The rationale of such pre-tests is to discover how the data collection code of behaviour and the survey instruments work in the real environment (Fowler 2002: 112).

The survey instrument used in this study was pilot-tested on academic colleagues in Dublin Institute of Technology. It was electronically distributed, accompanied by a cover letter which indicated that they were part of a pilot test and it also set a return date for the surveys. After the surveys were returned, a meeting was set up with some of the academics to discuss the results of the pilot test. Comprehensive probing of the questions, including phrases and words were executed. This proved to be a useful exercise as certain defects were highlighted. A number of questions were deleted due to their lack of relevance to the overall research objectives. It was also felt that the survey was too long and so it was shortened with the aim of curtailing any potential frustration for the respondents. Some ambiguities and drawbacks were also found and based on recommended adjustments a final survey was created **(see Appendix 1)**. The data from the pilot test was then entered into SPSS to test the coding of the data.

e) Define the sample

The sampling design process encompasses five steps, which are shown sequentially in **Figure 4.4**. Each step is directly connected to all aspects of the marketing research project, from problem definition to representations of the result (Malhotra and Peterson 2006: 325).

Figure 4.4

The Sampling design process

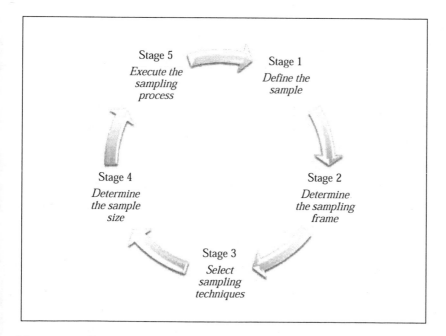

(Malhotra and Peterson 2006: 325)

A sample is a portion of elements taken from the population (Black and Champion 1976: 265) and is considered to be representative of that population **(Kerlinger 1973: 118 cited in Pizam 1994: 101)**

Saunders et al. (2003: 151) maintain that for some research questions it is possible to study an entire population (or complete a census) if it is of a controllable size. 'The population is the total group of people from whom information is needed' (McDaniel and Gates 1993: 457). In spite of this, it should not be assumed that a census survey would essentially offer more constructive results than a well-planned sample survey. Sampling provides a legitimate substitute to a census when it would be unfeasible for the whole population to be assessed. Financial and time restrictions can prevent the entire population from being surveyed or also when the results are swiftly required (Saunders et al. 2003: 151). There are four main advantages of using samples rather than populations (Pelegrino 1979: 74).

- It is less costly.
- It allows speedier processing of information and presentation of results.
- It can obtain more data per euro from one single investigation.
- It enables precision, which may be specified beforehand and calculated from the sample itself (Pizam 1994: 101).

A sample is at all times seen as a general calculation of the whole population rather than as a whole in itself (Pelegrino 1979: 74). Sarantakos (1998: 139) defines a sample as a selection of subjects or units from the overall population. When outlining a sampling plan, three decisions should be taken, which the researcher contemplated preceding undertaking this tourist survey: Who is to be surveyed, how many people should be surveyed and how should respondents be chosen? (Proctor 2005: 107–108). There are two sub populations of interest to this particular research *study: tourists* to Yorkshire and the tourism and film stakeholders involved in developing the Yorkshire brand. The researcher was interested in surveying tourists to Yorkshire and to verify the film induced images that they presently have of the county. Ideally, the researcher would have liked to survey all members of the tourist population, but this was not practical due to their temporary disposition and the multifaceted nature of the industry.

f) Determine the sampling frame

A sampling frame is 'the list that represents all members or units of a study population' (Neuman 2000a: 201). It may be a database or a list of names or telephone numbers. The frame classifies the sampling unit applied in the design of the sample. Fowler (2002: 12) believes that the initial step in appraising the quality of the sample is to identify the sample frame. Most sampling frames fall into the following generic classes:

- A relatively complete list of individuals in the population to be considered;
- A set of people, who go somewhere or do something that allows them to be sampled;
- Is done in two or more stages, with the first stage concerning sampling something excluding the individuals finally chosen (Fowler 2002: 12).

Tull and Hawkins (1984: 384) describe the idyllic sampling frame in which each element of the population is represented only once. In the case of the target population being tourists to Yorkshire a list is not available. For that reason, the sampling frame used in this study was the annual number of tourists to Yorkshire's Tourist Information Centres[27] (TIC) in 2002. As the survey was of the general tourist population, it was carried out at a number of TICs across Yorkshire.

g) Select sampling techniques

The sampling technique categorizes the way the sample is to be selected. This might be probability or non-probability based sampling. Probability sampling is a controlled procedure that each population element is given a known non-zero chance of selection (Churchill 1987: 299). Probability samples can be subdivided into four specified techniques: cluster sampling, stratified sampling, simple random sampling and systematic sampling (Pizam 1994: 101). Non probability sampling is subjective, thus it is not as reliable as it permits human judgement in the selection of those to be included in the study (Cooper and Emory 1995: 202). Non probability samples have no basis for establishing how closely the sample characterizes the features of the population from which the sample was taken (Black and Champion 1976: 267). Non probability samples can be broken down into three key techniques: convenience sampling, judgemental sampling and quota sampling (Pizam 1994: 102).

The sampling techniques selected for researching the tourists to Yorkshire was a probability based stratified random sample, which is one of the most popular forms of probability sample (Kerlinger 1973: 118). This is essentially a sampling method in which each probable person; establishment or

27 The TICs provide the public with information on the tourist facilities and services in Yorkshire.

house for instance has the same chance of being selected as every other individual case (Cannon 1994: 132). In this sampling type, the population is separated into sub groups and a sample is taken from each one (Aaker et al. 2004: 414). In this research, the sample was grouped and stratified to guarantee depiction of all tourist types. Such grouping means that the target population is first separated into mutually exclusive sub populations (Malhotra and Birks 2003: 370). The form of grouping employed for this research is area sampling, a common form of grouping in which geographical location characterizes the groups. The researcher conducted 300 tourist surveys at the TICs in Aysgarth Falls (representing *All Creatures Great and Small*), Holmfirth (representing *Last of the Summer Wine*), Whitby (representing *Heartbeat)* and York (regional capital) **(see Table 4.7)**.

A stratified sample happens when a sample is specifically planned so that exact known characteristics in the population under survey are represented in particular segments (Chrisnall 2001: 69). A stratified random sample was used to produce a true representation, thus minimizing sampling error. The steps in stratified sampling include:

- Separating the population into a number of subgroups;
- Developing a sampling frame for each subgroup (Churchill 1987: 317);
- Building a sample from each subgroup;
- Reconciling the individual samples onto one list (Jennings 2001: 143).

h) Determine the sample size

Proctor (2003: 127) insists that the *'size of sample affects the quality of the research data and it is not simply a question of applying some arbitrary percentage to a specific population. The sample size that needs to be taken should reflect the basic characteristics of the population, the type of information required and the costs entailed' (Proctor 2003: 127).*

Sarantakos (1998) claims that with qualitative research, it is the quality not the quantity of the data that decides the sample size. Qualitative methodologies as a rule concentrate on smaller sample sizes given that the intent is to collect in-depth information (Sarantakos 1998). Malhotra (1999: 332) advises that a sample size of at least 200 is sufficient for problem solving research, while Adam and Healy (2000: 71) encourage that on average more than a 100 legitimate surveys should be examined and any more than this will significantly reinforce the statistical analysis applied to the information. Saunders et al. (2003: 155–156) claim that in permitting a margin of error of 5% in a population of 10 million, a sample of 384 surveys needs to be conducted. This would support that a sample of 300 tourists, which were surveyed for this research is sufficient, to represent a target population of 4.4 million (Annual tourist numbers to Yorkshire's TICs in 2002) (YTB 2003), giving a 95% level of confidence, which is sufficient for the purpose of this study. This sample size was selected to allow for a clear representation of the tourist population and also helped minimize any bias (Saunders et al. 2003: 155–156).

i)   Execute the sampling process

'At this stage of the sampling design process all elements are implemented. The sample is defined, the sampling frame compiled and the sampling units are drawn using the appropriate sampling technique needed to achieve the required sample size' (Malhotra and Peterson 2006: 322-323). As stated earlier, the researcher conducted a stratified sample for the tourist surveys (300) which were conducted in Aysgarth Falls, Holmfirth, Whitby and York **(see Table 4.7)**. This represents the locations of three television series and also York, the regional capital. These locations represented the most popular TICs in the areas, where these television series were filmed **(see Table 4.7)**. The following table outlines the number of surveys completed in each location.

Table 4.7

Tourist survey sample

TIC	No. of surveys (300)	Overall % (100)
Holmfirth	20	7
Aysgarth Falls	40	13
York (De Grey Rooms)	80	27
Whitby	160	53

Aysgarth Falls is located to the North West in the Yorkshire Dales, Holmfirth in the southwest near Huddersfield, Whitby is on the east coast and York is in the centre of Yorkshire **(See Figure 4.5)**.

Figure 4.5

County Map of Yorkshire, UK

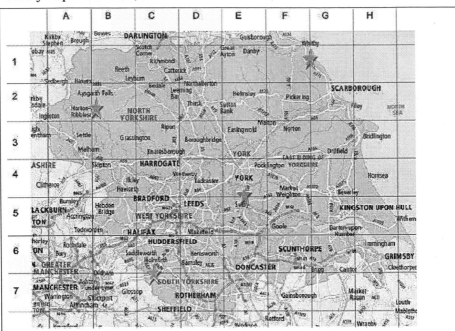

(Ford 2008)

The grid map **(see Figure 4.5)** shows the county of Yorkshire including the regions, principle towns and major roads including the locations surveyed – Aysgarth Falls, Holmfirth, Whitby and York.

4.8.2.3 Strategic conversations

a)   A theoretical perspective

The next stage of the research was to consider the views of the key stakeholders involved in the development of the Yorkshire brand **(See Table 1.2 – Research Objective 2)**. In the course of reviewing the academic literature on qualitative research techniques, it was shown that the mode of interview itself has moved away from a fairly structured format to a more unconventional, semi structured and unstructured procedure (Carson et al. 2001). The in-depth interview has now arrived at a stage where a more truthful and creative role is being played by the interviewer and this has been referred to as a 'strategic conversation' method (Ratcliffe 2002: 23). Ratcliffe (2002: 23) states that the term strategic conversation has been referred to by van der Heijden (1996) as the *'continuing process of dialect that takes place within an organisation as part of a scenario planning*

146

exercise to form a shared mental model of the organisation, its goals and the way in which it sets out to achieve them' (Ratcliffe 2002: 23).

Carson, Gilmore, Perry and Gronhaug (2001: 74) argue that with ability and good fortune, a researcher may be able to get an interviewee involved in a conversation sooner than an interview. The conversation can incorporate the general topic and associated questions, without the interviewee knowing they were actually premeditated. Subsequently, in a good 'conversation', the questions are often dealt with before they have to be directly asked (Carson et al. 2001: 74). The fundamental principle is that a strategic conversation leads to an outcome which is illustrated in **Figure 4.6**.

Figure 4.6

Art of the strategic conversation

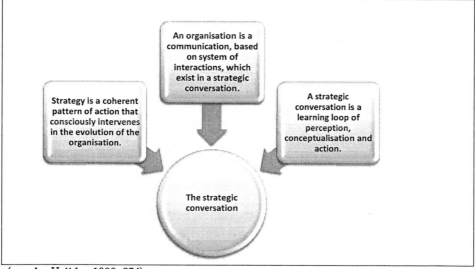

(van der Heijden 1996: 274)

Miles, Munilla and Darroch (2006) state that strategic conversations are multi-directional multi-dimensional communication devices for determining and incorporating the strategic intent of management with both the firm's capabilities and the competitive realities they encounter. For strategic conversations to be successful in strategy making, communications must clearly include both talking and contemplative listening by all participants. Characteristically, they have been used to produce open channels of unfiltered information between managers and ground level employees (see Kochan et al. 2003). They also help the employees to appreciate the strategic intent of management while at the same time facilitating managers to acquire a richer and more truthful understanding of both the possible future the company faces and the ability of the company to align itself with its desired future (Miles et al. 2006).

Strategic conversations have been used to bring into line the perceptions, values and concerns of management (see Chesley and Wenger 1999; Liedtka and Rosenblum 1996), insignificant work has been done on leveraging strategic conversations to better support the aspirations of management and other stakeholders (see Brann and Brann 2003). In actual fact, without employing stakeholders in strategic conversations, management runs the risk of isolating the stakeholders and its own employees, forming an attitude that advocates a limited perspective of the company, its abilities, and potential futures (Miles et al. 2006).

Ratcliffe (2002: 23) highlights many reasons why a researcher may prefer the strategic conversation as the interview tool, namely to

- Understand the models of the decision makers;
- Convey the trend breaking developments;
- Be familiar with new external signals of potential change;
- Extract strategic insights and perceptions;
- Determine the future concerns of key stakeholders;
- Corroborate issues and trends;
- Help in understanding predictability, impact and improbability;
- Detect a variety of perspectives;
- Attempt to reduce any difficulties;
- Establish definite competencies;
- Entrust decision makers to the planning process;
- Identify problematic respondents that might obstruct the process;
- Decide on the strategic agenda (Ratcliffe 2002: 23).

Up to now, the strategic conversation is a very much a practitioner-driven approach. Concerning further research on strategic conversations, there is a clear gap to be closed. A foundation for an evaluation could be to differentiate between content and process and to develop on that basis a method for evaluation. Secondly, strategic conversation often is deemed a tool for large global business. Finally, they can be enhanced if they are amalgamated with other potential methods such as creativity techniques (Miles et al. 2006). In contrast to these cited strengths, Mietzner and Reger (2005) maintain that strategic conversations have many weaknesses including:

- This interviewing technique can be very time-consuming.
- A more qualitative approach needs to put a firm weight on the selection of appropriate interviewees and in reality this is not an easy task to accomplish.
- A profound knowledge and familiarity of the field under examination is crucial.
- Information and data from different sources have to be collected and interpreted which prolongs the strategic conversation even more.
- It may be hard not to concentrate on black and white scenarios or the most likely scenario during the interviewing process (Mietzner and Reger 2005).

Ratcliffe (2002: 23) determined that there is in fact no set process for the performing of strategic conversations or rules regarding participants. However, a few comments can be made in the light of some recent studies (van der Heijden 1996), which the researcher put into practice in conducting the strategic conversations in Yorkshire.

- It is imperative that several strategic conversations are held, as these will determine the strategic vision. For the purpose of this research study, data was collected via 28 strategic conversations with the key stakeholders behind the development of the Yorkshire brand.
- The nature of the strategic conversation obviously changes as the number of interviews carried out increases. Through the tourist survey and the literature review, several themes and issues emerged that needed to be explored further and these were adapted for each individual strategic conversation undertaken.
- Certain potential respondents cannot be ignored when choosing interviewees, either by way of their power or because of the information they can make available. All respondents chosen for this study had extensive and specialist knowledge of the specific matters pertaining to the Yorkshire brand as it was felt that they were the most effective source for obtaining detailed in-depth information.
- It is vital that the researcher is professed as credible, so as to gain the trust of the interviewee. An in-depth knowledge of the subject matter being investigated is vital, as this will allow the researcher to gain respect and also challenge or even explore what the interviewee presents. Telephone calls were made to each interviewee to confirm details and an email was also sent to them with a list of themes to be reviewed during the strategic conversations. The purpose of this was to highlight the aims of the forthcoming strategic conversation, the background to the

research study being undertaken and the future plan for the dissemination of the results. This allowed the participants to prepare themselves for the discussion. The themes and issues **(see Figures 4.1)** identified for discussion, emerged from a combination of the secondary data reviewed and the tourist survey undertaken.

- Perhaps, the most critical feature of the strategic conversation compared with other forms of in-depth interview is the personality and function of the researcher. There has to be communal respect and understanding between the interviewee and the researcher and also an ability for each to communicate with equal appreciation of the other's knowledge and experience (Ratcliffe 2002: 23).

Ratcliffe (2002: 24–25) proposes a few broad guidelines, which the researcher considered when trying to undertake successful strategic conversations.

- The strategic conversation must start by outlining the motive behind the research, the method being used and the way in which the collected data will be disseminated. The issues identified included the extent of the respondent's consultation with tourists and film stakeholders, the strength of the Yorkshire brand, future marketing strategies, the impact of film induced tourism on the county and its linkages with destination branding.
- They should be performed with a wide line of inquiry, intended to endorse a free flow of conversation. The conversations in this research followed this structure, a loose but semi structured approach based on questions of a general nature derived from a review of the literature and the tourist survey. The issue of brand monitoring was explored, as it is unclear if this has been carried out in Yorkshire to date. Also more detailed qualitative research explored the extent to which tourism related branding and imagery reflected the wider image which the county wishes to portray in its ATPs.
- Strategic conversations are best conducted in an environment familiar to the interviewee. They should also be carried out at a time suitable for the interviewee. The strategic conversations were carried out at a suitable time and venue instigated by the interviewee.
- The suggested time for a strategic conversation is typically set at an hour but in reality, most surpass this. The researcher made the interviewee aware of the time commitment required and scheduled a time suitable for both the interviewer and the interviewee. The conversations took between 1-2 hours to complete. Telephone interviews were arranged with those individuals where a face-to-face meeting was not possible.
- It is essential to stress the classified nature of the interview. This was highlighted prior to the commencement of the interview.

- The examination of the conversations can be a very lengthy process. It is normal to set aside quite a few hours to evaluate each interview. Interviewee responses were documented in written and oral form which were electronically resent to the interviewee for further editing and clarification. This was a lengthy process, taking a number of hours to complete each individual interview.

- The best way of starting a strategic conversation is to present a brief set of questions such as: *How did you arrive in your present position?* An appropriate way of closing a strategic conversation may comprise a question like What might you have done differently? (Ratcliffe 2002: 24–25). As the conversations were conducted with a number of experts behind the Yorkshire brand, comparison of responses revealed a variety of different interpretations of the issues and so it was concluded that the interview format did not lead to any biases.

Ratcliffe (2002: 30) proposes that the unusual nature of strategic conversations does not mean that the scrutiny is any less thorough than the conventional interview findings. In contrast, the results from strategic conversations necessitate a regimented approach towards both process and substance (Ratcliffe 2002: 30). Additionally, strategic conversations can look into the hows and whys plus the whats of experience (van der Heijden 1996). In this study, the strategic conversations enabled the researcher to explore the emergent themes and issues mentioned previously.

Non probability judgemental sampling or purposive sampling was selected to explore the tourism and film stakeholders. This requires the researcher to make a decision about who will be incorporated into the study (Jennings 2001: 139). Judgemental sampling is a sampling procedure in which the representativeness of the sample is based on an evaluation by the researcher or some other expert (Cox 1979: 369). In this research study the researcher used expert judgement as to which stakeholder to pick, and chose only those who meet the aims of the study (Kerlinger 1973: 129). Neuman (2000b) calls to mind that judgemental sampling enables the researcher to use their judgement to select cases that will best allow them to answer their research questions and thus facilitate meeting their objectives. This form of sample is often used when using small samples like with case study research (Saunders et al. 2003: 175) which is also supported by Aaker et al. (2004: 388). The next stage of the research was to consider the views of the key stakeholders involved in the development of the Yorkshire brand.

b)   The Yorkshire based strategic conversations

Since research on destination branding for regional tourism locations has been in short supply, an exploratory research design was implemented to explore the changes and opportunities in designing a consistent branding strategy for up-and-coming regional destinations.   The issue of brand monitoring was explored, as it is unclear if this has been carried out in Yorkshire to date. Also, more detailed qualitative research explored the extent to which tourism related branding and imagery reflected the wider image, which the county wishes to portray in its Area Tourism Partnerships[28] (ATP). These strategic conversations enabled the researcher to explore the emergent issues which were outlined earlier in **Figure 4.1**. It was also helpful that the researcher is not from or living in Yorkshire, therefore possible interviewer bias was minimized.

Strategic conversations were deemed appropriate as they provided the opportunity to strike a rapport with interviewees so as to obtain relevant information. They were undertaken to extract ideas, obtain insights and generate discussion around a number of issues that emerged from the preliminary phase of the primary research, which were integrated into the strategic conversations. Issues arose from the original research questions thus particular questions arose that needed to be answered. These issues had to be customized for the different interviewees since each stakeholder, depending on their knowledge and experience of the several areas under review, could tackle specific issues better.

Data collection via strategic conversations with the key stakeholders behind the Yorkshire brand was undertaken in July 2006 **(see Table 4.8)**. All of the respondents had extensive and specialist knowledge of the specific matters pertaining to the Yorkshire brand and thus, they were the most effective method of obtaining detailed in-depth information.   The 28 stakeholders were chosen based on their current positions to facilitate representing the views of the film and tourism industry in Yorkshire.   While this method is subjective, the researcher picked the most well-informed tourism and film stakeholders that represent an industry based perspective **(see Table 4.8)**. Issues for discussion materialized from the original research questions in addition to those which emerged from the design of the survey data, resulting in particular questions arising that needed to be answered. These issues had to be customized for the different interviewees, since each stakeholder, depending on their knowledge and experience of the several areas under review, could tackle specific issues more fittingly.

---

28 The ATP is a regional tourism partnership, which is in place in each of Yorkshire's tourism regions and it comprises of representatives from the public and private sectors, as well from Yorkshire Forward, Yorkshire Culture and the YTB.

Table 4.8

Strategic conversations with Tourism and film stakeholders interviewed

Stakeholder	Name	Position	Organization's role
VisitBritain	Ms Claire Hancer	England Sales and Marketing Manager	VisitBritain, the national tourism agency, promotes the UK internationally in 36 markets and England in the UK, France, Germany, Ireland and the Netherlands (VisitBritain 2008).
	Mr Michael Clewley	Film and Media Consultant	
	Ms Seren Welch	Head of International Brands	
	Mr Vineet Lal	England Brand Manager	
Yorkshire Forward	Ms Alison Barker	Tourism and Culture Manager	Yorkshire Forward is the Regional Development Agency, charged with improving the Yorkshire and Humber economy (Yorkshire Forward 2008).
Yorkshire Tourist Board (YTB)	Ms Amanda Smyth	Marketing Campaigns Manager	The YTB is the official tourism agency responsible for representing and helping to generate sustainable tourism for the Yorkshire tourism economy, while representing the whole of the Yorkshire and northern Lincolnshire's tourism industry (YTB 2008).
	Ms Lesley Wragge	Press Officer	
National Park Authority (NPA)	Mr Andy Guffogg	Head of Sustainable Tourism, Peak District	The North York Moors National Park (NYMNP) /National Parks are run by the NPA, who have twin purposes of preserving and enhancing the UK's natural beauty while promoting their enjoyment to the public (National Park 2008).
	Mr Bill Breakell	Transport and Tourism Officer, North Yorkshire Moors	
	Ms Julie Barker	Sustainable Tourism Manager, Yorkshire Dales	
	Ms Catherine Storey	Sustainable Tourism Officer, Yorkshire Dales	
The National Trust	Mr Harvey Edgington	Broadcast and Media Liaison Officer	The National Trust is responsible for conserving and enhancing natural beauty, wildlife, culture and heritage in the UK. The National Trust also promotes opportunities for understanding and enjoyment of the special qualities of the National Parks by the public (The National Trust 2007).
Tourism Information Centre (TIC)	Ms Christine Morton	Manager, York	This TIC provides the public with information on tourist facilities and services in Yorkshire.
	Ms Geraldine Coates	Manager, Aysgarth Falls	
	Ms Sue Rhodes	Manager, Holmfirth	
UK Film Council	Mr David Steele	Head of Research and Statistics Unit	The UK Film Council is the Government backed strategic agency for film in the UK (UK Film Council 2008b).

Stakeholder	Name	Position	Organization's role
Regional Tourism Authority (RTA)	Mr David Shields	Tourism Manager, Hambleton District Council (The Moors and Coast Area Tourism Partnership – ATP)	The Moors and Coast ATP is responsible for the promotion and development of tourism in the Hambleton area.
	Ms Helen Rowe-Marshalls	Senior Tourism Officer, Kirklees Council (West Yorkshire ATP)	The West Yorkshire ATP is responsible for the promotion and development of tourism in the Kirklees area.
	Ms Kay Hyde,	Public Relations Manager, York Tourist Bureau (York ATP)	The York Tourist Bureau is responsible for the promotion and development of tourism in city of York.
	Mr Mark Kibblewhite	Project Development Officer, Tourism and Leisure Services, Scarborough District Council (The Moors and Coast ATP).	The Moors and Coast ATP is responsible for the promotion and development of tourism in Scarborough area.
Northwest Regional Development Agency (NWDA)	Mr Peter Dodd	Marketing Director	The NWDA leads the economic development and regeneration of England's Northwest which includes Yorkshire (NWDA 2008).
Screen Yorkshire	Ms Jacky Dickins	Marketing and Communications Manager	Screen Yorkshire is the regional screen agency[29] (RSA) for filming, broadcasting and digital media industries in the Yorkshire and Humber region and is part of the Regional Screen Agency network which covers the whole of the UK (Screen Yorkshire 2008).
	Ms Kaye Elliott	Production Liaisons Manager	
Screen East	Ms Kerry Inze	Head of Locations and Inward Investment	Screen East is the RSA for the East of England.
Screen South	Ms Jo Nolan	Chief Executive Officer	Screen South is the RSA for the South East of England.
EM-Media	Ms Emily Lapin	Head of Communications	EM-Media is the RSA for England's East Midlands.
Screentourism.com	Mr Martin Evans	Director	Screentourism.com is the first marketing agency in the UK to specialize in the fast-growing sector of film and television tourism (Screentourism.com 2008).
University of Nottingham / UK Film Council	Ms Anita Fernandez-Young	Film Induced Tourism Project Manager	Co-ordinator of the UK Film Council's funded research study into the impacts of film induced tourism in the UK.

---

29 The UK Film Council invests STG£7.5 million a year into regional film activities through the Regional Investment Fund for England (RIFE), which supports the nine Regional Screen Agencies (RSA) providing a variety of resources aimed at developing public access to, and education about, film and the moving image. (UK Film Council 2008a).

4.8.2.4 Fieldwork

As already mentioned, the most appropriate data collection methods for this research included tourist surveys and strategic conversations with the tourism and film stakeholders behind the Yorkshire brand. This combination of methods maximizes the accuracy of the results achieved, with qualitative research providing a deeper understanding of the issues being explored by quantitative research.

a) Tourist survey

Once the pilot study was completed and suggested alterations made, the survey was implemented over a seven day period in July 2003. Only first-time tourists were considered, as previous visitation can influence one's perception of destination (Fakeye and Crompton 1991). It was undertaken during the daytime and included both the weekdays and the weekend.

b) Strategic conversations

Yin (2003b: 114) states that detecting the unit of analysis is a vital part in completing a case study. This characterizes what is to be investigated and over what timeframe. The unit of analysis of this study is the stakeholders who are involved in the development of Yorkshire who are embracing the film tourism concept in recent years. Yin (2003b: 145) indicates that where a small number of case studies are used, the tactic of undertaking separate cases and looking for patterns across them can be used. The researcher used this cross case analyses, i.e. a small number of case studies were reviewed as individual case studies. Then, an amalgamation of them was undertaken to discover what impacts materialized and what lessons can be learned (Yin 2003b: 145).

The Yorkshire case study discussed earlier utilizes a range of research methods that include observation of the tourist, informal discussions (strategic conversations) with the tourism and film stakeholders, a survey of tourists to the county, and other secondary data. Beeton (2001a: 20) recommends that by encompassing such an assortment of methods within the overall case study method, a wealth of information may arise. Within this study there has been a deliberate attempt to remain impartial, however, when using and interpreting formal conversations, personal research bias may be evident. This does not detract from the significance of the findings but rather is a fundamental aspect of case study work (Beeton 2001a: 20).

4.9   Data Analysis

Data analysis in mixed methods research concerns the type of research strategy selected for the procedures (Creswell 2003: 220).   Accordingly, in a proposal, the procedures should be acknowledged within the design.   Nonetheless, analysis occurs both within the quantitative and the qualitative approach and often between the two approaches.   Some of the more popular approaches in this regard have been highlighted by Caracelli and Green (1993), and Tashakkori and Teddlie (1998). A feature of data analysis in mixed methods research is the series of steps which check the validity of both the quantitative data and the precision of the qualitative findings (Tashakkori and Teddlie 1998).   For both qualitative and quantitative data, the strengths that should be employed to check the accuracy of the findings should be stated (Creswell 2003: 221).

The final steps in a tourism research study that should be premeditated before the actual carrying out of the study are the processing and analysing of the data (Pizam 1994: 102).   The data gathered from the qualitative methods was evaluated using Malhotra and Birks' (2003: 207) model, which portrays the four stages in the process of analysing qualitative data **(see Figure 4.7)**.

Figure 4.7

Stages of qualitative data analysis

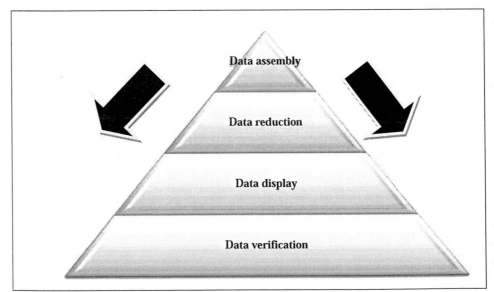

(Malhotra and Birks 2003: 207)

4.9.1 Data assembly

The process begins with data assembly. This includes collecting data from the tourist surveys and the strategic conversations. All of the tourist surveys and the strategic conversations were recorded (either written down or on a dictaphone) with the permission of the interviewees to ensure the precise reporting of the data (Malhotra and Birks 2003: 206–207).

4.9.2 Data reduction

This involves the organization and formation of data. Malhotra and Birks (2003: 208–212) claim that data reduction requires coding. Coding involves breaking down the data into pieces of data and assigning a reference to those pieces (Malhotra and Birks 2003: 208–212). It entails the reduction of the collected data to a form that will allow statistical tabulation, ease of storage and access for future use (Selltiz et al. 1976: 434). The researcher used a documentary style of analysis, which is the assessment of the strategic conversation transcripts, theme by theme, issue by issue and the comparison of the answers to specific questions given by the interviewees.

Documentary analysis starts by abstracting from each document those elements which are considered to be crucial, by mutually grouping these findings or setting those alongside others believed to be related (Blaxter et al. 1996: 190). Saunders et al. (2007: 480) insist that the themes and issues chosen need to partake in a coherent set so that they provide the researcher with a logical analytical framework to pursue their analysis. This process of reduction was completed manually by the researcher, who was mindful of the fact that this is a selective process but was steered by the rationale of the research and the in-depth understanding of the research under investigation (Saunders et al. 2007: 480).

Pizam (1994: 102–103) advocates that data processing can be completed either manually or with the help of a computer. To arrange the data for accurate processing, the researcher should code the data. The process of coding entails the conversion of data into symbolic form by using numbers. Coding is done at the end of the data collection. However, the preparation and development of the coding scheme are done when the research instrument is created. The coding scheme is an outline that depicts what is coded and how it is to be coded. If the processing is to be done by computer, then the researcher should plan and develop not only a coding scheme but also a way of converting the data that allows it to be analysed, stored and retrieved by the computer. As the sample in this research study is 300, the survey results were recorded and analysed using SPSS, a quantitative analysis software programme. The data from the surveys were utilized to inform the development of items for inclusion in the strategic conversations. These items were merged with items generated from the literature (for example, Beeton 2000; Mintel 2003; Mordue 2001; Riley 1994). Subsequent to each strategic conversation, the tape was transcribed. Applicable sections were then extracted and filed under each theme and in turn issue.

The aim of data analysis is to review the complete data in such a way that it generates answers to the research questions. Like data processing, data analysis is performed after the data has been gathered, while the planning for analysis needs to be done in the earlier stages of the study. This planning should state the several forms of tabulation expected and the type of statistical analysis that is to be carried out. Once the data processing and information analysis plans have been finished, the process of planning a tourism research system is concluded. What remains to be done, is the actual collection of data, its processing, analysis, the interpretation and drawing of conclusions (Pizam 1994: 102–103).

4.9.3   Data display

The researcher must engage in the writing process of which several models exist. Murray (1982: 15) indentifies the three stages in the writing process – pre-writing, writing and reviewing. Graves (1984) also utilizes three phases – rehearsal (pre–writing), composing and post-writing (all actions after the first draft is completed).

Macrorie (1980: 297) employs a four phase model – gathering, imitating, reworking and writing. In reality, all are describing the same process, one in which one-off writing is seldom the norm (Jennings 2001: 25). The process entails summarizing and presenting the data in a structured manner (Malhotra and Birks 2003: 212). The data collected from the strategic conversations and the tourist surveys is included in **Chapter 5**.

Brannick (1997: 27) states that the organization of a research report depends on its intended audience. Data displays, focus on details, length and graphics will also be a function of the audience. Despite the fact that report writing needs to be customized to meet the needs of both research purpose and audience, certain basic qualities are fundamental to all written report.

4.9.4   Data verification

This involves the support of qualitative data findings through alternative data findings (Malhotra and Birks 2003: 214–215). Malhotra and Birks, (2003: 214–215) also make clear that this can be accomplished by the use of theory from secondary data and also from similar research findings.

4.10   Research Limitations

During the course of conducting this study, the researcher has noted a number of potential research limitations, which have the possibility to diminish the quality and accuracy of the findings presented in this research study.

- *The academic literature* While there is a plethora of information available on tourism destination marketing, as well as tourism performance statistics at international and national level, the amount of research data available about film induced tourism and related destination branding material is limited.   Subsequently, the researcher diversified into the areas of destination branding and imagery to substantiate the research under consideration.
- *The case study* Yorkshire was selected as the case study area, due to the high numbers of film induced tourists that visit its many film sites. It cannot be assumed that the results from this research could automatically be used to benchmark other such destinations on how to brand themselves based on the film induced tourism concept as each destination has variables to manage such as political and government enforced strategies and plans.
- *Further assumptions* Tourist attitudes and views could be measured through the survey and that the sample represented the attitudes and views of Yorkshire's tourist population. However, interviewees could have provided inaccurate answers out of context, yet all interviewees were expected to give truthful answers.
- *Exploratory research* It should be noted that the research design for this study was exploratory. Such research is conducted on a small and non-representative sample, in this case a stratified random sample (tourist survey) and a judgemental sample (strategic conversations), so the findings should be regarded as tentative and used as building blocks for further research.
- *Survey research* A limit of survey research is the level to which people are able and willing to provide the researcher with data in the context of the survey.
- *Stratified random sampling* As a stratified random sample was chosen over a survey of all tourists to Yorkshire, the research may have suffered from non-response error. The responses of those who were not interviewed may have differed from those who did.
- *Sampling* Blaxter *et al.* (1996: 200) suggest that samples, by their very nature are subject to the potential error of chance variations. The sample size chosen for this research study was sufficient for the purpose of statistical analysis. Yet, using a larger sample may have minimized potential error.
- *Sample size* Given the small size of the tourist survey sample (300) there will be a degree of error in all statistics calculated. As mentioned earlier in this chapter, it is estimated that in a heterogeneous population with a sample size of 300 at a 95% confidence level, there will be

sampling error of 5%. For this reason, the statistics do need to be treated with a degree of caution (Saunders *et al.* 2003: 155–156).

- *Strategic conversations* The key stakeholders were aware of the other participants being interviewed and as a result their responses may have been articulated to reflect this.
- *Judgemental sampling* The judgemental sampling method used in the strategic conversations diminishes the generalizability of findings (Creswell 2003: 148). This research study is not generalizable to all aspects of film induced tourism, even within Yorkshire.
- *Validity* The validity of the research was strengthened by the multi-method approach used and in particular the strategic conversations were strengthened by the findings from the tourist survey.
- *Qualitative findings* As with all qualitative research investigations, the interpretation of the findings is based on the researcher's own knowledge, background and expertise; however, in this mixed methods study the triangulation of quantitative and qualitative findings could reduce subjectivity interpretation (Kunes 1991: 21–22).

To sum up, this chapter has endeavoured to show the sequential steps in conducting a tourism research study. These steps, as stated previously, need to be planned well before their implementation to guarantee consistent, cost effective and legitimate results.

4.11   Final Thoughts on Research Methodology

4.11.1 Survey error

The lack of attention to the important aspects of data collection regularly creates survey data that lacks credibility or does not meet high standards for dependability and consistency (see Bailar and Lanphier 1978; Turner and Martin 1984). How accurate and replicable a research study should be depends on the problem to be tackled and how the data will be used. Reducing error in surveys is commonly done at a cost. In some cases, the best probable measurement is not worth the cost (Fowler 2002: 164).

4.11.2 Future research area

Due to tourism's strong growth in the global economy, the call for related research is essential (Jennings 2001: 414). This would ensure that planning for tourism service provision would be effective and forward directed rather than reactive to past trends.

The enhancement of information technology also influences the conduct of tourism research. Jennings (2001: 414) suggests that Information and Communications Technology (ICT) affords a better research plan and analytical tools for gathering data. ICT provides another medium for accessing research participants via online research technologies and methods of conducting research.

On the whole, tourism research needs to move to the stage of being a discipline in its own right. Ultimately, it should value qualitative as well as quantitative research methodologies in developing this tourism phenomenon even further (Jennings 2001: 414).

Elsworth, Yoon and Bai (1999: 173–174) contend that for tourism research to receive the much needed attention and as a result funding from the public and private sectors, the significant research which is being carried out needs to be published. As supplementary research in other areas is completed, the necessity for existing tourism journals to focus on special types of publications may arise. Academics who contribute to tourism research should review these publications and identify areas of interest with the intention of strengthening the body of literature in tourism research (Elsworth et al. 1999: 173–174).

4.11.3 The mixed methods approach

With the development and recognition of qualitative and quantitative research in the social sciences, mixed methods research using both forms of data collection is growing. New publications promoting mixed methods research exist as channels for discussions about such research. With increasing frequency, such articles are emerging in social science journals in many varied disciplines. Complete books now exist about measures for carrying out mixed methods studies, whereas comparable books were not available a decade ago (Green and Caracelli 1997; Newman and Benz 1998; Reinhardt and Rallis 1994; Tashakkori and Teddlie 1998). These procedures developed from a need to explain the aim of mixing qualitative and quantitative data in a single study. With the addition of multiple methods or multiple forms of analysis, the difficulty of these designs calls for less ambiguous measures. These measures also developed to some extent to assist researchers to create logical designs out of intricate data and analysis methodologies (Creswell 2003: 208).

4.12   Conclusion

Chapter 4 has provided the theoretical background for this study's research objectives (**see Table 1.2**). This chapter has focused on the methodology required to inspect and document the film induced tourism phenomenon. A research plan followed from the extensive literature review and research questions were created to investigate the theoretical findings of the study (Morse 1991). Chapter 4 describes the model within which the study has developed, providing details on the research design chosen and details of the methodology used to carry out the research. It has examined the means by which data was obtained and analysed, to answer the research questions and objectives. Secondary data sources used were outlined and primary survey methods, survey instruments and sampling techniques were detailed. This chapter has also introduced the importance of the case study as a research method.

Chapter 4 has provided an operational definition of the case study and has identified some of the variations in case studies. It has attempted to distinguish the case study from alterative research strategies, indicating the situations in which using a case study may be more suitable than doing a survey, for example, as the strengths and weaknesses of the various strategies may overlap. The chapter also discusses some of the major criticisms of case study research and has suggested that some of these criticisms are misdirected.

In **Chapter 5** the results of this research study will be presented. It will be two-phased with the first (quantitative) results displaying and discussing the role of film induced tourism and destination brand from the tourist perspective. Then, the qualitative based case study results will be presented in terms of themes and issues supported by the literature. The resultant amalgamation of quantitative and qualitative findings will take place. In this discussion, the researcher will highlight the quantitative results and the problems that surfaced in relation to these in **Chapter 5** (Creswell 2003: 223).

CHAPTER 5

SURVEY RESULTS AND DETAILED ANALYSIS OF STRATEGIC CONVERSATIONS WITH TOURISM AND FILM STAKEHOLDERS IN YORKSHIRE

5.1 Introduction

Chapter 5 presents a discussion on the integration of film induced tourism and destination branding in locations such as Yorkshire **(See Table 1.2 – Research Objective 2).** As mentioned earlier, Yorkshire has been the film location for a number of popular English television series and as such is the subject of much location research within the tourism discipline (Mordue 2001). As stated in **Chapter 4**, the sites studied are Aysgarth Falls (*All Creatures Great and Small*), Holmfirth (*Last of the Summer Wine*) Whitby (*Heartbeat*) and York (county capital). The main objective of this research is *to develop a model to be used as a best practice framework for the successful integration of film induced tourism in a destination marketing strategy.* This was initially investigated using a survey of tourists to Yorkshire in 2003.

The review of the existing literature identified a gap in previous investigations; that there has been little research on the impacts of a film or a television series on the branding of a destination. The tourist survey undertaken was an initial attempt to fill this gap. The findings of the tourist survey and the issues which arose from the literature review highlighted a number of implications for the future development of such destinations. To proceed to the next stage of research, the key tourism and film stakeholders behind the Yorkshire brand were interviewed (strategic conversations[30]). The findings from both the tourist survey and the strategic conversations are discussed in this chapter which in turn reflects the expected outcomes in **Table 1.2.**

5.2 Survey Results

The main aim of the survey was to assess the linkages between film induced tourism and destination branding and to identify research issues in relation to these. This was completed by surveying a sample of the general tourist population. The survey undertaken by the researcher and outlined in **Chapter 4** was an initial attempt to fill this gap. The findings of this survey are outlined in this chapter and have a number of implications for the future branding of destinations based on film imagery.

5.2.1 Destination branding: empirical research

5.2.1.1 *Yorkshire and its brand image*

The aim of the question was to identify if the tourists had any image of Yorkshire before they arrived at their destination, and more specifically, if the image that they had was related in any way to a television series filmed in the region. The tourists were simply asked if they had an image of

---

30 Footnotes have been used to reference the strategic conversations in this research study. In some instances, the footnote (number) may appear to be out of sync. This is due to the footnote having been referenced earlier in this chapter.

Yorkshire before they arrived and what that image consisted of. This was an open-ended question and it was envisaged that if branding based on the television series was strong, then images associated with these would be mentioned. The results of this question are outlined in **Table 5.1.** The phrases illustrated in **Table 5.1** and **Table 5.5** originated from film and tourism image research studies such as Beeton 2005; Bolan and Davidson 2005; Busby and Klug 2001; Connell 2005a, 2005b; Croy and Walker 2001; Echtner and Ritchie 1991, 1993; Fakeye and Crompton 1991; Fernandez-Young and Young 2006; Gallarza *et al.* 2002; Hede and O'Mahony 2004; Hudson and Ritchie 2006a, 2006b; Iwashita 1999, 2003, 2006; Jones and Smith 2005; Kim and Richardson 2003; Lam and Ap 2006; Macionis 2004a, 2004b, 2005; Mintel 2003; Mordue 1999, 2001; Morgan and Pritchard 1998, 1999; Morgan, Pritchard and Piggott, 2002, 2003; Morgan, Pritchard and Pride 2002, 2004; Riley and Van Doren 1992a; Riley *et al.* 1998; Riley 1994).

Table 5. 1

Image before Arrival

Image	Yes (%)	No (%)	Total 100%[31]
Rural Countryside (Moors and Dales)	37.8	62.2	100
Old English Way Of Life	19.1	80.9	100
Quaint Villages	16.9	83.1	100
Good Food and Drink	10.6	89.4	100
Similar To The West Country / The Lake District	6.6	93.4	100
Lived In Yorkshire All Of My Life	6.2	93.8	100
Peace And Quiet	5.9	94.1	100
James Herriot Books	5.3	94.7	100
Friendly People	5.3	94.7	100
Good Walking Routes	5.0	95.0	100
Slow Pace Of Life	4.4	95.6	100
Television Portrayed Image	4.1	95.9	100
Nice Coastline	3.8	96.2	100
Emmerdale	3.1	96.9	100
Farming	2.8	97.2	100
Not Very Built Up	2.2	97.8	100
Very Different From Home	1.9	98.1	100
Heartbeat	1.6	98.4	100
Last of the Summer Wine	0.9	99.1	100
All Creatures Great And Small	0.6	99.4	100

(n=300)

The results show that the Yorkshire related television series have had little impact on the actual perceptions of the place or location in the minds of the general tourist population. It is worth noting that general Yorkshire associated factors, such as 'Rural Countryside (Moors and Dales)', 'Old English Way of Life' and 'Quaint Villages' were the images, which rated highly among the sample **(See Table 5.1)**. The 'Rural Countryside (Moors and Dales)' was the main image (37.8%) that

---

31 The results are out of 100% as this question was asked by the researcher; therefore a definite answer was achievable.

tourists associated with Yorkshire prior to their trip. It is worth noting that demographic profile of the survey respondents was considered during this research study. When considering the image of Yorkshire prior to tourist arrival, the older respondents highlighted the traditional images mentioned previously.

It had been envisaged that the region's reputation as a filming location would be a high image recognition factor but the results show that this was not the case, as only 4.1% of the tourists stated that they had any film induced image of Yorkshire. It is worth noting that the literary image tends to be a more influential image recognition factor than film, with 5.3% of tourists mentioning literary images, in this case the *James Herriot* books. If we look at the television series themselves, we can see that they have a very low image recognition factor as only 3.1% of the sample mentioned *Emmerdale* as an image they had before arrival, 1.6% *Heartbeat*, 0.9% *Last of the Summer Wine* and 0.6% *All Creatures Great and Small* **(See Table 5.1)**.

5.2.1.2 *The strength of the Yorkshire brand*

This question identified whether or not the tourists' image of the destination prior to arrival corresponded to what they found on arrival at their destination. It was hoped that this would evaluate how effective the marketing and the branding of the region has been. It is very interesting to note that over half (66%) of tourists stated that Yorkshire was not different in reality to the image and perception they had before arrival, which would indicate that the general image of the region being branded is what the tourists actually experienced. Some 9% stated that it was prettier than they thought it would be, but 7% stated that it was busier and 4% (11% negatively overall) claimed that it was not as quaint. The results of this question are presented in **Figure 5.1**.

Figure 5.1

Yorkshire Different in Reality

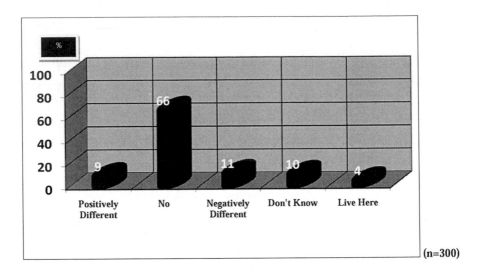

(n=300)

5.2.2 Film induced tourism: Empirical research

A number of questions included in the survey were more direct in their exploration of the effects of film induced tourism. The first question outlined in this section tried to establish what imagery, if any, the tourists associated with the television series, which are based in Yorkshire. The second question explores how effective the direct marketing of the television brand had been by asking tourists directly if they had received any information regarding the association of the region with television and/or film. The final question explored in **5.2.2** was included towards the end of the survey to ascertain the extent to which tourists were actually aware that certain television series were based and filmed in Yorkshire.

5.2.2.1 *Television series imagery*

The aim of this question was to identify the images, if any, which tourists associated with the Yorkshire based series mentioned. This was an open-ended question where tourists were asked to comment on the imagery that the following Yorkshire based series portrayed: *All Creatures Great and Small, Emmerdale, Heartbeat, The Royal* and *Last of the Summer Wine*.

There was only limited opportunity to ascertain the imagery, which the tourists associated with the series highlighted, as they were unaware of the series or did not recollect watching it. Of the tourists, 33% had no image of *All Creatures Great and Small*, 49% of *Emmerdale* and 41% of *Heartbeat*, despite *Heartbeat's* popularity and weekly broadcasts. The majority of the tourists (53%) had no image of *Last of the Summer Wine*, while a substantial 69% had no image of *The Royal*. This is unsurprising as at the time of the survey (2003) it was relatively new to the viewing public. No new research studies have been carried out in Yorkshire since 2003, so the researcher cannot identify if these images have altered.

Tourists who watched the series most frequently outlined a number of images with the series. The images associated with *Emmerdale* and *All Creatures Great and Small* were specific rural Yorkshire based images, with the tourists mentioning them as 'Yorkshire based dramas', 'set in the Yorkshire Dales/Rural Yorkshire' and 'Typical Yorkshire villages'. The images associated with *Last of the Summer Wine* were 'comedy' (13%) and 'the old way of life' (10%) and it is not really seen as having a strongly related Yorkshire image, rather it is its characters, who are most memorable.

5.2.2.2 *Promotional material based on television imagery*

The main aim of this question was to ascertain whether or not any of the tourism information that tourists had received had mentioned the region's association with television. The tourists were asked to highlight which tourism information magazines, newspapers, tourist brochures and media related advertisements, they had seen before their arrival and if this tourism information had mentioned Yorkshire's association with filming.

The tourists had received most of their tourism information from the following sources: Radio (36.9%), TICs (23.7%) and Friends and Relatives Recommendation (21%) **(See Table 5.2).** Other sources identified included Newspaper/Magazine Advert (14.1%), and Signposting (8.1%). Only 5.3% of the tourists stated that television had been a source of information. (It should be noted that it is unclear whether this was television series or television adverts.)

Table 5.2

Information Received Before Arrival

Source	Yes (%)	No (%)	Total 100%3
Radio	36.9	63.1	100
Newspaper/Magazine Article	24.1	75.9	100
Tourism Information Centre	23.7	76.3	100
VFR Recommendation	21	79	100
Newspaper/Magazine Advert	14.1	85.9	100
None	14.1	85.9	100
Signposting	8.1	91.9	100
Live In Yorkshire	6.9	93.1	100
Television	5.3	94.7	100
Previous Visit	3.4	96.6	100
Regional Leaflet At Accommodation	3.4	96.6	100
Guidebook	3.1	96.9	100
Other	2.2	97.8	100

(n=300)

If the results are looked at in more detail, in relation to whether Yorkshire's association with television series was apparent, either before or during their visit, it can be seen from **Figure 5.2** that the majority of the tourists had received no information regarding the region's association with television and/or film. The main source of tourist information regarding television series was books (12%). It is unclear whether this refers to guidebooks or the *James Herriot* books, as it represents books in general. While it may be a reference to guidebooks, it is probably more likely that tourists are aware that the *James Herriot* books have been televised and this is their primary information source **(See Figure 5.2).**

Figure 5.2

Television Series Related Information

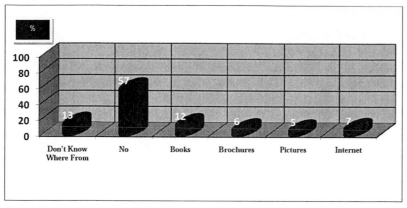

(n=300)

5.2.2.3 *Recognition and Yorkshire based television series*

The final question measured the influence of television on Yorkshire. It aimed to identify if the tourists were aware if any of ten listed television series were filmed in Yorkshire (**See Table 5.3** for the list of television series included).

Table 5.3

Possible Series Filmed in Yorkshire

All Creatures Great and Small		Heartbeat	
Brookside		Hollyoaks	
Coronation Street		Last of the Summer Wine	
Eastenders		The Royal	
Emmerdale		Peak Practice	

The aim of this question was to identify if the tourists associated any of the previously mentioned television series with Yorkshire. It was interesting to see that 69.1% recognized that *All Creatures Great and Small* was filmed in Yorkshire. In relation to the other Yorkshire based series, 64.7% stated that *Heartbeat* was Yorkshire based, 33.8% said *The Royal* was Yorkshire based, 58.8% stated *Emmerdale* was filmed in Yorkshire and 56.9% correctly identified that *Last of the Summer Wine* was filmed in the region (**see Table 5.4**). Of all of these series, *All Creatures Great and Small* is the oldest but still is at the forefront of people's minds. It is also the one of the only series,

171

which has not been filmed for many years, unlike some of the other series which are still in production namely, *Heartbeat*. The level of recognition of *All Creatures Great and Small* may in fact be due to the previously mentioned point, that the *James Herriot* books, on which the television series was based, are still famous and loved worldwide. As these television series have been running for many years and are not set in current times, these responses were generally from the older tourists.

Table 5.4

Television Series Filmed In Yorkshire

Television Series	Yes (%)	No (%)	Total 100%3
All Creatures Great and Small	69.1	30.9	100
Heartbeat	64.7	35.3	100
Emmerdale	58.8	41.3	100
Last of the Summer Wine	56.9	43.1	100
The Royal	33.8	66.3	100
Peak Practice	2.5	97.5	100
Coronation Street	2.2	97.8	100
Hollyoaks	1.3	98.8	100
Eastenders	1.3	98.8	100
Brookside	0.3	99.7	100

(n=300)

5.2.3 Yorkshire's tourism product

5.2.3.1 *The key success factors of Yorkshire tourism product*

A final question was included to highlight the key success factors of Yorkshire tourism product. Once again, it was included to evaluate the extent to which television series/locations had influenced tourists' visits to Yorkshire or had been a highlight. As can be seen from the results outlined in **Table 5.5,** television had a very limited impact as the Yorkshire based television locations were only referred to by 4.7% of tourists **(See Table 5.5).** It is worth considering if 'Beautiful Rural Countryside' (24.1%) and 'Friendly People' (20.9%), which were the highlight of many tourists to Yorkshire, were as a result of the general branding of Yorkshire rather than branding based on a television location. Seeing the *Herriot Country* brand was deemed to be the highlight for 3.1% of tourists, illustrating the strength of literary imagery and the fact that the *James Herriot* books are published worldwide. Their recognition is global and more widespread than the impact of an English language television series.

Table 5.5

Reasons for Visiting Yorkshire

Source	Yes (%)	No (%)	Total 100%3
Beautiful Rural Countryside	24.1	75.9	100
Friendly People	20.9	79.1	100
Visitor Attractions	12.5	87.5	100
Pubs and Restaurants	11.6	88.4	100
Relaxing Atmosphere	9.4	90.6	100
Weather	8.8	91.3	100
VFR	7.5	92.5	100
Not Far From Home	6.3	93.8	100
Walking / Cycling Routes	4.7	95.3	100
Seeing Television Filming Locations	4.7	95.3	100
Beaches	4.7	95.3	100
Peace and Quiet	4.4	95.6	100
Area Quaintness	4.4	95.6	100
Variety Of Scenery	3.4	96.6	100
Value For Money	3.4	96.6	100
Seeing *Herriot Country*	3.1	96.9	100
Clean And Tidy Destination	3.1	96.9	100
Good Kids Facilities	2.8	97.2	100
Lovely Food And Drink	1.6	98.4	100
Getting Away From It All	0.6	99.4	100

(n=300)

Research on the impact of filming and the branding of a destination has been limited to date. While the researcher can corroborate the existence of the branding that exists in Yorkshire, the survey results on the influence of television were limited. This contrasts with the findings of Mordue's (1999, 2001) and Beeton's (2005) research. Then again, the previous existing research focuses more on the residential impacts of filming and not on how successful destinations can be in branding themselves based on this concept. This may be a reason why the empirical research carried out in Yorkshire for the purposes of this research study produced very different results to those which had been outlined in previous research.

5.3   Detailed Analysis of Strategic Conversations

As themes and issues **(see Figure 4.1)** arose from the original research questions, plus the design of the survey data, particular questions emerged that needed to be answered.   These had to be customized for each stakeholder, since each stakeholder depending on their knowledge and experience of the several areas under review, could tackle specific issues more fittingly **(see Table 5.6)**.   **Table 5.6** indicates the level of agreement and disagreement for each issue raised with the stakeholders.

Table 5.6

General summary of results of strategic conversations with tourism and film stakeholders in Yorkshire

Issue	Agree	Disagree	No Comment	Responses
a) Yorkshire's Tourism Industry				
Tourists want to experience the authenticity of the tourism product.	19	3	6	28
Tourism is important to the wider development of the region.	16	0	12	28
b) Branding				
Destinations cannot afford to overlook branding, as it offers a valuable tool with which emotional links can be established with the potential tourist.	12	0	1	13
The challenge for destination marketers is to find the best way to use images and to build the destination brand.	4	2	2	8
A destination brand can be developed in many ways.	7	0	0	7
It takes time and patience to create brand reputations.	8	0	1	9
The brand name must represent your tourism product.	10	2	2	14
Most DMOs have limited budgets.	6	2	0	8
The strength of VisitBritain's brand should be regularly monitored.	6	0	2	8
Yorkshires brand is the 3rd most recognizable tourism brand in England, as per VisitBritain.	5	0	3	8
It is necessary that destinations use successful film induced branding examples to initiate their own strategies.	11	0	3	14
The increasing amounts of visual media exposure may lead to the belief that the images portrayed in film/television play an important role in shaping a destination's image.	4	1	2	7
UK brand should be exclusively based on films and/or television series.	3	2	3	8
Yorkshire's regional brand has been successful to date.	11	0	2	13
The Yorkshire brand should be exclusively based on films and/or television series.	11	14	0	25
The media associated brands associated with Yorkshire are the most effective brands to use.	10	6	4	20

Issue	Agree	Disagree	No Comment	Responses
c) Imagery				
Destination marketers need valid and reliable research to make both imaging and branding decisions.	9	0	2	11
Tourism destinations are one of the most difficult products to promote, involving many stakeholders and a brand image over which a destination has very little control.	9	1	0	10
The strongest tourism motivator is 'the destination brand image'.	16	9	3	28
The image perceived by potential tourists is very important.	11	0	1	12
The promotion of a strong image is the key to successful branding.	23	2	3	28
Destinations need to create their own distinctive image.	13	0	1	14
Visual images play a central role in promoting a destination's image.	18	1	1	20
Films and television series can encourage people to visit destinations.	12	0	2	14
Well-liked images portrayed in films and television series play a fundamental role in determining tourist's expectations of a particular destination.	22	0	3	25
Television commercials can directly influence the tourism image.	21	2	0	23
Some destinations are over-using television and film imagery in their marketing.	13	2	0	15
The images that Yorkshire wants to portray include the rural idyll, small villages and community life, which are depicted in many of the television series filmed in Yorkshire.	11	2	0	13
The UK is presently portraying a strong image.	9	0	2	11
Yorkshire is presently portraying a strong image.	20	3	2	25
Some communities have been able to prevent negative film images of their community.	0	1	2	3
British based television series have been successful in changing the image of the UK.	6	1	1	8
Yorkshire based television series have been successful in changing the image of Yorkshire.	10	9	0	19

Issue	Agree	Disagree	No Comment	Responses
d) Film induced tourism				
People currently read less, so what is shown in films and television is becoming even more important.	23	3	2	28
Film induced tourism can have a long-term effect.	9	1	0	10
Film induced tourism will continue to grow as films / television series are distributed worldwide.	14	3	2	19
Films and television series are recognized as an incentive that can induce people to visit destinations.	14	0	4	18
Film allows destinations to boast their tourism potential.	22	2	4	28
Tourist awareness has been little influenced by films or television series.	5	2	0	7
Research has shown that film induced tourism can benefit the development of a destination.	22	2	3	28
Marketers are increasingly working with film producers to promote their destinations as possible film locations.	15	4	1	20
Film can be an effective tool to help place images and affect the audience's interest in visiting the destination.	8	0	2	10
The emergence of movie maps has been a positive development.	18	4	6	28
There are many drawbacks to film induced tourism.	22	3	3	28
Television series tend to have a greater impact than films due to their prolonged existence.	21	5	2	28
The influence of filming in re-imaging rural areas has proven to be very important.	13	4	6	23
Re-runs of a television series or a further series helps the image remain longer.	15	0	6	21
Displacement (film / television series filmed in one location but set elsewhere) is commonplace.	16	2	2	20
British based television series attract extra tourists to the region.	8	0	0	8
Film induced tourism has impacted Yorkshire.	4	0	2	6
Yorkshire based television series attract extra tourists to the county.	21	0	0	21
An influx of tourists is not always beneficial to Yorkshire.	19	6	3	28

Issue	Agree	Disagree	No Comment	Responses
e) Stakeholder involvement				
Tourism stakeholders should appreciate the local image and the impact that tourism can have on the community.	12	4	5	21
The current Tourism Marketing strategy intends to build on the strength of the Yorkshire Brand.	14	0	3	17
Consultation with the relevant stakeholders occurred for Yorkshire's Tourism Marketing Strategy 2006–2010.	4	0	0	4
The Regional Economic Strategy 2003–2012 has realized the value of Yorkshire being used as both a film and television location.	3	0	2	5
Tourist agencies should be aware of the possible benefits for featuring positive images of a destination in a film or television series.	3	2	2	7
Planning needs to adopt a long-term consideration to the image of film.	19	2	7	28
The tourism and film stakeholders in Yorkshire have linked up with the Yorkshire Tourist Board / VisitBritain in the development of their media related brands.	18	2	5	25
There is a major buy in from the NTOs to its association with a film or a television series.	4	4	2	10
The tourist authorities and the film councils need to work together.	15	5	4	24
Tourism organizations cannot influence how their image is depicted until they financially contribute to filming.	26	1	1	28
It has become evident that some agencies are over-using film and television imagery in their regional promotion.	6	7	4	17
It is crucial that film/television is included into tourism/destination marketing planning.	14	4	4	22

These key results are now examined in detail.

5.3.1 Yorkshire's tourism industry

5.3.1.1 *The authenticity of the destination's tourism product*

Nowadays tourists are looking for an authentic tourism product more than ever before. People's perception of what is 'authentic' can be different depending upon their expectations **(see 3.6.1).**

Through the ages there have been multiple influences on the landscape, culture and heritage buildings. Some people wish to preserve, rather than conserve and this can result in conflict where a tourist wants to see or experience what they perceive to be authenticity, whereas local people might want to take advantage of new technology and fashion. Tourism can also change the face of a destination as it evolves into a tourism attraction, whereas in most instances the local people would prefer to keep it the way it was before the tourists arrived. It can of course alter so dramatically, that its original appeal disappears. Many tourists want to experience the destination in the way they have envisaged it to be, that does not necessarily mean that the product they experience is classed by others as authentic but they may perceive it to be so.[32]

Some of the stakeholders **(See Table 5.6)** mention that tourists want to experience the authenticity of Yorkshire's tourism product[33,34,35] even more so, as the media are bringing more knowledge to the tourists.[36] They want to see something that is real and they also want story based marketing.[37] York is an authentic tourism product due to its historical background[38] while the authenticity of Scarborough's tourism product is very much part of their tourism strategy, as they are trying to move away from an artificial tourism product.[39] An overlap between an authentic and an artificial tourism product may not work, but audiences understand that representations in film and television might only tell part of the story. Film induced tourists can be attracted to an area not only through 'positive' images but also through the characters of the film/television series that makes them want to see where the characters

---

32 Inze, Ms Kerry; Head of Locations and Inward Investment, Screen East (31st July 2006).
33 Coates, Ms Geraldine; Manager, Aysgarth Falls Tourist Information Centre Manager (18th July 2006).
34 Rhodes, Ms Sue; Holmfirth Tourist Information Centre Manager (31st July 2006).
35 Morton, Ms Christine; York Tourist Information Centre Manager (7th August 2006).
36 Barker, Ms Alison; Tourism and Culture Manager, Yorkshire Forward (20th July 2006).
37 Dodd, Mr Peter; Marketing Director, England's North Country (31st July 2006).
38 Hyde, Ms Kay; PR Manager, York Tourist Bureau (20th July 2006).
39 Kibblewhite, Mr Mark; Project Development Officer, Tourism and Leisure Services, Scarborough District Council (8th August 2006).

'live' and where the story is set. Even true life stories can provide a positive image to a film tourist through engagement with the story40 as tourists to Holmfirth want to experience the *Last of the Summer Wine* phenomenon. Yorkshire is trying to present a more modern image than the old traditional one that can be seen currently in its television series *(Heartbeat* and *Last of the Summer Wine)*. A modern image may cause tension in the future progression of the Yorkshire image.[41]

5.3.1.2 *The increased dependence on tourism as an alternative source of income in Yorkshire*

The marketing of tourism destinations is gradually becoming more competitive. Destinations need to take full advantage of their visual identity, for example aligning with relevant film and television assets.[42] VisitBritain has received funding from the Department of Culture, Media and Sport[43] (DCMS) and also raises non-government funding of around €3m annually.[44,45] VisitBritain has a small budget compared to their competitors but they try to counteract this by working in conjunction with the film studios and thereby minimize their costs.[46] The YTB also has a limited budget of €4.6m in comparison to some of their competitors, i.e. Scotland.[47] The successful British film, *The Full Monty* (1997) gave Sheffield worldwide exposure and *Calendar Girls* (2003) gave the impression that Yorkshire was a warm friendly place. Scotland also has a very strong brand at present aligned with a considerable budget to finance its development.[48]

VisitBritain is currently re-launching its website, as it is a very cost-effective marketing tool which will facilitate the fine tuning of its target audience. Another reason for this is that printed material is costly. All of VisitBritain's marketing and press communication represent the brand (corporate logo, direct marketing, exhibition, imagery, online content and print material). Radio, television, the internet and printed literature are the main media sources used by VisitBritain. It also publishes supplements in the national press. The YTB partners VisitBritain through ongoing brand awareness campaigns (national press advertising, public relations and television)[43]

40 Elliott, Ms Kaye; Production Liaisons Manager, Screen Yorkshire (9th August 2006).
41 Rowe-Marshall, Ms Helen; Senior Tourism Officer, Kirklees Metropolitan Council (20th July 2006).
42 Clewley, Mr Michael; Film and Media Consultant, VisitBritain (1st September 2006).
43 The DCMS is responsible for Government policy on the arts, sport, the National Lottery, tourism, libraries, museums, galleries, broadcasting, film, the music industry, press freedom and regulation, licensing, gambling and the historic environment (YTB 2006).
44 Hancer, Ms Claire; England Sales and Marketing Manager, VisitBritain (27th July 2006).
45 Lal, Mr Vineet; England Brand Manager, VisitBritain (2nd August 2006).
46 Welch, Ms Seren; Head of International Brands VisitBritain (27th July 2006).
47 Smyth, Ms Amanda; Marketing Campaigns Manager, Yorkshire Tourist Board (31st July 2006).
48 Wragge, Ms Lesley; Press Officer, Yorkshire Tourist Board (20th July 2006).

VisitBritain has developed both the British and English brands but not the Yorkshire brand as this is the responsibility of the YTB. Yorkshire has many of the brand attributes of the UK and England brands[48] and VisitBritain claims that Yorkshire has been triumphant in its branding and identity creation through its alignment to its core visual appeals and representation of this on screen *(Calendar Girls, Heartbeat)*. This could always be improved if Yorkshire used a more integrated representation of its contemporary, urban culture in its branding as YTB are presently trying to implement.

Both Holmfirth and York TICs claim that tourism's ability to generate repeat business tourism is vital given the decline of Yorkshire's local industries. It also contributes €6.15 billion annually to the local economy.[49] In Scarborough, tourism employees make up 18% of the workforce, while this is only 8% nationally. Tourism has also aided regeneration as it helps diversify agriculture. In the Peak District, tourist spending in pubs and restaurants is important, as 33.3% of all jobs are based in the tourism industry.[50] In 2005, York city alone attracted four million tourists, produced revenue worth €172 million and created 9,561 jobs.[51]

5.3.2 Film Induced tourism and destination branding: The emergent themes and associated issues
5.3.2.1 *Theme: Branding*
a) Issue 1 – The development of a strong brand is vital for future success of a destination
VisitBritain's current domestic brand is to be in place for three years. Its logo is *Real, Fun, Indulgent*. The ATPs will assist with this, as brand and image are key elements but the needs of the locals from a social and economic perspective also need to be considered. The target is to raise their brand position and to increase their competitiveness in the domestic market. The YTB feels the image portrayed and perceived by potential tourists is very important and as a result should be given special attention in destination management planning.[47] This can be achieved through careful research and segmenting the market, matching and tailoring what is on offer to what the target markets desire[49]

VisitBritain46 and Scarborough District Council39 argue that branding cannot be ignored. Once it is established, the brand needs to evolve with the product and Yorkshire is trying to do this through its new ATP. To facilitate the development of a recognized brand, a collective understanding and awareness of the brand by its target audience is required. The huge increase in both television channels

17 Nolan, Ms Jo; CEO, Screen South (5th October 2006).
50 Guffogg, Mr Andy; Head of Sustainable Tourism, Peak District National Park (17th July 2006).
51 Tempest, Mr Ian; Tourism Manager and Secretariat to the Executive, York City Council (21st July 2006).

and the internet means that it is becoming even more difficult to develop brands based on television experiences due to audience diversity, fragmentation and reduction. Subsequently, television induced brands as opposed to film induced brands are likely to become niche products, rather than universally recognized products.

A brand needs to reflect the destination, otherwise it will weaken and return visitation will invariably decline.[52] Tourism professionals want images created by other sectors, such as the film industry, to reflect and support the brand, not weaken it. So as to maximize effectiveness, the strong image of the destination should be aligned to the destination branding from the DMO. They can then make the best out of the free advertising. With films or television this may not always be possible as no one really knows how powerful the production will be until it is transmitted, nor will they know whether the images portrayed therein will reflect the destination brand. Production companies do not consider destination marketing when they make a film or television series as they are looking for locations that reflect a script and the director's perception of how the story line should be portrayed. For that reason, there is the possibility that the images can be powerful, but the destination may not be portrayed in accordance with the destination brand. This is supported by some of the stakeholders **(See Table 5.6)** interviewed.[32,46]

Scarborough District Council states that the Goathland brand is very specific.39 The Yorkshire Dales brand does indeed reflect their tourist product33 and was very successful when the television series *All Creatures Great and Small* was first broadcast53 (see Beeton 2001a, 2005; Mintel 2003; Mordue 1999, 2001; O'Connor and Flanagan 2000; O'Connor *et al.* 2005, 2006; Tooke and Baker 1996). The long-term exposure from television is the main benefit of hosting a show rather than the short-term location fee. For the internationally acclaimed film *Pride and Prejudice* (2003), the National Trust's tourism product was featured on the DVD, film website, movie map and contractually got the film production company, 'Working Title Productions' to provide a costume exhibition. That explains why, wherever the marketing of the film went, so did the Peak District's tourism brand.[50]

---

52 Inze, Ms Kerry; Head of Locations and Inward Investment, Screen East (31st July 2006).
53 Shields, Mr David, Tourism Manager, Hambleton District Council (Herriot Country) (18th July 2006).

The National Trust claims that if the image portrayed in advertising the experience is totally different to the brand image, this will lead to bad publicity through word of mouth. It would appear that Yorkshire as a whole portrays a strong image.[54] This is very much the case in the Scarborough district as two of Yorkshire's most successful television series, *The Royal* and *Heartbeat*, are set there. It is felt by stakeholders **(See Table 5.6)** that a strong image does not matter so much to the domestic market as domestic tourists tend to take shorter breaks.[43] Viewers can become interested in a destination through the story and the characters but the aim of this is to sell the overall Yorkshire experience.[43]

The power of the brand is crucial. National Park amenities, towns and villages are all unique as are their festivals and markets[50] Destinations need to create a unique image and brand to differentiate themselves from their competitors. This will help them compete with their European competitors, who have increased since the emergence of budget airlines and the enlargement of the European Union (EU).43 France and Italy are the UK's main competitors, while VisitBritain forecasts that China will be a much stronger competitor after the 2008 Summer Olympics in Beijing.[48]

The development of a strong image can fill the gaps through assessing the films and then add to that slowly as has happened in the recent British based films; *Elizabeth II* and *Henry VII*. York's image is important but it could be argued that the reality has to at least match and preferably exceed people's expectations once they get there.[51] The Peak District National Park Authority recently completed a brand analysis on the strength of its brand. They found that their image was positive but they need to ensure what is on offer meets the brand promise.[50]

b) Issue 2 – Film induced tourism has very much influenced the strength of the Yorkshire brand
Many academic researchers (Beeton 2001a 2005; Mintel 2003; Mordue 1999 2001; O'Connor 2000; O'Connor *et al.* 2005 2006 and Tooke and Baker 1996) have studied Yorkshire as a film induced tourism destination. Film media is an important way to gain new audiences, such as ethnic minorities and television series are also influential.[55] Screen Yorkshire indicates that such branding can be highly successful. It was also suggested by Screen East[32] that films are free marketing opportunities. They should be considered within a destination marketing strategy with the purpose of strengthening the brand. Screen South[49] feel that it is probably not essential but good partnership marketing can assist regional development. On the other hand, if a destination has as much tourism as its infrastructure can

---

54 Barker, Ms Julie; Sustainable Tourism Manager, Yorkshire Dales National Park (18th July 2006).
55 Edgington, Mr Harvey; Broadcast and Media Liaison Officer, The National Trust (9th August 2006).

cope with, as seen in Goathland, then perhaps it would be unwise to advertise extensively that successful films have been shot in key locations. It can be beneficial to incorporate film and television into tourism destination marketing and planning as seen with the success of the collaboration between *The Lord of the Rings* and TNZ. The YTB could profit from doing this but so far has not been that proactive considering the number of film and television series **(See Table 1.1)** that have put the county on the map.

Currently, film induced tourism is not a strategic priority for the YTB and it has no plans to use it in its future marketing and/or branding campaigns even though this research has shown that the imagery that tourists tend to associate with Yorkshire for example are rural countryside and old country way of life). In relation to YTB's current brand, its objective is very generic ...*to position the Yorkshire brand* as *a destination of choice for priority target markets with respect to key competitors and achieve measurable increases in awareness of key sub-regional destination brands.* This objective is to facilitate the development of a new brand image (fun, hip, modern and vibrant) of Yorkshire for both the business and leisure traveller. As seen earlier, many of these images were created through the media (DVD, film, the internet, and television). The responsibility for delivery of this objective is split between the YTB, RTA, LA and the private sector who use a variety of marketing communications tools to brand the region. These include;

- Business Tourism Liaison Forum;
- Conference & Incentive Yorkshire - the annual regional business tourism publication;
- Familiarisation visits for conference buyers;
- Websites; Conference www.venueyorkshire.com, Group travel www.yorkshire.com and e-newsletter and itineraries www.yorkshire.com/grouptravel;
- Regular news stories and photocalls to showcase Yorkshire as a destination;
- e-newsletter to buyers and conference organisers;
- Target magazines (Conference an Incentive Travel, Meetings and Incentive Travel, Conference News, Meet Britain's annual publication, Corporate Hospitality Monthly, Headquarters, Incentive Travel Corporate Meetings, Group Leisure, Destinations UK, Coach Touring and Coach Monthly);.
- Exhibitions (UK and international trade);
- 'Make Yorkshire Yours' marketing campaign[38, 39, 41, 47, 48, 51, 53, 54, 61, 62.]

Previously, the board used it when it devised the *Yorkshire on Screen Film Trail* (2001/2002), but it was not seen as financially viable for the publication to continue. The use of the film induced tourism phenomenon seems to have been a success in recent times as seen with *Pride and Prejudice* where the agencies such as the Peak District National Park have worked with their RSA, EM-Media, and responded to the demand and produced materials to encourage tourism. This is supported by some of the stakeholders **(See Table 5.6)** interviewed.[50] Ideally, multiplier effects should be considered at the time of shooting of a film or television series. Screen East claims that the moving images tend to strengthen the brand they are trying to portray. This can become even more successful if the tourist board and the local tourism officers work collaboratively with their RSA.

York and Aysgarth TICs argue that the Yorkshire brand should be based on film/television and be part of a wider brand as both of these bring in tourists, whereas VisitBritain suggests that a wider brand tends to deliver more than what is shown on screen.46 The main aim of using films is the free public relations, however there is only a very narrow window from production to release. The integration of film induced branding into the wider brand can be very productive but the success of a production needs to be realized first, otherwise there would be too much risk. Nevertheless, that does not mean to say that preparations should not be made in anticipation of the demand. A brand needs to continually reinvent itself. Screen South and The Peak District National Park advocate that as long as a film or television series has a large popular viewing audience that is likely to visit, the brand can be based around these.[49,50] This can happen if the brand is powerful enough, but it is more productive for it to be part of a wider brand. It would be a mistake to give the media brand a narrow focus as it should be part of a wider brand.[56] Tourists visit a destination for different reasons and not all of them watch the films or television series that a destination-marketing agency may use. Also, a film or television series may only reflect one or two aspects of an overall brand.

There have been a lot of very successful television series set in Yorkshire over the last 50 years so the British themselves have an image of Yorkshire **(see Table 5.2)**. Like any destination that has only been experienced through a film and/or television series, it only tells part of the story. Yorkshire is a big county and is effective in attracting tourists.[41] There are lots of sides to Yorkshire that tourists who have never visited would not be aware of.[39] Kirklees Metropolitan Council supports the idea that Yorkshire's Unique Selling Point (USP) is its tourism product; beaches, food, mountains, people, sea

---

56 Steele, Mr David; Head of Research and Statistics Unit, UK Film Council (27th July 2006).

and shops. The YTB suggests that Yorkshire is presenting a positive image through a strong portrayal of adventures, community, experiences, family values and roaming countryside.[47]

Yorkshire's television series have reinforced the traditional core values associated with a rural county.39 The county is not always portrayed as very traditional and can be given a negative slant as in Sheffield and *The Full Monty* (1997).[50] Then again, the Yorkshire based television series, have primarily raised awareness and shown a positive image of the county.57 Historically, Yorkshire has been represented as mostly rural and is often portrayed on screen in this manner. The YTB is trying to change this so it can attract a younger audience and instead it reinforces the concept of the county being beautiful.[48]

Nonetheless, over the last couple of years, Yorkshire has been home to new gritty urban television series like *No Angels* (2004–2006) and *Bodies* (2004–2006), hence a new television image of the county is starting to emerge, which the YTB very much supports. It is bringing in new tourists as *Heartbeat* continues to perpetuate the traditional image.[41] The image of the county is continually reinforced through television series like *All Creatures Great and Small*, *Heartbeat* and *Last of the Summer Wine*. It would be true to say that the face of some destinations within the county have been altered after the increase in tourism. For example, the village used in *Heartbeat* has turned into a tourism product itself.[48] Kirklees Metropolitan Council claim that the way forward is to get away from the traditional image. The North of England's marketing consortium, The Northern Way, is trying to encourage such growth as it seems to be a very media-led world today.[57]

The use of media brands should be cost effective as the film company is providing free marketing. It is not only branding but it is one of the most effective ways to market the county.[40] Portmeirion (Wales) plays down its links to the television series, *The Prisoner* (1967–1968) as it is felt that the village's strengths are greater than having been in a cult show.[55] In the case of Yorkshire, however, the YTB and RTA have recognized the strength of certain brands, for instance the *Herriot* and *Heartbeat Country* brands, help raise the profile of the destination and encourage tourists. The popularity and longevity of these productions have contributed to the creation of successful media-related brands, both domestically and internationally.

---

57 Evans, Mr Martin; Director, The Tourism Business (Film Induced Tourism Consultancy Business) (21st July 2006).

5.3.2.1 *Theme: Imagery*

a) Issue 1 – The brand image can be a strong tourism destination motivator

Yorkshire has a strong positive brand image through its television series, films, books and a general feeling of nostalgia for the county in the way that it is portrayed by the YTB. Many tourists are looking for something different, so what the brand says about a destination can either encourage or discourage tourists. Once the destination is decided upon, secondary factors like cost are considered, as people decide where to stay and what sort of experience they want in the destination. There are a variety of factors that increasingly use brand image as a key differentiator for tourist destinations. Television brings in well-versed tourists who have researched their trip on websites and they can be very informed. Television series have changed people's perception of Yorkshire as people want a quality experience and good facilities, for example, restaurants, public toilets and car parking.[50]

Most of the stakeholders **(See Table 5.6)** concur that visual images or symbols play important roles in promoting a destinations image.[58] Film and television exposure can have a big impact on the UK as it receives much of global media related coverage. VisitBritain maintains that news programmes portray the British as being bureaucratic, heritage lovers, honest, humorous, reliable and trust-worthy.[46] The positive portrayal of destination icons can also reaffirm the status of destination.[42] They create the experience and set the tourist agenda, i.e. who would go to Paris and not go to the Eiffel Tower or London and not visit Buckingham Palace.[55] The perception that people have of the UK is of a wealth of historic buildings and quaint villages. The power of visual images or symbols can be significant in promoting a destination both nationally and internationally. It was put forward by VisitBritain that when appropriate images appear in a moving image, such as a powerful film or even a well-shot commercial, the image can create the desire to visit.[46]

The National Trust maintains that the media portrays Blackpool as a family fun destination, Ireland as a destination full of bars with red heads serving Guinness, Scotland as full of mountains, and Australia is the big adventure. VisitBritain, in developing images, has started tourism-related theme days, such as the royal and stately homes days which have been well-received by tourists; also the British heritage, scenery, cream teas and quaint villages help to build this image. In Yorkshire, brand image is not perhaps the most important factor for success as it should be noted that 85% of its tourists are repeat

---

58 Fernandez-Young, Ms Anita; Film Induced Tourism Project Manager , University Of Nottingham / UK Film Council (17th July 2006).

visitors.39   The tourist image of the city of York itself changes once tourists arrive, as they are surprised by how vibrant and modern it actually is.   York has a very distinctive brand which seems to be stronger than the Yorkshire brand itself and York City Council is very keen to work with the YTB on developing the branding even further.[51]

b) Issue 2 – The images portrayed in films/television play an important role in influencing travellers' expectations of Yorkshire

The National Trust has allowed several documentary programmes to be filmed on its properties for free as it recognizes this sort of exposure is worth many millions in advertising value.   Due to this collaboration, tourist numbers have increased, particularly when the National Trust linked its tourist advertisements to the many popular films and television series and film set on its properties[55.]

People are reading more and if the books tie in with a film they are even more successful, such as the *Master and Commander* (2003), Dickens and *Bleak House* (2005) novels.   It would appear that young people are reading less and watching more television than the older generations, however research is needed to support this[51]   The popular Scottish television series *The Monarch of the Glen* was only meant to be a pilot.   The series tried to link with original books but was unsuccessful, maybe due to the fact that it was filmed in a private house.   On the other hand, it should be noted that one of the strongest international products for Yorkshire is the Brontë connection and has been for centuries.[48]

The tourist industry is actually cutting down on its printed material and putting more time and money into website development, which seems to be the most appropriate way forward.[59]   Group-travel type tourists still read brochures, while independent travellers rely more on web-based information.   Screen East insists that the power of the moving image will continue to provide a strong influence. Promotional literature can portray a destination through people's imagination whereas film, DVD and television can depict a more realistic visual portrayal of a destination.

A positive portrayal of destinations through television series can certainly influence the image and hold up well for repeat viewing.[42]   Screen Yorkshire mentioned that if the tourist advertisement has the right image it can dramatically increase people's desire to visit. Many different types of series can showcase destinations.58   The *Picture of Britain* (2005) and *Coast* travel series, the popular television series, *The*

---

59 Hancer, Ms Claire; England Sales and Marketing Manager, VisitBritain (27th July 2006).

Royal and *Heartbeat* are examples of this, but it is very hard to quantify as Scarborough District Council have focused.

It is believed that more and more young people are using the internet as an interactive source. In China, there are only twenty international films shown annually (which is changing due to piracy laws). It is imperative therefore, that the UK Film Council gets some British based films shown there as they have the power to change the image of a region.[56]

The numerous series based in the Yorkshire Dales portray the area very positively and the stakeholders **(See Table 5.6)** would like to continually use them,[34] however, sometimes this image can also be negative as seen with the film *Little Voice* (1998) and Scarborough.[39] The positive images portrayed in the media can also attract attention to the city and the surrounding areas, not just the beautiful scenery. In addition, it is important to promote the home produced food (Yorkshire Lamb and Wensleydale Cheese) and the farmers markets.[57] Most definitely Yorkshire is about the outdoors but images should be more vibrant than is currently portrayed in terms of culture, heritage and quality. Yorkshire is trying to re-image itself, especially the cities such as Leeds and Sheffield with their 'Café Culture'.[41] There is also Yorkshire's history and culture. The York Tourist Bureau is currently working to promote York as a lively, vibrant, historic city.[51] The county's tourist product should also change in collaboration with any change in brand. It was argued that as a county Yorkshire has a very diverse offering and although the brand values associated with this rural image are very strong and attractive, the YTB would ideally like this to be portrayed in a manner, which is aspirational and portrays the region as high quality and contemporary.[48]

With the positive portrayal of locations in a dramatic and inspirational way, and the association of popular actors, the right film can have the effect of shaping images of a destination to a captive audience.[42] The scenes portrayed in films certainly play an important role in both shaping images and influencing travellers' expectations of Yorkshire due to the power of the media. The northern city of Newcastle has successfully managed to improve its image in the last few years due its positive portrayal in the media.[46] The images portrayed in films and television create awareness, and positive attractive images are very beneficial.[48]

Screen Yorkshire proposes that if an iconic image such as Big Ben appears in a film then it tends to strengthen the London brand. Tourists now have more access to sources of media information. VisitBritain suggests that a high proportion of the developed world is exposed to increasing amounts of visual images from the big screen to their mobile phones. Websites also play a big part but they have to be easy to navigate and if a Yorkshire related article appears in a national newspaper, it can have a big knock-on effect to the county.[33]

Although *Heartbeat* has influenced people's perception of Yorkshire, it is important to remember that lots of programmes contribute to this perception. For Yorkshire there is also *Emmerdale*, the *Last of the Summer Wine* and *Where the Heart Is*, and a popular film or television series can give exposure to an area like no marketing drive. Yet, Screen Yorkshire states that it is up to the tourist/marketing boards to capitalize on the exposure and market it appropriately.[47]

VisitBritain, the YTB, the National Trust and the National Park state that the influence of re-imaging rural areas through film is not that important, as tourists know what is real and what is fictional. It hardly works in reverse as most of the images of New York come mainly from crime shows but tourism is hardly affected. On the other hand, the re-imaging of rural areas has already proven to be effective, certainly in the case of *The Lord of the Rings*; the trilogy provided New Zealand with substantial destination marketing opportunity at each screening which maximized the attractiveness of the country to the tourist. Nonetheless, not everyone who visited New Zealand would have watched the film, but they might have seen the trailer. Subsequently, each time the production is screened on the small screen; it could well provide another stimulus **(see Chapters 2 and 3)**. Television is just one of a number of media that allow people to get an impression of what the city of York is like. This is mainly done through regional news coverage rather than advertising.[51]

5.3.2.3 *Theme: Film induced tourism*

a)   Issue 1 – Challenge of sustaining the benefits of film induced tourism

Some of the stakeholders **(See Table 5.6)** claim that film induced tourism can create mass appeal and awareness. It contributes financially and it is an ongoing positive occurrence for the little villages of Yorkshire, however, these economic impacts are difficult to quantify. There is only anecdotal evidence that Holmfirth has financially benefited from the long-running television series the *Last of the Summer Wine* being filmed there.[57,58] Goathland is not really benefiting from the extremely popular television series *Heartbeat* as much as it could, as tourists are using Whitby as their base for touring the area.62

190

It is worth noting that it is generally becoming a very crowded market place.39,57 This is supported by some of the stakeholders **(See Table 5.6)** interviewed.

Several stakeholders **(See Table 5.6)** explain that extra tourism is induced by films and recommend that a film could be an effective tool to change place images and affect the audience's interest in visiting the place. Most stakeholders **(See Table 5.6)** claim that the phenomenon of film induced tourism will continue to grow as films are internationally distributed and viewed. Interestingly, it will continue to grow as the major films need bigger marketing campaigns to recoup their enormous costs. EM-Media claims that the quickest way of selling a destination is by being in a film especially as the directors can be encouraged (financially) to make it look wonderful.[60]

The multiplier effect continues as films are screened through the big screen, DVD and television. As long as the film remains popular there is likely to be some form of multiplier effect, as the production continues to provide a free promotional opportunity.[61] VisitBritain sees films and television series as a means of reaching new audiences in emerging markets and so film induced tourism is an excellent way to capitalize on the positive portrayal of destinations on the screen.[43]

With new technology, the exposure of films and television series has dramatically increased; children have portable DVD players for car journeys, iPods also give a good quality of image, digital television means that films or series can be selected and watched at any time. Screen South hase found that there is an increase in destinations wanting to encourage productions and many offer incentives (tax relief) to lure such film stakeholders.

The fact that Yorkshire based television series have increased tourists to the county was supported by many of the stakeholders **(See Table 5.6)** but it is very difficult to quantify. The success of the *Heartbeat* and the *Captain Cook Country* brands have been well publicized[37] as has the success of the hugely popular television series *Emmerdale* and *All Creatures Great and Small* which have attracted large numbers of tourists to the Yorkshire Dales area. Film induced tourism has not occurred in the city of York. This may be due to the fact that it tends to be used as a touring base. Goathland has had an increase in its tourist numbers, from 200,000 tourists annually when *Heartbeat* began in 1992 to 1.5 million at present. It should be noted that the newly developed television series *The Royal* has the

---

60 Lappin, Ms E.; Head of Communications, EM-Media (9th August 2006).
61 Barker, Ms Julie; Sustainable Tourism Manager, Yorkshire Dales National Park (18th July 2006).

same potential to develop such tourism, thereby resuscitating Holmfirth where *Last of the Summer Wine* television series is filmed.[62]

The National Trust (most of its properties are rural) can benefit from film exposure and it has documented an often dramatic increase in tourist numbers to its properties or villages when National Trust properties have featured in the media. A good example of this is the village of Laycock, which has been used for much filming and has seen a dramatic increase in family visits after it was featured in *Harry Potter* (2001–). The National Trust House, Basildon Park opened its door to filming for the first time with *Pride and Prejudice* (2005). The numbers of tourists increased by 500%. They took it a step further and laid on a special exhibition of costumes and memorabilia used in the film, which was highly successful and was due to be repeated in 2006, with over 100 coach tours booked a year beforehand.

Film induced tourism has also proven to be extremely important since the Foot and Mouth Disease (FMD) outbreak and is stronger than ever in Yorkshire.[33] Films and television such as *Mary Poppins* (1964) certainly have a longevity effect.[56] The popular television series *Heartbeat* and *All Creatures Great and Small* provide evidence for such a phenomenon, but there seem to be few measures in place to evaluate these impacts and in some instances the demand may not even be anticipated. In the case of some films such as *Calendar Girls* (2003), the economic impact is unknown. It was certainly a boost to the local economy but there was no monitoring mechanism in place to measure the tourism multiplier effect.[54]

b) Issue 2 – Controlling film induced tourism – positive and negative tourist management issues

• Positive tourist management flows

Depending on the strength of the production, there are many positive benefits for the tourist industry such as increased employment, product sales, new hotels and the production talent staying in the area, as has been seen in Yorkshire. Screen Yorkshire found that it has also extended the tourist season which is now from March to November,[54] boosted the morale of the community and increased a feeling of pride[40] in the area. It can heighten the appeal of a destination and make it more recognizable which is likely to be the case both from an economical and a sustainable community perspective.[41] The larger budget films often have scenes that require extras and this is where local residents can get involved, as well as potentially benefiting from location fees. Local businesses profit through the resulting tourism

---

62 Breakell, Mr Bill; Transport and Tourism Officer, North Yorkshire Moors National Park (19th July 2006).

multiplier effect after the television series has screened. Local residents continue to benefit, thereafter, as their feeling of pride intensifies when they see their locality on the screen. Nonetheless, problems can arise if the film or television series is a huge success and no infrastructure has been put in place to maximize the opportunity or manage the demand.[54]

- Negative tourist management flows
  - *Congestion*

An influx of tourists is not always welcomed with many towns and villages unsuited to supporting tourism growth because of their limited facilities, infrastructure and services. It depends on the film/television series and its individual impact.[38] Negative tourist management issues have arisen in Yorkshire,[54] for example congestion,[35] but this is specific to areas such as Aysgarth Falls and Goathland, rather than the county as a whole. Another negative impact which was highlighted was disruption to the locals.

There is a risk that a destination can become so popular that people are in danger of destroying the tranquil nature of an area in addition to spoiling the environment – by the erosion of footpaths for example. They simply cannot deal with the extra numbers. A huge influx of tour buses in areas that do not have the infrastructure in place to manage the tourists, the vehicles, or to maximize their presence in terms of tourism spend can cause irritation to the local community. This is very evident in conservation areas such as the small heritage market towns and villages of Yorkshire like Askrigg.

In the summer months, the fire risk to moor land in the Dales is a particular concern. Footpath erosion and car parking issues often occur in the small villages. This is the reasoning behind the development of a *Coach Driver's* map which helps manage tourists and keeps coaches off roads that could not cope with the increased traffic and size of vehicles.[54] Not only that but if there are no services when the tourists arrive, they tend to bring their own provisions, so their only spend may be on car parking and a postcard. The impact can be fairly significant in terms of road management, impact on local residents, road maintenance and waste management as seen in the Yorkshire Dales 'Honey Pots' areas (Askrigg, Kettlewell and Liddledale).54 Hambleton District Council does not see this as an issue in its region, as full tourist carrying capacity has yet to be reached.[53]

o *Resident negativity*

Tourism is highly interactive between people from diverse cultures. It has emerged as a forceful agent of change in many of the communities in which it has been encouraged (Ap and Crompton, 1993). The literature on tourist-host relationships is now a much larger, challenging and increasing useful area of academic activity (Pearce, 1998). Mathieson and Wall (1982) maintain that the consequences of tourism have been increasingly complex and contradictory and are manifest in subtle and often unexpected ways. Due to these findings, Pizam (1978) and Long, Perdue and Allen (1990) have carried out research over the last few decades on resident's perceptions of the impacts of tourism. Sheldon and Var (1984) argue that the seasonal nature of tourism is partly responsible for friction between residents and tourists (O'Connor, Flanagan and Bayliss, 2002).

VisitBritain deems that the negative effects of film induced tourism tend to come in spurts and can often overwhelm a smaller destination. If a series uses a location heavily, the disruption can be quite tiring for the residents. Goathland (*Heartbeat*) cannot cope with tourist influx, consequently carrying capacity problems are very evident with the daily arrival of the many tour buses. Congestion has had a major impact on the village. Tourists are also disappointed that Goathland is in the 21st century and not in the 1960s as *Heartbeat* is set. Even the signage has been changed from Goathland to Aidensfield (the name of the village in the television series) by the commercial sector.

If a private residence is used in a production (as with *The Monarch of the Glen*), tourists have been known to seek out the house and try to gain access which can have a considerable impact on the home owner.

There can also be resistance between residents and entrepreneurs, who financially gain from this phenomenon.[50] The issue seems to be that there are a large number of excursionists but they are low spenders (€11 per day) due to the Peak District's location near large urban areas such as Huddersfield, Leeds and Sheffield. The demand for holiday homes in the Dales has pushed house prices out of the reach of local people.[33] This in turn means that they are restricted to the main settlements through affordable housing. The NYMNP needs to get financial backing from ITV (Yorkshire Television), to aid its infrastructural improvements, which has not occurred thus far.[62]

○ *Authenticity and displacement*

Evidence for displacement is very strong in the case of *Braveheart* in Scotland and *Waking Ned* (1998) in the Isle of Man.[37] This refers to the aspect of a film being shot in one place but in reality representing somewhere else entirely. This also questions the authenticity of a destinations tourism product **(see 3.6.1.).** Many locations in the UK sometimes will double for locations overseas to reduce costs or because it would be impossible to film at the real location. Examples of this include Hylands House in Chelmsford, Essex (UK) which has doubled for the White House, a Norfolk (UK) farm for a Korean paddy field and a sand quarry for the Sahara. At a more local level, the film *Shadowlands* (1993) refers to the Golden valley in Herefordshire (UK) but was actually shot at Symonds Yat on the Herefordshire and Gloucestershire (UK) border.

The *Miss Potter* (2006) film did not use her real home but another home with a better setting, but both were part of the marketing campaign.[63] With the *King Arthur* (2004) film promotion, VisitBritain promoted the associated locations as the film was actually shot in Ireland. Screen South discovered that the popular television series *Band of Brothers* (2001) was shot entirely in Hertfordshire but depicted many French towns. This was well publicized and worked well for the county. Stanley Kubrick's *Full Metal Jacket* (1987) used Becton to double for Vietnam. This has been well documented and has become a very useful tool in underlining the versatility of the UK.

The final aspect is that the image reflected in the film may not be complimentary to the destination brand or accurately reflect the reality in the destination. Temporary sets are constructed and images can be manipulated or enhanced, so a film's location may appear different on the screen.51 A big issue which was highlighted is that the DMOs have no control over the image of the destination, as the director is more concerned about the film and the story than the tourism issues which may arise.[51] Sometimes films may raise an expectation, for instance in the British filmed *The Da Vinci Code* (2006) a sinister slant on innocent buildings is given.[55]

c) Issue 3 – The critical success of a film versus a television series

A filming location can attract extra tourists not just because something was shot there but also because the film shows somewhere that looks good and reminds people of destinations they might like to go back to. Wales has not maximized on the opportunity that it had recently with the tele-film *Very Annie*

---

63 Steele, Mr David, Head of Research and Statistics Unit, UK Film Council (27th July 2006).

Mary (2001).[58] Screen East claims that the film induced tourism phenomenon seems possible, given the number of enquiries that the TICs receive and the fact that tour operators have begun creating television branded tours to meet the demand. The YTB[48] and Screen Yorkshire found that the film *Calendar Girls* (2003) provided a great stimulus for people to visit the Dales[53] as do the *Heartbeat* (Goathland), *Herriot* (Yorkshire Dales), and *Summer Wine* (Holmfirth) Country brands which still encourage tourists to visit these areas and they also assist in the selling of English heritage aboard.

It is felt that films help a wider audience discover new areas – as with *The Lord of the Rings* and New Zealand, for example. The village in Scotland featured in *Local Hero* (1996) put a phone box in place to match the prop used in the film. This is an example of making the place fit the expectations. History influences perception of a destination. For example the North of England and the mining industry are very closely linked in people's minds, whereas in fact 70% of the Kirklees region (Northern England) is rural, and so the perceptions and image of Yorkshire that the media portrays are not necessarily true. The UK Film Council found that the critically acclaimed film *Bend It Like Beckham* (2002) was a big success in the Chinese black market, transforming the image/perception of the UK.[56]

The YTB maintain that positive coverage has a greater effect than negative coverage.[48], this is not supported by the literature review undertaken for the purpose of this study. The exception being a natural disaster but the primary cause of the negative effect is usually not the 'disaster' but the exaggerated media coverage and a tendency to sensationalize incidents and extend them beyond their true geographical context. The news media are more familiar with the geography of Afghanistan and Iran than they are with any domestic location outside of the M25 motorway.[48]

VisitBritain's research into domestic customer motivations shows that the incentive to visit a film or television location is low. As a result, the company probably is not going to use film induced brands as stand alone brands in the British market. These brands can be more useful as a basis for travel trade itineraries. Media brands used in specific international markets, where there may be a low awareness of Yorkshire, can be very influential but these are not the only brands that the tourism organizations can deliver. VisitBritain is currently conducting research into the '*Sunday night*' television effect when potential tourists are relaxing in their own environment, watching the positive portrayal of a destination. The scale and drama that a destination portrayal on the big screen can inspire can be a lot more productive. If the proposed *Brontë* film is recorded in Yorkshire, it should definitely be used to brand the county, as it has the strength to be a standalone brand.48 This has worked very well with *The Da Vinci Code* (2006) but not with the Rowan Atkinson's film *Johnny English* (2003)46 while the popular television series *Mr Bean* (1990-1995) is the most successful British television export in Canada and China due to its low translation costs. The marketing consortium England North Country are willing to work with VisitBritain on this, particularly as the film *History Boys* (2006) used Fountains Abbey, in Yorkshire.[55]

Certainly tourism induced by films and television series proposes that they can be an effective tool to help destination images and affect the audience's interest in visiting the place, as in *Pride and Prejudice*. The repeat viewing factor is a unique opportunity for destinations[42] to create an FMAP **(see Chapter 6)** for their area. The biggest development in the last twenty years has been the afterlife of films on cable, DVD, specialized channels and the internet.[54]

Popular films such as *Four Weddings and a Funeral* (1994), *Mary Poppins* (1964) and *Notting Hill* (1999) continue to portray a strong image of the UK through ongoing screenings on television which further attracts tourists to the destination. An even wider viewing audience through the continued screening of films and repeat television series will probably continue for some time without any efforts from the national tourism stakeholder, VisitBritain.[56]

An audience will continue to have exposure through the weekly viewing of a television series and as a result they may form a greater attachment to the story and the location. Audiences can view television series as extensions of their own lives, therefore the desire to see where the television series is filmed is greater due to their strong attachment. This can also be the case with very popular films, but as the viewers are not getting a weekly exposure to the story/location, the attachment weakens much quicker. This is substantiated by many of the stakerholders.[50,51,54] Castle Howard is still trading off the popular television series *Brideshead Revisited* (1979-1981). It was shown in the days of an average 10–18 million television audience per television series.

The UK Film Council maintains that films seem to be growing in their popularity, probably due to the emergence of the DVD and home cinemas.[56] DVDs have a better return and VisitBritain used them (e.g. *The Da Vinci Code* and the *Master and Commander*) to distribute their marketing material. *All Creatures Great and Small* is a great example of television longevity, while films like *The Sound of Music* (1965) are still attracting tourists to Salzburg some 40 years later.[56]

Generally, the Yorkshire based television series – *Emmerdale, Heartbeat* and *Last of the Summer Wine* have greatly influenced people's perceptions.[33] The UK Film Council suggests films (*The Sound of Music* and *Mary Poppins*) on the other hand have greater longevity than television series.[56] Television series can run for years, but popular films such as *Crocodile Dundee* and *Braveheart* also have considerable longevity,[54] although they are the exception rather than the rule.[56] They both have a huge impact as the exposure of a film will have an impact on a wider audience in many more countries than a television series but television series will possibly have longevity, due to repeat viewings.

d) Issue 4 – The effectiveness of the movie map as a marketing tool to promote a destination

Many stakeholders **(See Table 5.6)** endorse the use of movie maps as a marketing tool used by the DMOs to draw attention to areas within a region that have been used in a popular film or television series. As they are not economically viable, they are not widely used in Yorkshire.[41,50] The stakeholders **(See Table 5.6)** support their development especially if they are available online.[37] Their development needs to be monitored, controlled and facilitate the marketing of destinations that generally cannot afford to be reached. Generally, the tourist boards support their development and look towards specific market demographics for certain films.[55] The concept of a movie map as a tourism product is one that is of great interest, but it is expensive for it to be done an interactive basis. They can be used to promote locations for filming, by showing what an area has to offer as a destination marketing tool. VisitBritain has been producing movie maps for over ten years and fully recognizes their marketing and public relations value.[42] In future, the YTB intends to pool its resources into its website development, while its movie maps are likely only to appear online.[48] The *Pride and Prejudice* movie map cost over €200,000 to produce. It is a long-term investment and the Peak District National Park is using it as part of its cooperative marketing strategy.[50]

5.3.2.4 *Theme: Stakeholder involvement*

a) Issue 1 – Tourist stakeholders should be aware of the benefits of using positive
    destination images in a film or a television series

The promotional capability of films is not equal and some television series and films have little impact, while others may be both influential and memorable. This is supported by some of the stakeholders **(See Table 5.6)** interviewed. Those agencies that get to hear about films – DCMS, RSA and the television companies – should be encouraged to engage with the tourist stakeholders more. This has recently happened between the Peak District National Park Authority and Universal Studios with *Pride and Prejudice*.[50] The spin-off from film induced tourism can be wonderful but the tourist stakeholders

198

need to know what is being filmed in their area and to take an interest in it. Kirklees Metropolitan Council proposes that the tourist stakeholders need to be aware of the potential gain of featuring positive images of a destination in a film, which should also be part of the area's tourist strategy.[41] England's North Country feels that for any real maximization of potential, the tourist authorities and the RSAs have to work more closely together and the tourist authorities, in particular, have to take a more active strategic approach to the concept.[37] This is where the opportunity really lies[47] and it needs to be negotiated before cinematic release.[58] The UK Film Council maintains that its current film induced tourism research project integrates these.[56] Screen Yorkshire feels that it has never really had a strong working relationship with the YTB, whereas the York Tourist Bureau claims to work closely with both film producers and Screen Yorkshire in relation to possible film locations within the City of York. The YTB is currently developing a filming location pack for York for these producers and Screen Yorkshire to induce such tourism.[40]

The RTA needs to work with local councils to facilitate filming requests and to actually make it happen efficiently so that everyone has a positive experience. By working with the RSA, the RTA will develop a working relationship with the production companies. This will help them identify possible publicity shots as not all production companies are happy to give this information away and timing is crucial, so contact via a RSA is vital. Scarborough District Council has been doing this for the last few years with Screen Yorkshire, as they have found that the more they work with one other, the more the region benefits from the positive impacts of film induced tourism.[39]

As more destinations see the benefits of film induced tourism, marketers are getting more proactive and working closer with the film industry.[42] They have done this in the past as it seems to really work56 as with *Pride and Prejudice* and *The Da Vinci Code*[43] as previously mentioned. The producers of the *Miss Potter* film were considering using Scotland instead of Cumbria for the filming location but the Cumbrian Screen Commission lowered their location fees to attract the production. They were very proactive and they sent out a comprehensive guide to location managers and production companies to encourage filming there.[55] The Peak District National Park is also working EM Media, their local RSA, to promote their local film locations but it is only a small part of their overall work.[50]

b) Issue 2 – The importance of the financial contribution of film induced tourism to the destination

The suggestion that tourism stakeholders might financially contribute to filming so that they will gain the right to control how these images are portrayed in media is not likely, nor can this be financed on an individual basis by the local authorities. VisitBritain has developed close partnerships with film companies in relation to *Harry Potter* and *The Da Vinci Code*. The tourism stakeholders need to liaise with the production companies at the post film production stage, as the film stakeholders tend to be more concerned with their own needs and not those of stakeholders.

The RSAs are not always aware of what locations the film companies have decided to use until shooting begins, plus there is often only a certain amount of lead time and it can take years before the production begins to shoot. Once the production is secured and filming begins, the RSAs and the local authorities should work together to maximize the emerging opportunities. Nonetheless, Screen East has found that there is no guarantee that the film will be distributed widely, they are not always aware of the release date or aware of how successful it might be in the box office[40].

Many stakeholders **(See Table 5.6)** such as VisitBritain do not believe that getting directly involved in the production of a film is beneficial for the tourism stakeholders.[42] The buy-in from the NTOs into a film or television series can be very effective[37,39] especially if undertaken internationally as with *Pride and Prejudice*. Some stakeholders **(See Table 5.6)** have worked together successfully in the past but much of this depends on the tax breaks which endorse films as seen with *The Lord of the Rings* and TNZ but not with *The Da Vinci Code,* which was mentioned by only one stakeholder.[58]

5.4 Final Thoughts on the Survey and Strategic conversations

5.4.1 The study of film induced tourism

Numerous investigations such as Busby and Klug (2001) and Gartner (1996) are limited to descriptive understandings of the film induced tourism concept and do not give a theoretical insight as to why this phenomenon is happening. A small number of the studies give reasons for film induced tourism and suggest that a film could be an effective tool to change a destination's image and influence the viewer's interest in visiting the film location. It is clear from these studies that extra research is necessary to better understand the relationships between films and tourism (Kim and Richardson 2003: 232). Much of the up to date academic literature has not purposely added to the body of research, tending to concentrate on duplicating and reinforcing earlier studies, looking primarily at the marketing value of film induced tourism. If destinations are to successfully take advantage of their own attractiveness, but within a sustainable framework, private, public and community interests need to find harmony in setting fitting objectives to make the most of the benefits and reduce costs (Beeton 2005: 18).

5.4.2   The potential costs and benefits of film induced tourism

In the past, film induced tourism has been secondary to the film itself with little or no thought given to the enduring effects filming may have on a destination. While such tourism can present economic benefits to a destination, especially in a marginalized rural area, the destination may not be equipped or even prepared to deal with the alterations linked with film induced tourism. Through considering the possible costs and benefits of film induced tourism, Yorkshire has the potential to use the benefits to strengthen itself and deal with the costs (Beeton 2005).

5.4.3   The positive and negative impacts of filming

There are both positive and negative impacts of filming the various television series in Yorkshire. It contributes economically to the region and has led to a renewal and increase in employment but there is a need to compare with other film induced destinations most notably Australia and the USA. It would also be of interest to study the difference between the towns and villages that consistently succeed and those that do not. The research could assist in the setting up of a programme to minimize any friction that may arise in the future between tourists and residents. An overall plan for the development of the county as a tourist destination should be put in place to counteract the problems which other tourist destinations have faced in the past, possibly due to lack of planning (Beeton 2005).

5.5   Conclusion

Chapter 5 has drawn together the primary findings from this research study to facilitate tackling its main objectives stated in **Table 1.2**. The primary findings have been discussed throughout this chapter and the many themes and issues which emerged during the collation of both the primary and secondary data have been discussed. This has resulted in some key insights relative to the film induced tourism phenomenon. Such insights are advantageous, as they facilitate the advancement of more precise film related marketing strategies and models **(See Chapter 6).**

The findings of the tourist survey, strategic conversations and the issues which arose from the literature review highlight a number of implications for the future development of such destinations. These implications include the many positive and negative impacts of filming the various television series in Yorkshire and the use of destination branding in the promotion of a film location as found with *The*

Lord of the Rings and New Zealand. The tourist survey, strategic conversations and the literature review were undertaken to illustrate the effect of film induced tourism on a branding of a destination, namely Yorkshire. It has been shown that film induced tourism has the potential to offer many great opportunities but also creates many drawbacks. The perception of Yorkshire for film induced tourism is not widely welcomed by the stakeholders **(See Table 5.6)** and the implications are that maintaining a clear balance between Yorkshire's current tourism product and maximizing opportunities in new markets is the most appropriate way forward **(See Table 1.2 – Research Objective 2).** These were discussed through the emergent themes and associated issues in relation to destination branding, destination imagery and film induced tourism as applied to Yorkshire. In light of these results the following critical issues have arisen that need to be considered when developing a destination brand.

5.5.1 The potential of film induced imagery

It is imperative that destination brand is understood. The potential that television imagery has in the development of the brand should reflect the character of the destination. To a certain extent the YTB has done this, but the effect as evidenced by the survey results has been limited. The survey raises the issue of whether or not the general brand being developed by YTB is effective; the results do show that visitors have an image of the scenery and character of the area (outlined in **Table 5.1** and **Figure 5.1**), which is then substantiated by their visit. The question that this raises for the current research is: Should destination branding be based on film and television or simply be part of a wider brand and dovetail more coherently with this wider brand? The development of a strong image whether visual, vocal, personal, film or television related is the key to successful branding but the brand must reflect the destination, e.g. Las Vegas and entertainment, Paris and romance. The question that needs to be answered through further research is if the media associated images that Yorkshire partly uses to promote the region are the most effective brands to use in promoting the destination?

5.5.2 Closer collaboration between the film and tourism stakeholders

Closer collaboration with the RSAs and actively sponsoring their activities to encourage production, and being as film friendly as possible is crucial for continued success. Once it is secured, a closer collaborative partnership is essential in order to decide on a strategic approach to maximize the opportunities which emerge. The destination can then be ready to meet the demand following screening and the production can be woven into the destination brand itself. The tourist stakeholders should meet with the film stakeholders and work out how both sides can get the maximum exposure for their campaigns; working closer together can provide a fully effective, long-term partnership.[42] Film companies should be more forthcoming with publicity photos and clips while the filming destination should have a publicity clause in its contract with the studios.[55]

VisitBritain works closely with its strategic partners in relation to film induced tourism and plans to continue doing so to facilitate maximized effectiveness and inspiring people to visit what they have seen on the film screen.[42] It is essential to keep abreast of what is being filmed where, and initially maintaining the relationship between the tourism and film stakeholders, namely the production companies, the local authorities, tourism officers and the RSAs. It seems that once a release date is determined this is the point where planning should begin, so that promotional materials are ready to coincide with destination images appearing on the big screen.

5.5.3 The importance of effective branding

The key findings of this study support Gartner's (1996) argument that image formation agents like news and popular culture can alter destination images in a relatively short time period. The promoting of tourism destinations is turning out to be progressively more aggressive as destinations will need to find creative solutions to maximize their visual identity. In the YTB's strategy one of the aims is to increase domestic brand awareness even though the awareness of the Yorkshire brand is very strong. It is about making something different or providing an experience that cannot be gained elsewhere. For Kirklees Metropolitan Council, the brands that are currently being used are *Last of the Summer Wine* and the Pennine Yorkshire brands, whilst at a county level it is about displaying positive visions of Yorkshire and enabling consumers to *Make Yorkshire Yours* special to them.[41]

5.5.4 The association with a film or television series can be very effective

The evidence from some of the literature is that where there is a major buy-in from the national tourist organization to the association with a film or television series, the results can be very effective. As evidenced from the Yorkshire survey, tourist perceptions have been little influenced by the various television series. This may be because the level of branding based on these sources has been limited. A second issue is that film induced tourism has much more local and limited reach than tourism based in films and its impacts are thus circumscribed. The extent and importance of branding and film induced tourism was further explored in the strategic conversations. The results have shown that the media brand is currently subsumed within stronger general brand images. The issue of monitoring of the brand should also be explored, as it is unclear if this has been carried out in Yorkshire to date.

CHAPTER 6

THE FILM MARKETING ACTION PLAN (FMAP)

6.1   Introduction

The primary focus of Chapter 6 is to design a model for film induced tourism as a result of this research study.   This researcher's main objective is *to develop a framework to be used as a best practice framework for the successful integration of film induced tourism in a destination marketing strategy.* The other purpose of this chapter is to draw together the findings of this study which address the research questions and their associated objectives **(See Table 1.2)**. Therefore, it is important, to restate these once again:

- What are the film induced images that tourists presently have of Yorkshire? **(See Research Objective 1.)**
- What are the current and future tourism and marketing objectives and priorities of Yorkshire's key tourism and film stakeholders? **(See Research Objective 2.)**
- Are these stakeholders who are involved in the development of Yorkshire embracing the film tourism concept? **(See Research Objective 2.)**
- If so, is the film induced tourism concept successfully integrated into their destination marketing campaign? **(See Research Objective 2.)**
- Is the film induced tourism brand currently subsumed within Yorkshire's overall tourism brand? **(See Research Objective 2.)**
- Do the tourism and film stakeholders work in tandem? **(See Research Objective 2.)**
- What conclusions and recommendations emerge based on the research findings? **(See Research Objective 3.)**

These objectives **(See Table 1.2)** were investigated in the context of Yorkshire, which was used as the lens through which the film induced tourism phenomenon was observed. This discussion will draw on and try to understand the most pertinent findings from the literature and where relevant, some new sources of secondary information will be utilized. For the purpose of this research a model will be devised through the creation of an FMAP.

6.2 Journey of Theoretical Thinking

The 'Journey of theoretical thinking' that the researcher undertook for this work is clearly illustrated in **Figure 6.1,** which shows the process through which the FMAP was conceived and the research questions investigated **(See Table 1.2)**. This journey began when the researcher reviewed the secondary research on destination branding **(See Chapter 2)** and film induced tourism **(See Chapter 3)**. This was undertaken from many different perspectives including examining the impact of film induced tourism on a destination and also by reviewing the current theoretical and empirical branding literature with special emphasis on destination branding, destination image and how it is applied to film induced tourism related branding.

Figure 6.1   Journey of Theoretical Thinking

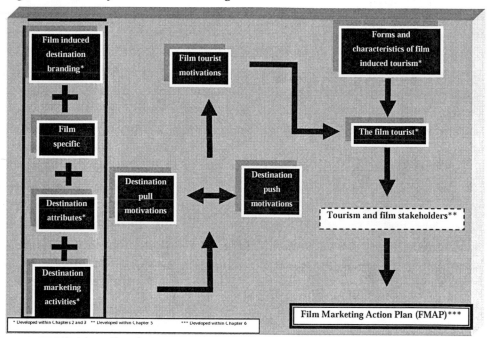

At the beginning of the framework three factors – film specific factors, destination attributes and destination marketing activities – inspire the tourist who is motivated to visit a destination through various push or pull motives. In turn, the forms and characteristics of film induced tourism emerge, as well as the identifiable characteristics of the film induced tourist. These issues were discussed at length with the tourism and film stakeholders **(see Chapter 5),** which led to the formation of the FMAP **(See Table 1.2 – Research Objective 3)**.

Chapter 5 revealed the impacts of film induced tourism on a destination (Yorkshire in this instance) and its related effects. Film induced tourism has the potential to offer many great opportunities but also creates many challenges which were demonstrated in **Chapter 3**. The concept of film induced tourism is not widely welcomed by the stakeholders in Yorkshire and the future task is to retain a transparent balance between Yorkshire's current tourism product and making the most of the opportunities that arise in new markets, to identify the most appropriate way forward (Connell 2005a: 774).

6.3   The FMAP

In developing a model for the integration of film induced tourism in a destination marketing strategy, in addition to reviewing the current literature on the topic, the researcher specifically looked at other frameworks that would help create the FMAP **(see Table 6.1)**. **Table 6.1** represents a chronological history of the development of destination branding, destination imagery and film induced tourism related frameworks, which in turn have facilitated the creation of the FMAP. These models originated from both the marketing and film induced tourism literature, most notably Beeton 2002; Hudson and Ritchie 2006a, 2006b, and Macionis 2004a **(See Chapter 3)**. Beeton (2002: 5) introduces a model for an *integrated marketing de-marketing strategy* to tackle issues like detrimental imagery of destinations while Hudson and Ritchie (2006a: 258) devised a *'conceptual framework for understanding the film induced tourism phenomenon'*. A variation of this is *'film tourism; a model for exploiting film tourism marketing opportunities'* which looks at their earlier model but from a marketing perspective (Hudson and Ritchie 2006b: 390). Macionis (2004a: 22) created a *'continuum of film induced tourism motivation'*, which is a practical classification for examining film induced tourism motivations, as it emphasizes the specific media representations and attributes that are imperative for film tourists. Whilst formulating the FMAP **(see Figure 6.1)**, the researcher examined these models, paying special attention to Hudson and Ritchie's model (2006b: 390).

Table 6.1

FMAP – Chronological Additions to Theoretical Thinking

Anon 2004	Beeton 2002, 2005	Benfield 2001	Borkowski 1994	Butler 1990	Clements 1989
Cohen 1986	Connell 2005a, 2005b	Corlett 1998	Croy and Walker 2003	Demetriadi 1996	Gilbey 2004
Grihault 2003	Hall 2003	Hudson and Ritchie 2006a, 2006b	Kim and Richardson 2003	Kindra and Taylor 1990	Klenosky 2002
Kotler and Levy 1971	Mitchell 1998	Macionis 2004a	Malhotra 1990	Mordue 2001	Mintel 2003
Morgan and Pritchard 1998, 1999	Morgan et al. 2002	Nielson 2001	O'Connor and Flanagan 2000	Reddy 1989	Riley et al. 1998
Riley and Van Doren 1992a	Swan 2003	Tooke and Baker 1996	Urry 1990	Woodward 2000	WTO 2006

Table 6.2 suggests that each of the stakeholders – Local Authority (LA), National Park Authority (NPA), National Tourism Authority (NTA), Regional Screen Agency (RSA), and Regional Tourism Authority (RTA) – can use a variety of marketing activities both before and after release of a film and/or televisions series. The focus of this new model **(Table 6.2)** is the destination marketing activities related to film induced tourism. In spite of suggestions that destination marketers have discarded this very useful form of publicity (Cohen 1986), a re-examination of the film induced tourism literature indicates that some destinations have leveraged the visibility that films provide and benefit by representing a considerable rise in tourist numbers subsequent to a film's release (Hudson and Ritchie 2006b: 388–389)

Table 6.2

The FMAP

	A	B	C
Phase ➡	Before Release	After Release	After Release
Management Action ➡	Planning	Maximize Positive Impacts	Minimize Negative Impacts
Control Mechanism ➡	Marketing	Marketing	De-marketing
	Workforce support	*Brand marketing*	*Business*
	Competitive business	*Co-operative marketing*	*Economic*
	Destination images	*Online marketing*	*Environmental*
	Marketing strategy	*Marketing campaign*	*Quality*
	Media coverage	*Marketing research*	*Social*
	Post-production exposure	*Product marketing techniques*	
	Production action plan	*Relationship management*	
	National promotion		
	Studio relations		
	(See Figure 6.2a)	**(See Figure 6.2b)**	**(See Figure 6.2c)**

Table 6.2 outlines the optimum marketing factors that encourage film tourists to visit destinations which are portrayed in films and/or televisions series. Therefore, **Table 6.2** is one of the first theoretical models to illustrate the optimum marketing factors that encourage film tourists to visit destinations which are portrayed in films and/or televisions series. The researcher suggests that the model for exploiting these film tourism marketing opportunities **(see Table 6.2)** should be divided into three phases:

- Before Release (A) **(See Figure 6.2a)**;
- After Release (B) **(See Figure 6.2b)**;
- After Release (C) **(See Figure 6.2c)**.

These phases represent when each element of the FMAP should be implemented for best results. Within these phases, three management actions are in place to capitalize on the film induced tourism phenomenon:

- Planning **(See Figure 6.2a)**;
- Maximize positive impacts **(See Figure 6.2b)**;
- Minimize negative impacts **(See Figure 6.2c)**.

These management actions should have a control mechanism in place; marketing and de-marketing **(See Chapters 2 and 3)**. The marketing and de-marketing elements of the FMAP are divided into headings to reflect their associated impact and/or action (for a more detailed analysis of these, refer to **Figures 6.2a, b and c**).

Figure 6.2a

Before Release – Planning

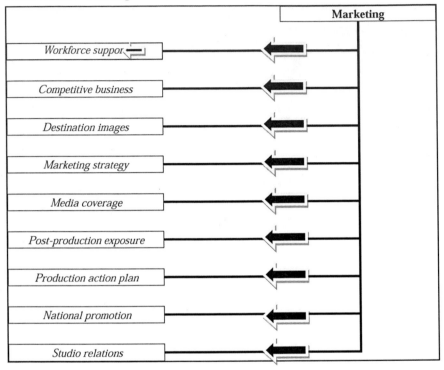

Figure 6.2b

After Release – Maximize Positive Impacts

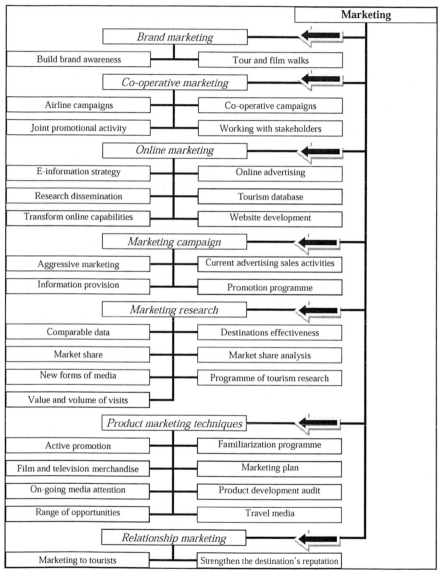

Beeton (2002: 3) introduces a model of an *integrated marketing de-marketing* **(See 3.7.4)** *strategy* to tackle issues of such detrimental imagery of destinations. Initially, the de-marketing concept was developed by Kotler and Levy (1971) and it can be applied to film induced tourism by way of a series of strategies consisting of behavioural education, entry controls, pricing strategies and a decrease in destination marketing (Beeton 2002). In exploratory research, Beeton (2002: 3) examined the degree to which de-marketing tools are used to counteract the negative film induced destination images in destinations associated with films like *Witness* (1985) and *Field of Dreams* (1986). Resident frustration relating to greater than before tourist volumes and anxiety over unwanted imagery of their community is widespread at many film induced tourism destinations.

An integrated marketing de-marketing model could be launched, which could help in the future planning at tourism destinations influenced by such film tourism visitation (Macionis 2004b: 13–14). As problems are becoming apparent at some film destinations, little is being done to proactively manage some of the sites, with tourism and film stakeholders, focusing first and foremost on the associated economic benefits. As with film and television series, de-marketing techniques are proposed as management and re-imaging strategies in film indeed tourism destinations due to their capability to access and influence visitors prior to their visit (Beeton, 2002:2.3), much the same as a film or television series. **Figure 6.2c** illustrates the de-marketing strategies that destinations could be put in place to minimise the film induced tourisms associated negative impacts on a destination **(see 3.7).**

Figure 6.2c

After Release – Minimize Negative Impacts

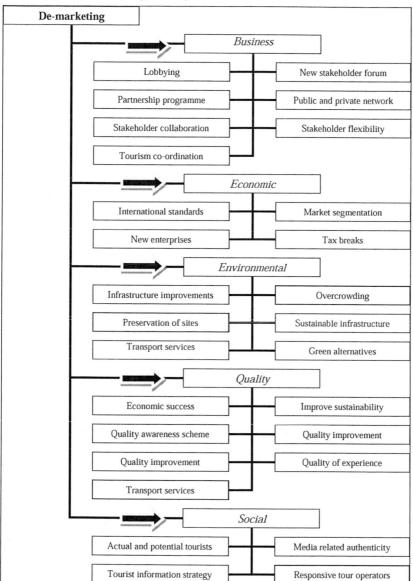

6.4 Key Issues, Strategic Interventions, Actions and Responsibilities of the FMAP

One of the first things to note is the lack of a physical sequential structure to the FMAP **(see Table 6.3a)**. It consists of a much simpler appearance than other models. The first of these columns represents a summarized version of the impacts of film induced tourism on a destination. The second column is a brief overview of the strategic interventions that could be used to maximize (positive impacts) or minimize (negative impacts) such impacts. The third column is the proposed action (response) that the FMAP recommends to put in place to meet these strategic interventions. The fourth and final column is 'responsibility', which identifies the stakeholder, who should implement each strategic intervention.

Table 6.3a   FMAP – Key Issues, Strategic Interventions, Actions and Responsibility

Issue	Strategic Intervention	Action	Responsibility
		Before Release Planning	
Marketing			
Workforce support	Define role of the FMAP.	FMAP will act as a 'front door' for businesses to access advice, business support and aid workforce skills.	All
Competitive business	Boost key sectors of regional significance.	Encourage national and regional co-operation between stakeholders through better integration.	All
Destination images	Create destination images for media inclusion.	Supply promotional images of the destination to media / tour operators e.g. cd-rom, website.	RTA
Marketing strategy	Devise a marketing strategy before release.	Assertively market the destination as a prospective filming location to film studios, through on-going relationship marketing.	RTA
Media coverage	Minimize displacement occurring.	Informative marketing will ensure media exposure cites the destination of the film or television series to curtail the occurrence of displacement.	RSA/RTA
Post-production exposure	Consider the impacts of post-production exposure.	Meticulously predetermine both the positive and negative post-production exposure impacts, by examining the film induced tourism literature.	NPA/RSA/RTA
Production action plan	Increase the value of tourism earnings, through aiming to become a leading filming destination.	Devise a detailed post-production plan of action.	RTA
National promotion	Research the viability of national promotion.	Strongly promote the destination as a feasible filming location to national stakeholders via a national promotion campaign.	RTA
Studio relations	Improve the relations with the film stakeholders.	Employ a marketing expert to liaise directly with film and/or television studios.	NTA/RSA

217

Issue	Strategic Intervention	Action	Responsibility
	After release	**Maximize (Positive impacts)**	
Marketing			
Brand marketing			
Build brand awareness	Publicize the destination as a business destination.	Form an international and domestic marketing campaign.	NTA/RTA
Tour and film walks	Devise tour and film walks for the destination.	Provide 'movie maps' and guided tours of film and television series, set in the destination.	RSA/RTA
Co-operative marketing			
Airline campaigns	Increase co-operative airline campaigns.	Lobby for direct access to the destination at government level.	NTA/LA
Co-operative campaigns	Execute new co-operative campaigns with industry stakeholders.	Operate with international stakeholders to deliver global support of communication plans for films launches.	RSA
Joint promotional activity	Joint promotional activity should involve the film studios.	Participate in joint promotional activity with film and television studios such as destination information on DVDs.	RSA/RTA
Working with stakeholders	Raise awareness of the tourism product with stakeholders.	Identify and minimize any negative perceptions of the destination, through working with stakeholders to stop their reoccurrence.	RSA/RTA
Online marketing			
E-information strategy	Cultivate an e-information strategy.	Appoint an e-business consultant to form an e-information strategy.	RTA
Online advertising	Increase the budget spend for online advertising.	Produce a mini destinational based film to deliver the destinations brand for use at exhibitions, online and television advertising.	RSA/RTA
Research dissemination	Ensure that any research and analysis produced is widely dispersed.	Dissemination may be done through a e-newsletter.	RTA
Tourism database	Improve the gathering, interpretation, provision and use of information.	Set up a common tourism database and website to interlink all public tourism facilities with tourism businesses and provide an integrated tourist booking system.	RTA
Transform online capabilities	Construct the website to transform online capabilities.	Put the website at the heart of the marketing strategy.	RTA
Website development	Sustain the film and television website.	Design the film and television website, to allure potential tourists to the destination.	RSA/RTA

Issue	Strategic Intervention	Action	Responsibility
Marketing campaign			
Aggressive marketing	Strengthen the destination marketing plan.	Apply a more aggressive advertising campaign.	RTA
Current advertising sales activities	Evaluate all current advertising sales activities included in the marketing plan.	Approve actions and objectives to meet targets. Achieve forecasted targets and agree future models of revenue generation.	RTA
Information provision	Support honest marketing.	Ensure the best information provision for tourists before, during and after their visit.	RTA/NPA
Promotion programme	Provide a series of guidelines on good environmental management practice.	The tourism stakeholders should create a top-class environment awareness and promotion programme.	All
Marketing research			
Comparable data	Complete destination wide research.	Provide comparable, competitive and consistent marketing research data.	RTA/NPA
Destinations effectiveness	Explore the effectiveness of the destination.	Complete an evaluation of the destination's effectiveness.	RTA/NPA/LA
Market share	Improve the destination's market share.	Detect the marketing approaches that best serve repeat tourists and acquire new tourists through an evaluation of the marketing strategies.	NTA/RTA
Market share analysis	Reduce emergent negative trends.	Monitor market share performance of all markets with a view to the information gathered, being used by the stakeholders as a trigger for review, analysis and action response, where negative trends emerge.	All
New forms of media	Research new forms of media related tourism products.	Identify the strengths of these new forms of media tourism products and capitalize on these in all of the destination marketing campaigns.	NTA/RTA
Programme of tourism research	Create a co-ordinated programme of tourism research.	Monitor the economic, environmental and social impacts of tourism.	RTA
Value and volume of visits	Increase the value and volume of tourists.	Using focused high quality marketing activities and work with other stakeholders as appropriate.	All

Issue	Strategic Intervention	Action	Responsibility
Product marketing			
Active promotion	Film induced tourism offers free promotion of the destination.	Film induced tourism can continually promote the destination through both DVD and television release.	RSA/RTA
Familiarization programme	Improve product knowledge of the destination.	Set up a familiarization programme to improve product knowledge of the destination among stakeholders.	RSA/RTA /LA
Film and television merchandise	Assess the importance of using merchandise as a marketing tool for the destination.	Build exhibitions of film and television series memorabilia and sell related merchandise.	RSA/RTA
Marketing plan	Prepare a marketing plan.	Consult with stakeholders in the preparation of the destination marketing plan.	All
On-going media attention	Encourage continuous media attention of the destination at any given opportunity.	Use DVDs/videos to maintain destination visibility in the mind of the prospective consumer.	RTA
Product development audit	Plan an audit of product development needs of the destination.	Complete an audit of product development needs with reference to current and emerging market requirements and expectations.	NTA/NPA/RTA
Range of opportunities	Increase range of opportunities.	Carry out press, radio, television and other media related direct marketing campaigns.	NTA/RTA
Travel media	Use the film premiere for more publicity.	Invite the travel media to the film premiere.	RTA
Relationship Management			
Marketing to tourists	Seek to clearly understand the tourists' perspective.	Produce a brand strategy and hierarchy, which will allow effective marketing of the destination, maintain existing markets and enhance key market segments.	NTA/RTA
Strengthen the destination's reputation	Provide a communications manual.	Run events, which strengthen the destination's reputation and relevance to stakeholders.	RTA

Issue	Strategic Intervention	Action	Responsibility
	After release	Minimize (negative impacts)	
De-marketing strategies			
Business			
Lobbying	Endorse the importance of film induced tourism.	Campaign for this at government level.	RSA/RTA
New stakeholder forum	Facilitate the effective co-ordination of tourism.	Form a new stakeholder forum to assist local tourism businesses.	All
Partnership programme	Evaluate current stakeholder partnership programmes.	Expand any existing partnership programme to include all potential stakeholders.	All
Public and private network	Reinforce the public and private network at the destination.	Make better use of the public and private network by referring to them for advice on how to maximize on the film induced tourism phenomenon.	LA
Stakeholder collaboration	Interact with the tourism and film stakeholders.	Co-operate with all tourism and film stakeholders to endorse film locations.	All
Stakeholder flexibility	Enhance the capacity of the stakeholders.	Respond to unforeseen and market changes at home and overseas by putting contingency plans in place.	All
Tourism co-ordination	Operate strategically with other tourism stakeholders.	Ensure co-ordination within regional and sub-regional programmes.	All
Economic			
International standards	Seek quality, world class investment, innovation and product development.	Extend international standards to all accommodation, activities, amenities and attractions.	NTA/NPA/RTA /LA
Market segmentation	Maximize the economic benefit of tourism.	Target segments that will balance maximum economic benefit with minimal environmental and social impacts.	NTA/RTA
New enterprises	Promote new enterprises.	Sustain a prosperous and flourishing economy that will sustain high employment rates.	LA
Tax breaks	Investigate the importance of tax breaks for filming studios.	Ensure the film industry receives attractive tax breaks, to allow destinations to compete with emerging competitive filming locations.	RSA/RTA

Issue	Strategic Intervention	Action	Responsibility
Environmental			
Green alternatives	Limit times for car access to congested or environmentally fragile areas.	Offer green alternatives, e.g. park and walk, free public transport buses.	LA
Infrastructure improvements	Organize associated infrastructure improvements.	Infrastructure improvements, e.g. coach drop / pick-up points; signage should be implemented.	NPA/LA
Overcrowding	Design initiatives to ease overcrowding.	Introduce initiatives such as pay parking, park & ride and restricted access.	LA
Preservation of sites	Continual upkeep of heritage sites.	Put restrictions in place at heritage sites to make them more sustainable.	NPA/LA
Sustainable tourism infrastructure	A new programme of community planning with residents should be reviewed.	Put an improvement plan for tourist facilities and services into practice.	All
Targeted campaigns	Contrive a targeted marketing campaign to enhance the value of tourism to the sub-region.	Business tourism, conversion of excursionists to overnight stays; group travel marketing will support this.	RTA
Quality			
Economic success	Foster the economic success of the tourism industry while enhancing the quality of life of local people and safeguarding the environment.	Help operators to maximize their effectiveness by improving the quality and scope of the tourism product.	All
Improve sustainability	Facilitate marketing and database management co-ordination.	Impart information to stakeholders to raise quality and improve sustainability.	RTA/LA
Quality awareness scheme	Establish the provision and quality of the tourism product.	The quality awareness scheme should recognize and promote excellence.	LA
Quality improvement	Enrich the destination's quality.	Corroborate improvement in destination quality through paid employment and in the performance of small businesses enabling on-going investment and high standards of customer care.	NPA/RTA/LA
Quality improvement and customer	Formulate initiatives to improve product quality.	A key role would be to support businesses, ensure high standards of environmental management and reward good practice.	All

service			
Quality of experience	Maximize the satisfaction and quality of experience of tourists.	Raise awareness and demand for the quality through multi-media campaigns by building relationships with TICs and via the website.	NTA/RTA
Transport services	Transport stakeholders should work in close association with each other.	Improve the quality of transport services from, to and within the destination.	LA
Social			
Actual and potential tourists	Ensure that destination product is appropriate to their needs.	Determine what the actual and potential tourists' needs and wants are.	NTA/NPA/RTA
Media related authenticity	Preserve film and television authenticity.	Reproduce film and television icons/sites/scenes/sets to promote authenticity.	RSA/RTA
Tourist information strategy	Investigate the viability of implementing a long-term tourist information strategy.	Utilize the long-term tourist information strategy in the destination which should be familiar to all of the stakeholders.	All
Responsive tour operators	Back any responsive tour operators.	Support certified tour operators, special packages deals to promote sustainability.	NPA/RTA

6.5 Applying the Model

The next challenge for this model would be to find a destination where the stakeholders are willing to test the model. Testing would necessitate a comprehensive collection of the quantifiable impacts summarized in the model to determine the current state of the film induced tourism industry. Subsequent to this, the model would be used to detect and examine trends of each impact. Depending on the situation in which the model is used, the positive or negative movement of tourists could be used to indicate a move towards or away from the film induced tourism goals that the stakeholders have in place (Flanagan *et al.* 2007). Hence, in its simplest form, the FMAP acts as a benchmark against which changes (resulting from film induced tourism) in the destination can be measured. In a destination where there is an apparent concern for the lack of such tourism, more resources would firstly be spent on the first part of the model (Before Release – Planning), while this may not be an initial concern for other destinations. In actual fact, the only aspects of the model to be used may be those within **Table 6.3a**. The manner in which the model is adopted will result from the tourism marketing strategy in which it is operationalized, but in order to be seen as a true model of such tourism, all aspects of **Tables 6.3a and 6.3b (see Appendix 3)** should be implemented.

6.6 Implementing the Model

Flanagan *et al.* (2007) argue that tourism marketing and management are currently experiencing great change. As a result, the internet is being used increasingly as a travel planning tool, which is important for both the tourist and the stakeholder. It allows them both to acquire instant access to more information about tourism destinations than ever before and tourism stakeholders are marketing their products faster and cheaper and in a progressively more targeted way. In this research study, the stakeholders are responsible for the delivery of tourism in some form, from the NTA to the smaller stakeholders. The FMAP therefore could be considered as a sustainable tourism model for film induced locations. Thus, Denman's (2006) key stages for implementing sustainable tourism management can be used for implementing sustainable tourism management, which can be adapted for usage in the case of the FMAP:

- Form a multi-interest working group;
- Agree on preliminary topics to examine;
- Embark on extensive consultations;
- Plan a situation analysis, comprising destination performance, needs and opportunities;
- Settle on key issues and priorities;
- Decide on strategic objectives;
- Cultivate an action programme;

- Ascertain and reinforce instruments to assist implementation;
- Execute actions;
- Observe results (Flanagan *et al.* 2007).

6.7   Implications

Proactively targeting film stakeholders is undoubtedly central at the pre-production stage and, in particular, some destinations are employing a public relations firm and becoming involved in location scouting. This supports a recent government report in New Zealand sponsored by the film stakeholders, which implied that getting involved at the beginning of film production is a key success factor for destinations (New Zealand Institute of Economic Research 2002). A further option is to offer film producers tours, which have been successful for some destinations. Such sales-focused initiatives should be performed by DMOs regularly and they should also be giving educational and scouting trips to film stakeholders (Hudson and Ritchie 2006b: 393–394).

Hudson and Ritchie (2006b: 393–394) state that at the pre-production stage DMOs should work together with film stakeholders because this is critical to film induced tourism success and corroborates earlier research (Grihault 2003). A further important element of film induced tourism success is the marketing of film locations themselves. Even though DMOs believe the generation of publicity to be the most significant factor for film induced tourism, they should think about placing more effort into having guided tours, film walks, advertising hotels and houses used in films, packaging attractions to extend stays, and constructing film and site maps for tourists. These activities seem to have more influence in attracting film induced tourists. This would respond to the obvious growing desire of film induced tourists to go to see locations that they have seen on the big screen (Riley *et al.* 1998).

Based on a methodical literature review, a regional survey and strategic conversations at a film induced tourism destination, this research has presented an invaluable insight into what Hudson and Ritchie (2006b: 395) describe as a comparatively new phenomenon which offers destinations the chance to create substantial additional income, economic development and tourist visits.

6.8 Final Thoughts on Film Induced Tourism

6.8.1   The concept of film induced tourism

It should also be acknowledged that film induced tourism is a complicated and vibrant concept and success depends on many factors beyond a destination's control. It was beyond the extent of this research to investigate these external factors in any real depth. Without a doubt, further research is necessary to scrutinize these and other factors relating to such tourism. There is also a need for more research into the emotional and behavioural aspects of film induced tourists. Several variables may affect a film's impact on viewers' attitudes toward a destination and as a result, the impact of tourism on these variables must be examined. It would be tremendously helpful to build an operational model to approximate the effects (both in terms of tourist numbers and spending) of choosing to use a specific destination for film or television. The model could analyse the effect and also could compute the potential value and the costs of a film or television series to the proposed destination. Such research could examine the impacts of different types of films and television series (Hudson and Ritchie 2006b: 395).

6.8.2 Growing body of research

Only a few years ago, there was a scarcity of academic research on the phenomenon of film induced tourism. A variety of studies have since examined this phenomenon and the benefits both before and after the cinematic release of a film for a host destination (Carl *et al.* 2007: 49). Busby and O'Neill (2006: 35) noted that travel inspired by the visual media has existed since the Grand Tour (17–19th centuries) (Butler 1990). Hudson and Ritchie (2006b: 388) suggest that there is a growing body of research related to film induced tourism (Beeton 2005) which can be categorized into four broad categories:

- *Film induced tourism as a destination motivator* (Bolan and Davidson 2005; Busby and Klug 2001; Riley *et al.* 1998; Riley and van Doren 1992a; Safari Kinkead 2002; Sharp 2000; Tooke and Baker 1996; Urry 1990)
- *The film induced tourist* (Macionis 2004a; Singh and Best 2004)
- *The impact of film induced tourism on both tourists and residents* (Beeton 2001a, 2001b, 2004a, 2005; Bordelon and Dimanche 2003; Busby *et al.* 2003; Connell 2005b; Cousins and Andereck 1993; Croy and Walker 2003; Gundle 2002; Iwashita 1999, 2006; Kim and Richardson 2003; Mordue 2001; O'Connor and Flanagan 2001; O'Connor *et al.* 2005; Sargent 1998; Schofield 1996; Stewart 1997; Torchin 2002)
- *Film induced destination marketing activities* (Beeton 2002; Cohen 1986; Connell 2005a; Frost 2004; Grihault 2003, O'Connor *et al.* 2006; Hudson and Ritchie 2006a, 2006b; Woodward 2000).

It is outside the scope of this research to appraise all of this literature and the focus of this research was on the latter two categories related to the impacts of film induced tourism and destination marketing. Nevertheless, it is evident from the preceding research, that film and television can both have a very positive impact on tourism to a destination (Hudson and Ritchie 2006b: 387–389).

6.9 Conclusion

Chapter 6 has brought together the overall findings of the research study. These were examined in conjunction with the main objectives of the study **(See Table 1.2)** which were investigated in the context of Yorkshire. The main objective for this chapter was to create the FMAP, which was the primary outcome of this research study **(See Table 1.2 – Research Objective 3)**. This was the final result of the research study and it will be used to guide the development of film induced tourism in a destination's tourism and/or marketing strategy. Consequently, this study contributes significantly to the existing knowledge base on the topic. Finally, Chapter 6 drew on and strived to appreciate the most significant findings from the literature and where appropriate, some new sources of secondary information were utilized. The last chapter **(Chapter 7)** will bring the research to a close by reassessing the most prevalent findings and investigating their contribution to the existing knowledge on film induced tourism. Additionally, the limitations of the research will be further outlined, and proposals for further investigation of the film induced tourism phenomenon are suggested.

CHAPTER 7

CONCLUSIONS AND RECOMMENDATIONS

7.1   Introduction

This research study examines the impact of film induced tourism and destination branding on locations featured in popular television series in Yorkshire. It also investigates the characteristics of film induced tourism, as the need for a thorough and comprehensive investigation of this phenomenon was particularly evident. In addition, Chapter 7 pinpoints the film induced images that tourists presently have of Yorkshire **(Research Objective 1)** and determines if the key tourism and film stakeholders support the integration of film into Yorkshire's tourism product **(Research Objective 2)**. A final result of this research is the creation of a model, the FMAP **(See Chapter 6)**, which will guide the development of film induced tourism in a destination's tourism and/or marketing strategy **(Research Objective 3)**. As a result, this study contributes significantly to the existing knowledge base on the topic.

7.2   Research Approach

To satisfy the research objectives of this study, an interdisciplinary approach was adapted. Insights from a variety of areas such as tourism and marketing were utilized and incorporated into the research framework. This gathering of data from a variety of disciplines was necessary given the nature of the topic being researched. Following an extensive review of the literature, it was noted that there was a significant research gap in relation to how film induced tourism could be used to market a destination. Most of the existing tourism decision models (see Beeton 2002: 5; Hudson and Ritchie 2006a: 258, 2006b: 390, Macionis 2004a: 22) did not reflect the present-day academic research and as such an updated model was required. In response to these primary gaps, a two phased approach was adopted: the first involved gathering and analysing quantitative data (tourist survey) regarding the film induced tourist, while the second phase consisted of strategic conversations with the key tourism and film stakeholders behind the Yorkshire brand. The approaches supplemented one another and each was successful in attaining the necessary information to satisfy the research objectives **(see Table 1.2)**.

7.3   Review of Research Objectives and Findings

The objectives of this research **(see Table 1.2)** guided and directed the research effort throughout. Apart from the last of the expected outcomes (see list below), all have been identified and evaluated at length in **Chapter 5**.

- Develop an initial understanding of the film induced tourism concept as applied to Yorkshire from the tourists perspective **(Research Objective 1)**.

230

- Determine if film induced tourism is a future priority for the stakeholders **(Research Objective 2).**

- Identify if the stakeholders accept that film induced tourism is a viable tourism product **(Research Objective 2).**

- Discover to what extent the integration of film and tourism has actually occurred in Yorkshire **(Research Objective 2).**

- See if film induced tourism can be used as a stand alone destination brand **(Research Objective 2).**

- Detect if the stakeholders work together **(Research Objective 2).**

- Recommend a final course of action through the creation of an FMAP **(Research Objective 3).**

The last and most important expected outcome was investigated in **Chapter 6,** which forms the conclusions to this research study. From the results of the research a large amount of data emerged, relating to many aspects of the film induced tourism phenomenon. Some of the most notable themes and issues will now be reviewed. Each has been examined in detail during this research study and therefore will be referred to here only in terms of the most prominent findings.

7.4   Emergent Themes and Issues

The emergent themes and associated issues which arose from the literature review and the tourist survey formed the basis of the strategic conversations. These were previously illustrated in **Figure 4.1**. The most important results **(see Chapter 5)** from the strategic conversations are outlined in the following sections.

7.4.1   The authenticity of the destination's tourism product **(Research Objective 1)**

Screen Yorkshire maintains that even films or television series based on a fictional way of life can provide a positive image to a film tourist through engagement with the story in much the way that tourists to Holmfirth want to experience the *Last of the Summer Wine* phenomenon. Kirklees Metropolitan Council suggests that Yorkshire is trying to present a more modern image than the old traditional one that currently can be seen in many of its television series (*Heartbeat* and *The Last of the Summer Wine*), which in many senses may not endorse the future progression of the Yorkshire image. The researcher found the idea of promoting a more modern Yorkshire to be solely endorsed by the YTB. The other tourism and film stakeholders felt that while it was necessary to develop the leading Yorkshire brand, the rural image that it currently has should be maintained in an 'if it's not broken don't fix it' mentality. Tourist belief in a destination brand is crucial if the brand is to be successful in promoting a destination; hence the researcher suggests that the tourism and film

231

stakeholders in Yorkshire should capitalize on its current image of a traditional rural destination which seems to be what tourists to Yorkshire are actually seeking.

7.4.2   Modernizing the Yorkshire brand **(Research Objective 2)**

VisitBritain has developed both the British and English brands but not the Yorkshire brand as this is the responsibility of the YTB.   The YTB feels that Yorkshire has many of the attributes characteristic of the UK and England brands.   VisitBritain claims that Yorkshire has been successful in its branding and identity creation through its alignment to its core visual appeals and the representation of this on screen (*Calendar Girls, Heartbeat*). This can always be improved if Yorkshire uses a more integrated representation of its contemporary, urban culture in its branding.

Tourism is Yorkshire's biggest income generator and as such it is crucial that all forms of tourism are seen as potential income generators. Yet, since O'Connor *et al.* (2006) have studied the impact of film induced tourism on Yorkshire, it has become increasingly evident that some of the stakeholders like the YTB are overusing the film and television imagery in their destination marketing. This in turn may result in considerable economic (e.g. the recession), environmental (energy shortages) and social (urban and rural dilapidation) problems (O'Connor *et al.*, 2006). These may threaten the future of Yorkshire's tourism industry.

The YTB is currently trying to re-launch Yorkshire's image as 'modern' and not as 'traditional' which comes across in its many television series. This has not really happened to date, which may be due to some of Yorkshire's enormously successful television series, *Emmerdale* and recent films like *Calendar Girls*, as these both reinforce the traditional image of Yorkshire. The issue here is if the YTB wants to brand Yorkshire as a modern vibrant tourist destination while its film and television series portray it as a rural and slow-paced location, the branding message may become blurred.

7.4.3   Development of a strong brand is vital for future success of a destination **(Research Objective 2)**

Screen East argues that the brand needs to reflect the destination otherwise it will weaken and return visitation will invariably decline. The Yorkshire Dales brand does indeed reflect the tourist product and it was very successful when the television series *All Creatures Great and Small* was first broadcast as per the respondents (see Beeton 2001a, 2005; Mintel 2003; Mordue 1999, 2001; O'Connor and Flanagan 2000; O'Connor *et al.* 2005, 2006; Tooke and Baker 1996).   Tourism professionals want images created by other sectors, such as the film industry, to reflect and support the brand not weaken it. So as to maximize effectiveness, the strong image of the destination should be aligned to the destination branding from the DMO. They can then make the best out of the free advertising. Nevertheless, with films or television this may not always be the case as no one will really know how powerful the production will be until it is transmitted, nor will they know whether the images portrayed therein will tally with the destination brand.

Production companies do not consider destination marketing when they make a film or television series as they are looking for locations that reflect a script and the director's perception of how the storyline should be portrayed. For that reason, VisitBritain feels that the images can be powerful, but the destination may not be portrayed in accordance with the destination brand. If both the tourism and film stakeholders are involved in the initial planning of the film and/or television related promotion, as occurred with VisitBritain and *The Da Vinci Code*, a more agreeable brand (from the destination's viewpoint) could be put forward. This in turn is more likely to be supported by the stakeholders involved in the branding of the destination, therefore a stronger brand will be in place to make the destination more competitive.

7.4.4   Yorkshire's tourism and film stakeholders should work in tandem **(Research Objective 2)**
Many academic researchers (Beeton 2001a, 2005; Mintel 2003; Mordue 1999, 2001; O'Connor and Flanagan 2000; O'Connor *et al.* 2005, 2006; Tooke and Baker 1996) have studied Yorkshire as a film induced tourism destination. They suggest that the YTB could benefit more from incorporating film and television into tourism destination marketing and planning, but so far they have not been very proactive considering the number of film and television series **(see Table 1.1)**, that have freely promoted Yorkshire to date. Currently, film induced tourism is not a strategic priority for the YTB and it has no plans to use it in its future marketing and/or branding campaigns. Previously, the Board had used it (when devising the *Yorkshire on Screen Film Trail* - 2001/2002), but it was not deemed financially viable to continue in the long term. The use of the film induced tourism phenomenon seems to have been a success in recent times, as seen with *Pride and Prejudice* where agencies such as the Peak District National Park have worked with their RSA, EM-Media. They responded to demand and produced materials to encourage tourism.

Unfortunately, in Yorkshire, the tourism and film stakeholders do not work together, even when a big budget film like *Harry Potter* is being produced there. This represents a failed valuable opportunity when the brand could be successfully integrated into any film promotion packages as seen in the Peak District. Ideally, the multiplier effects should be considered during the shooting of the film or television series. Screen East claims that moving image media tend to strengthen the brand they are trying to portray. It can become even more successful if the tourist board and the local tourism officers collaborate with their respective RSAs which presently is not happening in Yorkshire.

The popularity and longevity of a film or television production have contributed to the creation of successful media related brands, both domestically and internationally. In reality these brands have not been that successful, as witnessed in the tourist survey, but on the other hand it was found in the strategic conversations that the tourism stakeholders in particular feel that they have. This may be because these brands are used very much by Yorkshire based attractions and by the tourism stakeholders themselves but not so much in the promotional related literature.

Numerous authors (Morgan *et al.* 2002; Morgan *et al.* 2003; Piggott *et al.* 2004) have examined the impact of *The Lord of the Rings* trilogy on New Zealand with some suggestions on how the successful integration of a film into a destinations' brand can take place. This research shows how it can be beneficial to incorporate film and television into tourism destination marketing and planning.

7.4.5   Brand image can be a strong tourism destination motivator **(Research Objective 2)**
This study found that a strong motivator in creating interest is in fact the destination brand image; this concurs with studies undertaken by Awaritefe (2004), Bolan and Davidson (2005), Bordelon and Dimanche (2003), Lam and Ap (2006), Mayo (1973), Mayo and Jarvis (1981), Pearce (1982) and Ross (1993). Yorkshire has a strong positive brand image through its television series, films, books and a general feeling of nostalgia for the county in the way that it is portrayed by the YTB. The National Trust ascertains that many tourists are looking for something different, so what the brand says about a destination can either encourage or discourage them. The destination brand image shows that a place will appeal to whichever group of travellers it is aiming to attract.

Films and television series can act as a strong tourism destination motivator (see Beeton 2000, 2001a, 2001b, 2002, 2005; Butler 1990; Connell 2005b; Hudson and Ritchie 2006a; Macionis 2004a; Mishra *et al.* 2006 and Reeves 2003) but it should be noted that there is only a small amount of empirical data available to support this claim. This may be why film induced tourism is not being considered by the YTB as part of its overall tourism product.

7.4.6 The images portrayed in films/television play an important role in influencing travellers' expectations of Yorkshire **(Research Objectives 1)**

VisitBritain believe that the tourist industry is actually cutting down on printed material and putting more time and money into website development, which seems to be the most appropriate way forward. Group-travel type tourists still read brochures, while independent travellers rely more on web-based information. Screen East insists that the power of the moving image will continue to provide a strong influence. Promotional literature can portray a destination in a different way through people's imagination whereas film media (DVD, film and television) can portray a more realistic visual portrayal of a destination. The survey results showed that the television series examined have been running for many years and are not set in current times, therefore the respondents that indentified these as being set in Yorkshire were the older tourists.

7.4.7 Challenge of sustaining the benefits of film induced tourism **(Research Objective 2)**

As mentioned earlier, most film induced tourism research addresses relatively small tourism destinations where actual variation in numbers can easily be measure. The multiplier effect continues as films are screened through DVD and television. As long as the film remains popular there is likely to be some form of multiplier effect, as the production continues to provide a free promotional opportunity as per one of the respondents. VisitBritain indicates that the many ways people see films and television series are means of reaching new audiences in emerging markets and so film induced tourism can be an effective way to capitalize on the positive portrayal of destinations on screen. The benefits of this phenomenon are very much embraced by the UK Film Council and VisitBritain at a national level as they have invested a lot of time and money into the promotion of *Bond* films, for example. While all of the RSAs are trying to maximize on the benefits of film induced tourism, the YTB regards the phenomenon as economically unviable and not part of their overall tourism product now or in the future. This seems to be short-sighted and a lost opportunity for Yorkshire, as the limited research on film induced tourism has illustrated the phenomenon can indeed bring many positive benefits to a destination (see Beeton 2005; Riley *et al.* 1998) **(see Chapter 3)**.

7.4.8 Controlling film induced tourism impacts – positive **(Research Objective 2)**

Depending on the strength of the production, there are many positive benefits of film induced tourism which have been previously highlighted in **Chapter 3** (Beeton 2001a; Busby and Klug 2001; Butler 1990; Iwashita 1999, 2006; Morgan and Prichard 1998; Riley and Van Doren 1992a; Riley *et al.* 1998; Safari Kinkead 2002; Tooke and Baker 1996). These positive benefits include increased employment in the tourist industry, product sales, new hotels, and the production talent staying in the area as seen in Yorkshire. Screen Yorkshire found that it has also extended the tourist season which now stretches from March to November, boosted the morale of the community, and increased a feeling of pride in the area. It can heighten the appeal of a destination and make it more recognizable, which is likely to be the case both from an economical and a community sustainability perspective.

7.4.9   Controlling film induced tourism impacts – negative **(Research Objective 2)**

Problems can arise if the film or television series is a huge success and no infrastructure has been put in place to maximize the opportunity or manage the demand. This has occurred in Goathland (*Heartbeat*), where the local infrastructure cannot cope with the increased influx of tourists and there is open hostility between local residents and tourists. At the beginning of this research study, the researcher was advised by a key tourism stakeholder in Goathland not to survey the residents, as the level of hostility had reached record levels. The literature on film induced tourism reveals that films and television series have the strength to influence and even pull visitors to a destination (Riley and Van Doren 1992a). Alternatively, less attractive impacts are often generated by spontaneous increases in tourist demand within a short timeframe (Connell 2005b: 228).

7.4.9.1 *Congestion*

There is a danger that a destination can become so popular that people are in danger of destroying its tranquil nature in addition to spoiling the environment, for example, deteriorating footpaths. They simply cannot deal with the extra numbers. Screen Yorkshire advocates the fact that the NYMNP is not set up for coach tours. A huge influx of tour buses in areas that do not have the infrastructure in place to manage the tourists, the vehicles, or to maximize their presence in terms of tourism spend, can cause irritation to the local community. This is very evident in conservation areas such as the small heritage market towns and villages.

7.4.9.2 *Resident negativity*

VisitBritain deems that the negative effects of film induced tourism tend to come in spurts and can often overwhelm a smaller destination. If a series uses a location heavily, the disruption can be quite tiring for the residents. Goathland (*Heartbeat*) cannot cope with the increased tourist influx, consequently carrying capacity problems are evident with the daily arrival of many tour buses. Tourists are also disappointed that Goathland is in the 21st century and not in the 1960s, when *Heartbeat* is set. This supports Demetriadi's (1996) and Tooke and Baker's (1996: 72) research on Goathland and links in with Beeton's (2005: 19) analysis of film induced tourism on Barwons

236

Heads in Australia. If a private residence is used in a production (as with *The Monarch of the Glen*), tourists have been known to seek out the house and try to gain access which can have a considerable impact on the home owner.

Issues such as congestion, overcrowding and escalating property prices must be considered together, some of which arose in Yorkshire, due to the growth of film induced tourism. Through considering the possible costs and benefits of film induced tourism, Yorkshire has the potential to use the benefits to strengthen itself and minimize the costs. Such a solution may seem unsophisticated, which it is definitely not, as the complexities of these communities are continually escalating (Beeton 2005).

7.4.10 The critical success of a film versus a television series **(Research Objective 2)**

VisitBritain stated that tourism induced by films and television series proposes that they can be an effective tool to help destination images and affect the audience's interest in visiting the place, as in *Pride and Prejudice*. The repeat viewing factor is a unique opportunity for destinations to create an FMAP for their area. The biggest recent development has been the life after films on cable, video/DVD, specialized channels and the internet. Popular films, such as *Four Weddings and a Funeral*, *Mary Poppins* and *Notting Hill*, continue to portray a strong image of the UK through ongoing screenings on television which continues to induce tourists to the destination. Through the continued screening of films and repeat television series, this will continue for some time without any efforts from the tourism stakeholders.

The Sound of Music is often shown on television and this continues to be a big motivating factor for tourists to visit Austria. The same can be said for *Braveheart* and Scotland; *Crocodile Dundee* and Australia; *The Lord of the Rings* and New Zealand; *The Beach* and Thailand; *Sleepless in Seattle* and New York, USA; *Love Actually* (2003) and London, UK; *Gladiator* (2000) and Rome, Italy; *Gandhi* (1982) and India; *Doctor Zhivago* (1965) and Russia; *Out of Africa* and Kenya. This is also evident in the new wave of children's animated films – *Ratatouille* (2007) and Paris, France, or *Finding Nemo* and Australia. *The Full Monty* is a popular British film and is often repeated on television. Initially the residents hated it, as they thought it portrayed a depressing 1980s image, while Sheffield is now perceived and marketed to be a vibrant city. *The Full Monty* could have been set in any city as it was not intended to be a showcase for Sheffield. Nevertheless, there has been another spin-off, as there are creative/technical people now based in Sheffield, which has established a modest television/film industry in the city.

Audiences will continue to have even more exposure through the weekly viewing of a television series and as a result they may form a greater attachment to the story and the location. Audiences can view television series as extensions of their own lives, and as a result the desire to see where the television series is filmed is great due to their strong attachment. This can also be the case with very popular films, but as they are not getting a weekly exposure to the story/location, it is suggested that the attachment weakens much quicker. The main perceived difference between the results derived from research relating to television series versus a feature length film, is that television series have the advantage of repeat viewing and also may run for many years as seen with *Last of the Summer Wine*. With the growth of the internet e.g. YouTube and the increase in DVD sales, the longevity of the feature length film is rapidly increasing, therefore the impact of such films on a destination may increase either positively or negatively.

There are many examples of television series that have raised the profile of a destination: the very popular children televisions series *Balamory* (2003–) has certainly promoted Scotland in a positive light (Connell 2005a, 2005b), as has *Neighbours* (1985–) and Australia; *Eastenders* (1985–) and London, UK; *Heartbeat* and Yorkshire, UK (Beeton 2000, 2005; O'Connor *et al.* 2005, 2006; Tooke and Baker 1996); *Lost* (2003–) and Hawaii, USA (Kotler *et al.* 1993); *Dirty Sexy Money* (2007–) and New York, USA; *CSI* (2000–) and Las Vegas, Miami and New York. These television series are continually promoting these destinations internationally at no extra cost for the tourism stakeholders. Even television series that are no longer being filmed such as *All Creatures Great and Small*, *Magnum PI* (1980–1988) (Hawaii, USA) (Kotler *et al.* 1993), *Miami Vice* (1984–1989) (Miami, USA) (Chambers 1989) and *Sex and the City* (1998–2004) (New York, USA) (Torchin 2002) still continue to be shown on cable and mainstream television worldwide. These demonstrate the continuing impact that a television series can have on a destination.

7.4.11 The effectiveness of the movie map as a marketing tool to promote a destination **(Research Objective 2)**

With the convergence of RSAs, tourism promoters and media writers, the notion of film induced tourism has been established, even though little has been done to use this information until recently. Taking advantage of it has only happened in recent years when DVDs and movie maps have been produced by tourism stakeholders in the quest for attracting tourists. These marketing efforts have been taken on with the aim of profiting from film induced tourism (Riley *et al.* 1998: 920). Many of the stakeholders interviewed concur with this, supporting research carried out by Beeton (2005), Bolan and Davidson (2005) and Tooke and Baker (1996).

The YTB is not planning to produce any further movie maps as it is felt that the internet is a more effective marketing tool. This has also occurred in Ireland, where the Wicklow Film Commission (the RSA for County Wicklow, Ireland) produced its movie map several years ago but has no plans to update it (O'Connor *et al.* 2005, 2006). In contrast, Film London has recently successfully branded London as a film destination by devising a 'movie map' incorporating such films as *Closer* (2004), *Notting Hill* and *The Da Vinci Code*.

Yorkshire Forward suggests that a wider audience can be reached through the medium of television, the internet and tour operators. Key authors and books also seem to have a larger influence like James Herriot and the Brontë sisters. This is very evident with the *Harry Potter* series and the *Lord of the Rings* books and *Bridget Jones's Diaries* which have become very successful books and subsequently films in their own right. Busby and O'Neill (2006: 33) maintain that within the UK, the literacy tourism market is growing (DCMS 1999; Beeton 2001). The RTAs maintain that it is economically viable with brands such as *Agatha Christie Country* (Busby *et al.* 2003). *Shakespeare Country* alone generates an annual revenue of STG£135m for the Stratford-Upon-Avon economy (Andersen and Robinson 2002) and numerous locations have linked themselves to the incredibly successful *Harry Potter* books and films which are marketed through VisitBritain's *Potter Map* (Bentham 2001).

7.4.12 Tourist stakeholders should be aware of the benefits of using positive destination images in a film or a television series **(Research Objective 2)**

Tourist agencies should be aware of the possible gains from having positive images of a destination in a film (Bordelon and Dimanche 2003: 9). Then again, the promotional ability of each film is not the same, and some films and television series have little impact while others may be both powerful and unforgettable. This is supported by some of the stakeholders **(See Table 5.6)** interviewed. Agencies such as the DCMS, RSA and the television companies should be encouraged to engage with the tourist stakeholders more. This has recently happened between the Peak District National Park Authority and Universal Studios with *Pride and Prejudice*.

The spin-off from film induced tourism can be great but the tourist stakeholders need to know what is being filmed in their area and to take an interest in it. Kirklees Metropolitan Council proposes that the tourist stakeholders need to be aware of the potential gain for featuring positive images of a destination in a film, which should also be part of the area's tourist strategy. To support this idea, the film induced tourism concept could be developed as part of the destination's overall tourism product. This is based on the fact that tourist destinations can be a popular location for film and/or television filming, even more so in destinations which are looking for an alternative income due to the decline in local industries (agriculture, mining and steel) since the UK recession of the 1980s.

Destinations are also prone to external factors which are out of stakeholders' control. Constant consultation between the stakeholders could ease such problems like terrorism, as brands can change in accordance with the changing needs of the market. The researcher supports this initiative but this is not happening between the tourism and film stakeholders in Yorkshire. On the other hand, many film stakeholders constantly collaborate on any film/television related opportunities which arise throughout the UK.

Whilst some communities (Aidensfield – *Heartbeat*) have been able to minimisze the negative film images of their locality (Beeton 2000: 135), until tourism and film stakeholder organizations monetarily contribute to filming they will not have any rights to control how these images are represented in such media. What they do control though are their own tourism images, which may need to be customized in order to take full advantage of the opportunities presented in the increasing enthusiasm for film experiences (Beeton 2004: 134) **(see Chapter 3)**.

7.4.13 Tourism's collaboration with the film industry **(Research Objective 2)**

Collaborative campaigns with the film industry are a strong way to induce film tourists (Grihault 2003). DMOs are beginning to form relationships with the various film stakeholders, with the intention of pursuing productions and film releases, so they are in a position to act as soon as they see the signs of film induced tourism. Executives at VisitBritain try to plan with studios at least one year in advance of a film's release date. In the Bahamas, this is taken so seriously that their film commission is under the patronage of the Ministry of Tourism (Hudson and Ritchie 2006a: 259–260).

The tourism stakeholders need to liaise with the production companies at the post film production stage, as the film stakeholders tend to be more concerned with their own needs and not those of stakeholders. VisitBritain's continual collaboration with the film studios could be seen as a best practice framework for the other stakeholders in the UK to use, as this has been a very productive relationship especially for VisitBritain.

7.5   Contributions of the Study

The principle findings of this research add to the existing pool of knowledge relating to film induced tourism. As already outlined, the topic has been largely neglected by academic researchers with few detailed examinations of this phenomenon being undertaken. Thus, this research goes some way to filling this knowledge gap. Its principle value can be seen in the development of the model (FMAP) for film induced tourism. This researcher's main objective was *to develop a model to be used as a best practice framework for the successful integration of film induced tourism in a destination marketing strategy*. This objective was investigated in the context of Yorkshire, which was used as the case study through which the film induced tourism phenomenon was observed. Overall, the outputs (the FMAP) represent a considerable amount of insight into the film induced tourism phenomenon. This will not only contribute significantly to our existing knowledge on the topic but also stimulate further debate and research, something which is very much needed **(Research Objective 3)**.

7.6   Consideration on Research Methodology Used

As outlined in **Chapter 4,** the research methodology adopted for this research is a mixed method approach. This resulted in a two phased research approach being implemented in a sequential manner. Initially, the primary research consisted of a quantitative survey of 300 tourists to Yorkshire. This method proved successful for eliciting the necessary comparative data to examine the distinctiveness of the film induced tourism market **(See Chapter 4)**.

However, in order to achieve the principle requirement of the research study – *to develop a model to be used as a best practice framework for the successful integration of film induced tourism in a destination marketing strategy* – it was necessary to use both a quantitative and a qualitative approach. This was due to the nature of the specific data required. Thus, the second phase consisted of 28 strategic conversations with the tourism and film stakeholders in Yorkshire. Both phases complemented each other, with the survey setting the scene by building a picture of the film induced tourist and providing details which subsequently helped in the formation of the topics to be discussed in the strategic conversations **(See Figure 4.3)**. Subsequently, the quality and richness of the data from these allowed the relevant issues and themes relating to film induced tourism to emerge. Accordingly, when reviewing the results as a whole it can be maintained that both phases proved successful and justified the mixed methods approach adopted.

Following the findings of both phases of the research, it has become apparent that most of the film induced tourism models discussed **(see Chapter 6)** are inadequate in describing or explaining the film induced tourism process from a branding perspective. Thus, a new model which is more reflective of the process was constructed, using the main concepts and themes that emerged from the research findings. The FMAP provides a useful analytical tool for both academics and practitioners in terms of using the film induced tourism phenomenon to brand a destination. The following section describes the conclusions to each phase of the research findings and combines them to form overall recommendations **(Research Objective 3)**.

7.7 Overall Observations and Recommendations

Arising from the research, a number of observations are made and recommendations are proposed. The first of these focus on the research limitations, the others are more film related issues and finally recommendations for further study are explored.

7.7.1 Research limitations

Despite the overall success of the research methodology, a number of limitations were identified **(see Chapter 4)**. Probably the most significant of these relates to the generalizability of the results. Thus, the emphasis was placed on exploring issues and themes, rather than testing an existing hypothesis. Yet, because the primary research focus was on Yorkshire, the extent to which the findings are transferable to other destinations is not clear and for that reason caution needs to be considered.

Yorkshire was selected as the case study area as Yorkshire has been the film location for a number of well-known English television series, and high numbers of film induced tourists visit its film sites (see Beeton 2000, 2005; Mordue 1999, 2001; O'Connor *et al.* 2005, 2006, 2008). Although, there are reasons to be cautious about generalizing in relation to these findings, there is little doubt that many of the themes and issues could be applicable to other such tourism destinations, with some minor adjustments.

7.7.2 Recommendations for future study

This study intended to develop an appreciation of how film and television series can induce tourism based on an examination of Yorkshire. There is undoubtedly a drawback of the study in that it is selective instead of widespread or comprehensive. Consequently, it is acknowledged that generalization of the results would be speculative (Zikmund 1997). Additional research, encompassing a larger range of case studies, would be advantageous, to reveal more ways in which the media are used, or intervene, within the environment of the tourism industry. It is also anticipated that future research will focus on developing tactics regarding the media so that positive

242

relationships can be developed between the tourist and the stakeholder (Hede and O'Mahony 2004: 14).

Lam and Ap (2006: 167) argue that since film induced tourism is a comparatively new area of research it is imperative to recognize what the present literature has to say, ascertain gaps in the literature and look at future directions for such research. If film induced tourism as a field of research is not focused on, our appreciation of it will continue to be inadequate and its promise to mature as a tourist product in many destinations may not be fully understood, resulting in lost opportunities for destinations to strengthen their alluring pull factors.

Despite the fact that film induced tourism has regularly been overlooked by many internationally renowned destinations, for instance Hong Kong, researchers still have the opportunity to examine the possibility of developing such tourism in these destinations. Therefore, to facilitate a better appreciation of the film induced tourism concept, further study on this phenomenon as a tourism product in its own right and its power to increase the appeal and competitiveness of a destination is essential (Lam and Ap 2006: 167).

Whilst this research has contributed to the existing knowledge of film induced tourism, it would undoubtedly be beneficial to build on it through further research. In particular research that would examine whether the main findings identified here are more widely representative would be useful. A multi-destination research study could be undertaken in examining film induced tourism. This would provide rich, comparative data on the nature and characteristics of the phenomenon in other such destinations. These studies would add significantly to the concept of film induced tourism worldwide and more importantly would highlight the similarities and discrepancies between the different film induced destinations. However, such an understanding would need to be carefully co-ordinated with the intention of ensuring reliability across the different studies.

The existing research on film induced tourism is seemingly in short supply, in all probability due to its short history. Many destinations are presently putting efforts into developing such tourism. The changes taking place in the film induced tourism product of many destinations will subsequently provide various themes for interested researchers to investigate. An example is Busby and Klug's (2001) survey to assess the influence of the film *Notting Hill* (**see Chapters 2 and 3**) on tourists' decision to visit Notting Hill, London (UK).

7.7.3   Implementing the FMAP

A greater than ever number of marketers, irritated by waste and the lack of quantifiable results, are moving away from conventional marketing methods toward new communication concepts like product placement (Kaikati and Kaikati 2004). Hudson and Ritchie (2006b: 394) maintain that it is time for destination stakeholders to be more inventive in their marketing. The exposure that a film gives a destination is an advertisement potentially seen by millions of viewers, who cannot be reached through the traditional tourism promotions, hence the development of the FMAP.

In its simplest form, the FMAP forms a benchmark against which change (resulting from film induced tourism) in the destination can be measured. In a destination where there is an apparent concern for the lack of such tourism, more resources would firstly be spent on this aspect of the model, while this may not be an initial concern for other destinations. Depending on the destination in which the model is used, the positive or negative movement of tourists can indicate a move towards or away from the film induced tourism goals that the stakeholders have in place. In actual fact, the only aspects of the model to be used may be those within **Table 6.2a**. The manner in which the model is applied will result from the tourism marketing strategy in which it is placed, however, to be seen as a true model of such tourism, all aspects of **Table 6.2b (see Appendix 3)** should be implemented.

The model proposes that some marketing activities are more successful than others in attracting film induced tourists. Proactively targeting film stakeholders is undoubtedly central at the pre-production stage and in particular, employing a public relations firm and being involved in location scouting. This supports a recent government report in New Zealand sponsored by the film stakeholders which claims that getting involved at the beginning of a film's production is a key success factor for destinations (New Zealand Institute of Economic Research 2002). Another alternative is to offer film producers tours, which have been useful for some destinations (Hudson and Ritchie 2006b: 393–394). Hudson and Ritchie (2006b: 393–394) state that at the pre-production stage, DMOs should work closely with film stakeholders because this is vital for film induced tourism success (Grihault 2003).

7.8 Final Thoughts on the Factors and Variables Affecting Film Induced Tourism

Yorkshire has presented an insight into the film induced tourism phenomenon. This study has corroborated some of the preceding research on this topic, in particular supporting the influential effect that films and television series can have on a destination. It has shown that such tourism is a versatile and vibrant concept and success is reliant on many factors outside the destination's

244

control. Without a doubt, research is required to study these and other factors relating to film induced tourism. There is also a need for more research into the emotional and behavioural aspects of this tourism phenomenon. Many variables may affect the impact of a film or television series on a viewer's image of a destination and, as a result, their engagement with the destination through tourism. Responses to these variables merit further examination (Hudson and Ritchie 2006a: 266).

7.9 Conclusion

The tourism industry is a hugely competitive marketplace in which stakeholders are faced with the job of developing successful techniques to reach their target markets. The conventional tourism marketing media such as television promotion and literature have become dull and even though these media tend to be widespread, their success appears to be minimal compared to that of films. Tourists visiting a destination after having seen the location in a film or television series is an emerging phenomenon; and due to the perceived benefits, many films have had tourism stakeholders in their locations explore the issues relating to film induced tourism (Safari Kinkead 2002). Film induced tourism is partially based on tourist demands to escape reality, to the better world represented in films. By understanding the film tourist phenomenon, tourism and film stakeholders can better meet experiences, thus expanding on the positive impacts in such destinations (Carl *et al.* 2007: 60).

Beeton (2005: 5) suggests that the perception that de-marketing only relating to negative marketing sre still occurring. Nonetheless, in the healthcare sector, de-marketing has been perceived as a suitable tool to deter anti-social behaviour. While de-marketing has been seen as more a 'do not use our services' marketing, its real benefits will not be maximized upon. Film and television series are strong tourism inducers and image-makers and it would be beneficial for a destination to incorporate filming into destination marketing plans. Once a destination becomes aware of the nature of film-induced tourism, it is feasible to integrate suitable marketing and de-marketing strategies into the destinations marketing plans which will assist them in creating a sustainable tourism product (Beeton, 2005: 5).

The internet and indeed television offers great opportunities for creating a strong destination brand. There are numerous advantages associated with these interactive marketing tools over the traditional branding methods used to brand mainly the reduction in costs and lead times. Conversely, Palmer (2004) states that having a website in itself is not enough to promise continuous success of a tourist destination. In an age when each destination can create an interactive marketing tool, a website must be able to develop its market position and promote a strong electronic presence.

Never before have DMOs' had so many routes to reach their target markets and these should be maximized upon (Palmer, 2 004: 139). Tourism Australia[64] developed a marketing campaign for the recent film *Australia* (2008). They financed the film director Baz Luhramn to make a series of commercials generally related to the feature film to accompany its release. These commercials tried to recreate the films main themes (adventure, romance and transformation). Other marketing tools used in this branding campaign included billboards, themed postcards, a foldout movie map and a booklet containing motivational destination information (Roesch, 2009: 227-228).

The development of film induced tourism was reviewed and analyzed to provide an overview and evaluation of the present nature and status of film induced tourism. This research study also discussed possible directions and areas for future film tourism research. Studies on issues relating to film induced tourism, such as its nature, forms, characteristics, effects on the residents of destinations and tourist behaviour were not conducted until the mid-1990s. Following a broad search of the existing research on film induced tourism, it was observed that the academic literature on film induced tourism is somewhat scarce, which is in all probability due to its relatively short history (Lam and Ap 2006: 166).

The final chapter of this study provides the theoretical background for this study's research objectives (**See Table 1.2**). The issues which arose from the literature review and the findings of the tourist survey and the strategic conversations highlight a number of implications for the future development of such destinations. These implications include the many positive and negative impacts of filming the various television series and the successful use of destination branding in the promotion of a film location. It has been shown that film induced tourism has the potential to offer many opportunities but also has many potential risks.

---

64 Tourism Australia is the Government Statutory Authority who is responsible for promoting Australia to the international market.

REFERENCES

- Aaker, D.A. (1996) *Building Strong Brands*, Free Press: Sydney, Australia.

- Aaker, D.A., Kumar, V. and Day, G.S. (2004) *Marketing Research*, 8th edn, John Wiley and Sons: New York, USA.

- Adam, F. and Healy, M. (2000) *A Practical Guide to Postgraduate Research in the Business Area*, Blackhall Publishing: Dublin, Ireland.

- Adelman, C. Jenkins, D. and Kemmis, S. (1983) Rethinking case study: Notes from the second Cambridge conference, *Case Study Methods I*, 2nd edn, Waurn Ponds: Deakin University, pp. 1-10.

- Ahmed, Z.U. (1991) The influence of the components of a state's tourist image on positioning strategy, *Tourism Management*, 12(4), December: 334-340.

- Akama, J.S. and Kieti, D.M. (2003) Measuring tourist satisfaction with Kenya's wildlife safari: A case for Tsavo West National Park, *Tourism Management*, 24(1): 73-81.

- Allison, R.I. and Uhl, K.P. (1964) Brand identification and perception, *Journal of Marketing Research*, 1 (August): 80-85.

- Andereck, K.L. (2006) Publications in review – Film induced tourism, *Annals of Tourism Research*, 33(1): 280-282.

- Andersen, H.C. and Robinson, M. (eds.) (2002) *Literature and Tourism: Reading and Writing Tourism Texts*, Continuum: London, UK.

- Andreu, L., Bigne, J.E. and Cooper, C. (2000) Projected and perceived image of Spain as a tourist destination for British travellers, *Journal of Travel and Tourism Marketing*, 9(4): 47-67.

- Anholt, S. (2004) Nation-brands and the value of provenance. In Morgan, N.J., Pritchard, A. and Pride, R. *Destination Branding: Creating the Unique Destination Proposition*, 2nd edn, Elsevier Butterworth-Heinemann: Oxford, UK.

- Anon. (1996) Taking the less travelled road, *Brandweek*, 4 October.

- Anon. (2004) Movies that give Brits the travel bug, *The Guardian*, 28 September.

- Ap, J. and J.L. Crompton (1993) Residents strategies for responding to tourism impacts, *Journal of Travel Research*, 32 (1): 47-50.

- Ashworth, G.J. and Goodall, B. (1998) *Marketing in the Tourism Industry: the Promotion of Destination Regions*, Routledge: London, UK, pp. 1-17.

- Assael, H. (1984) *Consumer Behaviour and Marketing Action*, Kent Publishing: Boston, Massachusetts, USA.

- ATC (2008) Principles – Our role, http://www.tourism.australia.com/content/About%20Us/Annual%20Report2003.pdf (accessed 24/01/2008).

- Auckland Regional Council (2008) Council, http://www.arc.govt.nz/council/ (accessed 27/02/2008).
- Awaritefe, D.O. (2004) Destination image differences between prospective and actual tourists in Nigeria, *Journal of Vacation Marketing*, 10(3): 264–281.
- Bailar, B. and Lanphier, C. (1978) *Development of Survey Research Methods to Assess Survey Practices*, American Statistical Association: Washington DC, USA.
- Bailey, K.D. (1978) *Methods for Social Research*, Free Press: New York, USA.
- Baloglu, S. and McCleary, K. (1999a) A model of destination image formation, *Annals of Tourism Research*, 26(4): 868–897.
- Baloglu, S. and McCleary, K. (1999b) U.S. international pleasure travellers' mages of four Mediterranean destinations: A comparison of visitors and non-visitors, *Journal of Travel Research*, 38(2) (November): 144–152.
- Beeton, S. (2000) Its a Wrap! What happens after the film crew leaves? An examination of community responses to film-induced tourism. In *Travel and Tourism Research Association (TTRA) Conference Proceedings: Lights, Camera, Action – Spotlight on Tourism in the New Millennium*, Nickerson, R.N. and Moisey, N.P. (eds.) TTRA: Burbank, California, USA, pp. 127–136.
- Beeton, S. (2001a) Smiling for the camera: The influence of film audiences on a budget tourism destination, *Tourism Culture and Communication*, 3: 15–25.
- Beeton, S. (2001b) Cyclops and Sirens – Demarketing as a proactive response to negative consequences of one-eyed competitive marketing. In *TTRA 32nd Conference Proceedings: A Tourism Odyssey*, Moisey, R.N., Nickerson, N.P and Andereck, KL. (eds.), TTRA: Fort Myers, Florida, USA: 125–136.
- Beeton, S. (2002) A (de-)marketing approach to enhancing capabilities for film induced tourism. In *16th Australian and New Zealand Academy of Management (ANZAM) Conference Proceedings: Enhancing Business and Government Capability*, Bennington, L. (ed.), Beechworth, Victoria, Australia, pp. 1–8.
- Beeton, S. (2004) Rural tourism in Australia – Has the gaze altered? Tracking rural images through film and tourism promotion, *International Journal of Tourism Research*, 6(3): 125–135.
- Beeton, S. (2005) *Film Induced Tourism*, Aspects of Tourism (Series 25), Channel View Publications: Chichester, UK.
- Beeton, S. (2006) Location, location, location: Film corporations' social responsibilities. In *International Conference on Impact of Movies and Television on Tourism Conference Proceedings*, Chon, K. and Chan, A. (eds.), Hong Kong Polytechnic University: Hong Kong, China, pp. 7–16.

248

- Belch, G.E. and Belch, M.A. (2001) *Advertising and Promotion: An Integrated Marketing Communications Perspective*, 5th edn, McGraw-Hill: New York, USA.

- Benfield, R. (2001) Turning back the hordes, de-marketing research as a means of managing mass tourism. In *TTRA 32nd Conference Proceedings: A Tourism Odyssey*, Moisey, R.N. and Nickerson, N.P. (eds.), TTRA: Florida, USA.

- Bentham, M. (2001) *Harry Potter* called on to work his magic for tourism, *Daily Telegraph*, 5 August.

- Black, J.A. and Champion, D.J. (1976) *Methods and Issues in Social Research*, John Wiley and Sons: New York, USA.

- Blalock, H.M.J. and Blalock, A.B. (1968) *Methodology in Social Research*, McGraw-Hill: New York, USA.

- Blaxter, L., Hughes, C. and Tight, M. (1996) *How to Research*, Open University Press: Buckingham, UK.

- Bolan, P. and Davidson, K. (2005) Film induced tourism in Ireland: Exploring the potential. In *University of Ulster Conference Proceedings: Tourism and Hospitality Research in Ireland: Exploring the Issues*, Boyd, S. (ed.), University of Ulster: Portrush, Northern Ireland, pp. 1–19.

- Bolan, P. and Williams, L. (2008) The role of image in service promotion: focusing on the influence of film on consumer choice within tourism, *International Journal of Consumer Studies*, 32: 382–390.

- Bordelon, B. and Dimanche, F. (2003) Images of New Orleans: The relationship between motion pictures and tourists' expectations of a travel destination. In *34th Annual TTRA Conference Proceedings* (9 pages), Nickerson, N.P., Moisey R.N. and McGehee, N. (eds.), TTRA: Boise, Idaho, USA.

- Borkowski, N.M. (1994) De-marketing of health services, *Journal of Health Care Marketing*, 14(4): 12.

- Botha, C., Crompton, J.L. and Kim, S. (1999) Developing a revised competitive position for sun/Lost City, South Africa, *Journal Travel Research*, 37, May: 341–352.

- Brannen, J. (1992) Combining qualitative and quantitative methods: An overview. In Brannen, J. (ed.) *Mixing Methods: Qualitative and Quantitative Research*, Avebury: Brookfield, Vermont, USA, pp. 3–38.

- Brannick, T. (1997) An overview of the research process in business research methods: Strategies, techniques and sources. In Brannick, T. and Roche, W. (eds.), *Business Research Methods: Strategies, Techniques and Sources*, Oak Tree Press: Dublin, Ireland, pp. 1–30.

- Brewer, J. and. Hunter, A. (1989) *Multi-method Research: A Synthesis of Styles*, Sage Publications: Newbury Park, California, USA.

- Bronn, P.S. and Bronn, C. (2003) A reflective stakeholder approach: Co-orientation as a basis for communication and learning, *Journal of Communication Management*, 7(4): 291–303.
- Brontë Country (2005) Visitor attractions, http://visitbrontecountry.com (accessed 10/05/2005).
- Brown, F.E. (1980) *Marketing Research: A Structure for Decision Making*, Addison Wesley: Reading, Massachusetts, USA.
- Brown, G., Chalip, L., Jago, L. and Mules, T. (2002) The Sydney Olympics and Brand Australia. In Morgan, N.J., Pritchard, A. and. Pride, R., *Destination Branding: Creating the Unique Destination Proposition*, Elsevier Butterworth-Heinemann: Oxford, UK, pp. 163–185.
- Bryman, A. (1984) The debate about qualitative and quantitative methods: A question of method or epistemology? *British Journal of Sociology*, 35: 75–92.
- Bryman, A. (1988) *Quantity and Quality in Social Research*, Unwin Hyman: London, UK.
- Bryman, A. (1992) Quantitative and qualitative research: Further reflections on their integration. In Brannen, J (ed.) *Mixing Methods: Qualitative and Quantitative Research*, Avebury: Aldershot, Hampshire, UK, pp. 57–78.
- Buckley, K. (2004) DVD sets rules for Hollywood, *Financial Times Newspaper*, January 23, p. 12.
- Busby, G. and Klug, J. (2001) Movie-induced tourism: The challenge of measurement and other issues, *Journal of Vacation Marketing*, 7(4): 316–332.
- Busby, G. and O'Neill, K. (2006) Cephallonia and Captain Corelli's Mandolin: The influence of literature and film on British visitors, *Acta Turistica*, 18(1): 30–51.
- Busby, G., Brunt, P. and Lund, J. (2003) In Agatha Christie country: Resident perceptions of special interest tourism, *Tourism*, 51(3): 287–300.
- Butler, R.W. (1990) The influence of the media in shaping international tourist patterns, *Tourism Recreation Research*, 15(2): 46–53.
- Cai, L. (2002) Cooperative branding for rural destinations, *Annals of Tourism Research*, 29(3): 720–742.
- Campbell, D.T. (1975) Degrees of freedom and the case study, *Comparative Political Studies*, 8: 178–193.
- Campbell, D.T. and Fiske, D. (1959) Convergent and discriminant validation by the Multitrait-multimethod matrix, *Psychological Bulletin*, 56: 81–105.
- Cannell, C., Groves, R., Magilavy, L., Mathiowetz, N. and Miller, P. (1987) An experimental comparison of telephone and person health interview surveys, *Vital and Health Studies*, 2 (106), Government Printing Office: Washington DC, USA.
- Cannon, J.C. (1994) Issues in sampling and sample design – A managerial perspective. In Ritchie, J.R.B. and Goeldner, C.R. (eds.), *Travel, Tourism and Hospitality Research: A*

Handbook for Managers and Researchers, 2nd edn, John Wiley and Sons: New York, USA, pp. 131–146.

- Caracelli, V.J. and Greene, J.C. (1993) Data analysis strategies for mixed-method evaluation design, *Educational Evaluation and Policy Analysis*, 15(2): 195–207.

- Carl, D., Kindon, S. and Smith, K. (2007) Tourist's experiences of film locations, *Tourism Geographies*, 9(1): 49–63.

- Carson, D., Gilmore, A., Perry, C. and Gronhaug, K. (2001) *Qualitative Marketing Research*, Sage Publications: London, UK.

- Chambers, I. (1989) Popular culture: The metropolitan experience. In Fiske, J. (1992) *Reading the Popular*, Routledge: London, UK, p. 106.

- Chesley, J.A. and Wenger, M.S. (1999) Transforming and organisation: Using models to foster a strategic conversation, *California Management Review*, 41(3): 54–73.

- Chen, P. and Kerstetter, D.L. (1999) International students' image of rural Pennsylvania as a travel destination, *Journal of Travel Research*, 37 (February): 256–266.

- Chicago Film Office (2008) About us, http://egov.cityofchicago.org/city/webportal/portalContentItemAction.do?BV_SessionID=@@@@1317555157.1201175350@@@@&BV_EngineID=ccceadedeeeelgfcefecelldffhdfhl.0&contentOID=536926488&contenTypeName=COC_EDITORIAL&topChannelName=Dept&blockName=Film+Office%2FAbout+Us%2FI+Want+To&context=dept&channelId=0&programId=0&entityName=Film+Office&deptMainCategoryOID=-536893313 (accessed 24/01/2008).

- Chon, K. (1990) Tourism destination image modification process: Marketing implications, *Tourism Management*, 12(1) March: 68–72.

- Chrisnall, P. (2001) *Marketing Research*, 6th edn, McGraw-Hill: Berkshire, Vermont, USA.

- Churchill, G.A. Jr (1987) *Marketing Research: Methodological Foundations*, 4th edn, Dryden Press: Chicago, Illinois, USA.

- Clark, H. (2001a) *Some Facts about Lord of the Rings*, New Zealand Government announcement, http://www.executive.govt.nz/minister/clark/lor/lor.htm (accessed 07/11/2001).

- Clements, M.A. (1989) Selecting tourist traffic by de-marketing, *Tourism Management*, 10(2): 89–94.

- Cohen, J. (1986) Promotion of overseas tourism through media fiction. In *Tourism Services Marketing Conference Proceedings: Advances in Theory and Practice*, Benoy, J.W., Moutinho L. and Vernon I.R (eds.), Academy of Marketing Science: Cleveland, Ohio, USA, pp. 229–37.

- Connell, J. (2005a) Toddlers, tourism and Tobermory: Destination marketing issues and television induced tourism, *Tourism Management*, 26(5): 763–776.

- Connell, J. (2005b) What's the story in Balamory: The impacts of a Children's TV Programme on small tourism enterprises on the Isle of Mull, *Journal of Sustainable Tourism*, 13(3): 228–251.

- Cooper, D.R. and Emory, W.C. (1995) *Business Research Methods*, 5th edn, Irwin: Chicago, USA.

- Cooper, H.M. (1984) *The Integrative Research Review*, Sage: Beverly Hills, California, USA.

- Corlett, H.J. (1998) *The Influence of Television and Cinema on Tourism*, Unpublished M.Sc. Dissertation, University of Surrey, Guildford, UK.

- Coshall, J.T. (2000) Measurement of tourists' images: The repertory gird approach, *Journal of Travel Research*, 33(Winter): 21–27.

- COSMOS Corporation (1983) Case studies and organizational innovation, *Strengthening the Connection*, COSMOS Corporation: Bethesda, Maryland, USA.

- Couldry, N. (1998) The view from inside the 'Simulacrum': Visitors' tales from the set of *Coronation Street*, *Leisure Studies*, 17(2): 94–107.

- Cousins, A. and Andereck, K.L. (1993) Movie generated tourism in North Carolina: Two case studies, Poster presentation. In *TTRA 24th Annual Conference Proceedings*, TTRA: Wheat Ridge, Colorado, USA, pp. 81–88.

- Cox, E.P. III (1979) *Marketing Research: Information for Decision Making*, Harper and Row: New York, USA.

- Crandall, L. (1994) The social impact of tourism on developing regions and its measurement. In Ritchie, J.R.B. and Goeldner, C.R. (eds.), *Travel, Tourism and Hospitality Research: A Handbook for Managers and Researchers*, 2nd edn, John Wiley and Sons, New York: USA, pp. 413–424.

- Creswell, J. (1994) *Research Design: Quantitative and Qualitative Approaches*, Sage Publications: Thousand Oaks, California, USA.

- Creswell, J.W. (1999) Mixed method research: Introduction and application. In Cizek, G.J. (ed.) *Handbook of Educational Policy*, Academic Press: San Diego, USA, pp. 455–472.

- Creswell, J.W. (2003) Research design: Quantitative, qualitative and mixed method approaches, 2nd edn, Sage Publications: Thousand Oaks, California, USA.

- Crockett, S.R. and Wood, L.J. (2002) Brand Western Australia: Holidays of an entirely different nature. In Morgan, N.J., Pritchard, A. and. Pride, R., *Destination Branding: Creating the Unique Destination Proposition*, Elsevier Butterworth-Heinemann: Oxford, UK, pp. 124–147.

- Crompton, J.L. (1979) An assessment of the image of Mexico as a vacation destination and the influence of geographical location upon image, *Journal of Travel Research*, 18(10): 18–23.

- Crotty, M. (1998) *The Foundations of Social Research: Meaning and Perspective in the Research Process*, Sage Publications: London, UK.

- Croy, W.G. and Walker, R.D. (2001) Tourism and film: Issues for strategic regional development. In *New Dimensions in Managing Rural Tourism and Leisure* **Local Impacts** – Global Trends **Conference** *Proceedings*, Mitchell, M. and Kirkpatrick, I. (eds.), Scottish Agricultural College: Auchincruive, Ayr, Scotland.

- Croy, W.G. and Walker, R.D. (2003) Rural tourism and film – Issues for strategic regional development. In D. Hall, L. Roberts and Mitchell, M. (eds.) *New Directions in Rural Tourism*, Ashgate Publishing: Aldershot, Hampshire, UK, pp. 115–133.

- Davies, R. (2003) Branding Asian tourist destinations – Trends and brand recall, *Branding Asian Tourist Destinations – A Series*, http://www.asiamarketresearch.com/columns/tourism-branding.htm (accessed 11/06/2003).

- DCMS (1999) *Tomorrow's Tourism: A Growth Industry for the Millennium*, Department for Culture, Media and Sport: London, UK.

- de Leeuw, E.D. and van der Zouwen, J. (1988) Data quality in telephone and face to face surveys: A comparative meta-analysis. In Groves, R.M., Biemer, P.N., Lyberg, L.E., Massey, J.T., Nichols II, W.L. and Waksberg, J. (eds.), *Telephone Survey Methodology*, John Wiley and Sons: San Francisco, USA, pp. 177–196.

- Dees, R. (2000) *Writing the Modern Research Paper*, 3rd edn, Allyn and Bacon: Boston, Massachusetts, USA.

- Demetriadi, J. (1996) The tele tourists, *Hospitality*, October/November: 14–15.

- Denman, P. (2006) Tourism and sustainability: Objectives, policies and tools for sustainable tourism, *UNWTO Seminar on Tourism Sustainability and Local Agenda 21 in Tourism Destinations*, Jeddah, Saudi Arabia.

- Dibb, S., Simkin, L., Pride, W. and Ferrell, O. (2001) *Marketing Concepts and Strategies*, 4th European edn, Houghton Mifflin: USA.

- Dichter, E. (1964) *Handbook of Consumer Motivations*, McGraw-Hill: New York, USA.

- Dichter, E. (1985) What is image? *Journal of Consumer Marketing*, 2(1): 75–81.

- Dillman, D.A. (2000) *Mail and Internet Surveys: The Tailored Design Method*, John Wiley and Son: New York, USA.

- Domegan, C. and Fleming, D. (2003) *Marketing Research in Ireland: Theory and Practice*, 2nd edn, Gill and Macmillan: Dublin, Ireland.

- Dore, L. and Crouch, G.I. (2002) Promoting destinations: An exploratory study of publicity programmes used by national tourism organisations, *Journal of Vacation Marketing*, 9(2): 137–151.

- Dumfries and Galloway Tourist Board (2003) Richard and Judy invited to 2000 Acres Country, http://www.scotexchange.net (accessed 10/01/2003).
- Echtner, C.M. and Ritchie, B.J.R. (1991) The meaning and measurement of tourism destination image, *Journal of Tourism Studies*, 2(2): 2–12.
- Echtner, C.M. and Ritchie, B.J.R. (1993) The measurement of destination image: An empirical assessment, *Journal of Travel Research*, 31(3): 3–13.
- *Economist* (1998) United States: Lures and enticements, *Economist*, 346 (8059): 28–29.
- Elsworth, J.D., Yoon, B.J. and Bai, B.X. (1999) Analysis of papers published in the Hospitality research journal: Focus and trends of subjects, research designs and statistical designs. In Chon, K. (ed.), *The Practice of Graduate Research in Hospitality and Tourism*, Haworth Hospitality Press: New York, USA, pp. 163–175.
- Embacher, J. and Buttle, F. (1989) A repertory grid analysis of Austria's image as a summer vacation destination, *Journal of Travel Research*, Winter: 3–7.
- Evans, M. (1997) Plugging into TV tourism, *Insights March*, English Tourist Board: London, pp. D35–D38.
- Fáilte Ireland (2008) Our regions – Regional Development Directorate http://www.failteireland.ie/Our-Regions.aspx (accessed 24/01/2008).
- Fakeye, P. and Crompton, J. (1991) Image differences between prospective, first-time and repeat visitors to the Lower Rio Grande Valley, *Journal of Travel Research*, 30(2): 10–16.
- Feagin, J.R., Orum, A.M. and Sjoberg, G. (eds.) (1991) *A Case Study for the Case Study*, University of North Carolina Press: Chapel Hill, USA.
- Fernandez-Young, A. and Young, R. (2006) Measuring the effects of film and television in tourism to screen locations: A theoretical and empirical perspective. In *The International Conference on Impact of Movies and Television on Tourism Conference Proceedings*, Chon, K. and Chan, A. (eds.), The Hong Kong Polytechnic University: Hong Kong, China, pp. 125–147.
- Flanagan, S., Griffin, K., O'Halloran, E., Phelan, J., Roe, P., Kennedy-Burke, E., Tottle, A. and Kelly, D. (2007) *Sustainable Tourism Development: Toward the Mitigation of Tourism Destination Impacts*, Synthesis Report-Environmental RTDI Programme 2000–2006, Environmental Protection Agency, Dublin, Ireland.
- FNZ (2008) Welcome, http://www.filmnz.com (accessed 24/01/2008).
- Ford, D. (2008) Yorkshire Index Map, http://www.dave-ford.co.uk/Image_Map.htm (accessed 01/12/2008).
- Fowler Jr, F.J. (2002) Survey research methods, 3rd edn, *Applied Social Research Methods Series* vol. 1, Sage Publications: Thousand Oaks, California, USA.

- Frisby, E. (2002) Communicating in a crisis: The British Tourist Authorities' responses to the Foot and Mouth Outbreak and 11th September 2001, *Journal of Vacation Marketing*, 9(1): 89–100.

- Frost, W. (2004) Reshaping the destination to fit the image: Western films and tourism in Lone Pine, California. In *International Tourism and Media Conference Proceedings* (ITAM), Frost, W. Croy, G. and Beeton, S. (eds.), Tourism Research Unit, Monash University: Melbourne, Australia, pp. 61–68.

- Frost, W. (2005) Film-induced festivals: Reshaping destination image in small-town America, *Third International Event Management Conference*, University of Technology: Sydney, Australia.

- Gallarza, M.G., Saura, I.G. and Garcia, H.C. (2002) Destination image: Towards a conceptual framework, *Annals of Tourism Research*, 29(1): 56–78.

- Gardner, B.B. and Levy, S.J. (1955) The product and the brand, *Harvard Business Review*, 33(March/April): 33–39.

- Gartner, W. (1993) Image formation process, *Journal of Travel and Tourism Marketing*, 2(2/3): 191–215.

- Gartner, W. (1996) *Tourism Development: Principles, Processes and Policies*, Van Nostrand Reinhold: New York, USA.

- Gartner, W.C. and Shen, J. (1992) The impact of Tiananmen Square on China's tourism image, *Journal of Travel Research*, 30:47–52.

- Gibson, A. and Neilson, M. (2000) *Tourism and Hospitality Marketing in Ireland*, Gill and Macmillan: Dublin, Ireland.

- Gilbey, R. (2004) Who's the Daddy? *High Life* (November): 54–61.

- Gilboe-Ford, M., Campbell, J. and Berman, H. (1995) Stories and numbers: Coexistence without compromise, *Advances in Nursing Science*, 18: 14–26.

- Gill, J. and Johnson, P. (1997) *Research Methods for Managers*, 2nd edn, Paul Chapman: London, UK.

- Gilmore, F. (2002a) Branding for success. In Morgan, N.J., Pritchard, A. and Pride, R., *Destination Branding: Creating the Unique Destination Proposition*, Elsevier Butterworth-Heinemann: Oxford, UK, pp. 57–65.

- Gold, R. and Ward, S.V. (eds.) (1994) *Place Promotion: The Use of Publicity and Marketing to Sell Towns and Regions*, Wiley: Chichester, UK.

- Graves, D. (1984) The child, the writing process and the role of the professional. In Graves, D., *A Researcher Learns to Write: Selected Articles and Monographs*, Heinemann Educational Books: Exeter, UK, pp. 16–25.

255

- Green, J.C. and Caracelli, V.J. (eds.) (1997) *Advances in Mixed-methods Evaluation: The Challenges and Benefits of Integrating Diverse Paradigms*, New Directions for Evaluation, No. 74, Jossey-Bass: San Francisco, USA.

- Greene, J.C. Caracelli, V.J. and Graham, W.F. (1989) Toward a conceptual framework for mixed method evaluation designs, *Educational Valuation and Policy Analysis*, 11(2): 255-274.

- Grihault, N. (2003) Film tourism – The global picture, *Travel & Tourism Analyst*, 5: 1-22.

- Groves, R.M. and Kahn, R.L. (1979) *Surveys by Telephone*, Academic Press: New York, USA.

- Guba, E. and Lincoln, Y. (1988) Do inquiry paradigms imply inquiry methodologies? In Fetterman, D. (ed.) *Qualitative Approaches to Evaluation in Education: The Silent Scientific Revolution*, Praeger: New York, USA, pp. 89-115.

- Guba, E.G. (1990) The alternative paradigm dialog. In Guba, E.G. (ed.), *The Paradigm Dialog*, Sage Publications: Newbury Park, California, USA.

- Guba, E.G. and Lincoln, Y.S. (1994) Competing paradigms in qualitative methods. In Denzin, N. and Lincoln, Y. (eds.) *Handbook of Qualitative Research*, Sage Publications: Thousand Oaks, California, USA, pp. 105-117.

- Gundle, S. (2002) Hollywood glamour and mass consumption in post war Italy, *Journal of Cold War Studies*, 4(3): 95-118.

- Haire, M. (1950) Projective techniques in marketing research, *Journal of Marketing*, 14: 649-656.

- Hall, C.M. (1995) *Introduction to Tourism in Australia*, 2nd edn, Longman: Melbourne, Australia.

- Hall, C.M. (2003) Tourism issues, agenda setting and the media, *E-review of Tourism Research*, 1(3): 42-45.

- Hall, C.M. and Jenkins, J. (1995) *Tourism and Public Policy*, Routledge: London, UK.

- Hanefors, M. and Mossberg, L. (2002) TV travel shows: A pre-taste of the destination, *Journal of Vacation Marketing*, 8(3): 235-246.

- Harrill, R. (2004) Residents' attitudes toward tourism development: A literature review with implications for tourism planning, *Journal of Planning Literature*, 18(3) February: 251-266.

- Hawaii Tourism Authority (1999) *Ke Kemu:* Strategic Directions for Hawaii's Visitor Indurate, http://www.hawaii.gov/tourism (accessed 29/06/1999).

- Heath, E. and Wall, G. (1991) *Marketing Tourism Destinations: A Strategic Planning Approach*, John Wiley and Sons: New York, USA.

- Hede, A.M. and O'Mahony, G.B. (2004) The media and the development of the tourism industry during the 20th and 21st centuries: An analysis of four noteworthy cases. In the *ITAM*

Conference Proceedings, Frost, W., Croy, G. and Beeton, S. (eds.), Tourism Research Unit, Monash University: Melbourne, Australia, pp. 1–16.

- Hoaglin, D.C., Light, R.J. McPeek, B., Mosteller, F. and Stoto, M.A. (1982) *Data for Decisions. Information Strategies for Policymakers*, Abt Books: Cambridge, Massachusetts, USA, p. 134.

- Hochstim, J. (1967) A critical comparison of three strategies of collecting data from households, *Journal of the American Statistical Association*, 62: 976–989.

- Hsu, K.H.Y., Agrusa, J. and Park, B. (2006) The impact of Korean soap operas on Korea's image as a tourism destination. In *The 12th Asia-Pacific Tourism Association and the 4th Asia-Pacific Council on Hotel, Restaurant and Institutional Education (CHRIE) Joint Conference Proceedings*, Taiwan Hospitality and Tourism College: Hualien, Taiwan, pp. 859–872.

- Hu, Y. and Ritchie, J.R.B. (1993) Measuring destination attractiveness: A contextual approach, *Journal of Travel Research*, 32(2) Fall: 25–34.

- Hudson, S. and Ritchie, J.R.B. (2006a) Film tourism and destination marketing: The case of Captain Corelli's Mandolin, *Journal of Vacation Marketing*, 12(3): 256–268.

- Hudson, S. and Ritchie, J.R.B. (2006b) Promoting destinations via film tourism: An empirical identification of supporting marketing initiatives, *Journal of Travel Research*, 44 (May): 387–396.

- Hunt, J.D. (1975) Image as a factor in tourism development, *Journal of Travel Research*, 13(3): 1–7.

- Hydra Associates (1997) *The Economic and Tourism Benefits of Large Scale Film Production in the UK*, Scottish Tourist Board: Edinburgh, Scotland.

- Isaac, S. and Michael, W.B. (1971) *Handbook in Research and Evaluation*, Edits Publishers: San Diego, California, USA.

- Iwashita, C. (1999) *The Impact of Film Television and Literature as Popular Culture on Tourism and the Post-modern Gaze*, Unpublished M.Sc. Dissertation, University of Surrey: Guildford, Surrey, UK.

- Iwashita, C. (2003) Media construction of Britain as a destination for Japanese tourists: Social constructionism and tourism, *Tourism and Hospitality Research*, 4(4): 331–340.

- Iwashita, C. (2006) Roles of films and television dramas in international tourism: The case of Japanese tourists to the UK. In *The International Conference on Impact of Movies and Television on Tourism Conference Proceedings*, Chon, K. and Chan, A. (eds.), The Hong Kong Polytechnic University: Hong Kong, China, pp. 182–196.

- Jankowicz, A.D. (2000) *Business Research Projects*, 3rd edn, Thompson Learning: London, UK.

- Jeffery, F. (2004) Wishing on a star, *Travel Weekly*, 1731: 15–15.

- Jenkins, O.H. (1999) Understanding and measuring tourist destination images, *International Journal of Tourism Research*, 1(1): 1–15.

- Jennings, G. (2001) *Tourism Research*, John Wiley and Sons: Milton, Australia.

- Jick, T.D. (1979) Mixing qualitative and quantitative methods: Triangulation in action, *Administration Science Quarterly*, 24: 602–611.

- Jones, C.B. (1998) *The New Tourism and Leisure Environment*, A Discussion Paper, Economics Research Associates: San Francisco, USA.

- Jones, D. and Smith, S. (2005) *Middle Earth* meets New Zealand: Authenticity and location in the making of the *Lord of the Rings*, *Journal of Management Studies*, 42 (5): 923–945.

- Kaikati, A.M. and Kaikati, J.G. (2004) Stealth marketing: How to reach consumers surreptitiously, *California Management Review*, 46(4): 6–22.

- Kansas Travel and Tourism Division (2008) Welcome Kansas Tourism Industry Partners, http://www.travelks.com/s/index.cfm?aid=52 (accessed 26/02/2008).

- Katz, E. and Foulkes, D. (1962) On the use of the mass media as escape: Clarification of a concept, *The Public Opinion Quarterly*, 26(3): 377–388.

- Kennedy, M. (1998) Films brings tourist boast for stately homes, *Guardian*, 26 February, p. 8.

- Kennedy, M.M. (1976) Generalizing from single case studies, *Evaluation Quarterly*, 3: 661–678.

- Kerlinger, F.N. (1973) Foundations of behavioural research, 2nd edn, Holt, Rinehart and Winston: New York, USA.

- Kim, H. and Richardson, S.L. (2003) Impacts of a popular motion picture on destinations perceptions, *Annals of Tourism Research*, 30(1): 216–237.

- Kindra G.S. and Taylor W. (1990) A marketing prescription for Canada's health care, *Journal of Healthcare Marketing*, 15(2): 10–14.

- King, J. (2002) Destination marketing organisations: Connecting the experience rather than promoting the place, *Journal of Vacation Marketing*, 8(2): 105–108.

- Klenosky, D. (2002) The pull of tourism destinations: A means-end investigation, *Journal of Travel Research*, 40(4): 385–395.

- Kochan, T., Bezrukova, K., Ely, R., Jackson, S., Joshi, A., Jehn, K. Leonard, J., Levine, D. and Thomas, D. (2003) The effects of diversity on business performance: Report of the diversity research network, *Human Resource Management*, 42(1): 3–21.

- Kotler, P. and Armstrong, G. (1999) *Principles of Marketing*, Prentice-Hall: Upper Saddle River, New Jersey, USA.

- Kotler, P. and Gertner. D. (2002) Country as brand, product and beyond: A place marketing and brand management perspective, *Brand Management*, 9(4–5): 249–261.

- Kotler, P. and Levy, S.J. (1971) De-marketing, yes de-marketing, *Harvard Business Review*, 49(6): 74–80.

- Kotler, P., Haider, D.H. and Rein, I. (1993) *Marketing Places – Attracting Investment, Industry and Tourism to Cities, States and Nations*, The Free Press: New York, USA, p. 173.

- Kulshreshtha, S. and Akoijam, T. (2006) Destination branding: A complete 360° turnaround in consumers perceptions. In *Cutting Edge Research in Tourism – New Directions Challenges and Applications Conference Proceedings*, Papageorgiou, G. (ed.), School of Management, University of Surrey: Guildford, UK, pp. 1–7.

- Kumar, R. (1996) *Research Methodology: A Step by Step Guide for Beginners*, Longman: South Melbourne, Australia.

- Kunes, M.V. (1991) How the workplace affects the self esteem of the psychiatric nurse, Unpublished Proposal, University of Nebraska-Lincoln: Nebraska, USA.

- Lam, S. and Ap, J. (2006) Review and analysis of the film tourism literature. In *The International Conference on Impact of Movies and Television on Tourism Conference Proceedings*, Chon, K. and Chan, A. (eds.), The Hong Kong Polytechnic University: Hong Kong, China, pp. 166–181.

- Lawson, F. and Baud-Bovy, M. (1977) *Tourism and Recreational Development*, Architectural Press: London, UK.

- Lazarus, P.N. (1994) Location filming, *Florida Hotel and Motel Journal*, May: 20–22.

- Leiper, N. (1996) *Tourism Management*, RMIT Publications: Melbourne, Australia.

- Levy, S. J. (1959) Symbols for sale, *Harvard Business Review*, 37 (March/April): 117–124.

- Liedtka, J.M. and Rosenblum, J.W. (1996) Shaping conversations: Making strategy, managing change, *California Management Review*, (Fall): 141–157.

- Liu, B. and Liu, Q. (2004) On the present situation and trend of the development of China's movie & TV tourism [in Chinese], *Tourism Tribune*, 19(6): 77–81.

- Long, P., R. Perdue and L. Allen (1990) Rural resident tourism perceptions and attitudes by community level of tourism, *Journal Of Travel Research*, 28(3): 3–9.

- MacInnis, D.J. and Price, L.L. (1987) The role of imagery in information processing: Review and extensions, *Journal of Consumer Research*, 13 (March): 473–491.

- Macionis, N. (2004a) Understanding the film-induced tourist. In the *ITAM Conference Proceedings*, Frost, W. Croy, G. and Beeton, S. (eds.), Tourism Research Unit, Monash University: Melbourne, Australia, pp. 86–97.

- Macionis, N. (2004b) Film induced tourism: The tourist in the film place, *Placing the Moving Image, Symposium Proceedings*, Griffith Business School, Griffith University: Brisbane, Australia, pp. 1–14.

- Macionis, N. (2005) Lights! Camera! Tourist! In *Film and Media in Context*, Davies, E. and Moran, A. (eds.), Working Papers in Communication, No. 4/5, School of Arts, Media and Culture, Griffith University: Brisbane, Australia.
- Macrorie, K. (1980) *Telling Writing*, Hayden Book Company: Rochelle Park, New Jersey, USA.
- Malhotra, N.K. (1990) Reducing health care cost by de-marketing benefits, *Journal of Health Care Marketing*, 10(2): 78–79.
- Malhotra, N.K. (1999) *Marketing Research: An Applied Orientation*, 3rd edn, Prentice Hall: New Jersey, USA.
- Malhotra, N.K. and Birks, D.F. (2000) *Marketing Research: An Applied Approach*, European edn, Prentice Hall: Harlow, Essex, UK.
- Malhotra, N.K. and Birks, D.F. (2003) *Marketing Research: An Applied Approach*, 2nd edn, The Financial Times Press: London.
- Malhotra, N.K. and Peterson M. (2006) *Basic Marketing Research – A Decision Making Approach*, 2nd edn, Prentice-Hall: Upper Saddle River, New Jersey, USA.
- Mangione, T., Hingson, R. and Barrett, J. (1982) Collecting of sensitive data: A comparison of three survey strategy, *Sociological Methods and Research*, 10(3): 337–346.
- Mansfeld, Y. (1992) From motivation to actual travel, *Annals of Tourism Research*, 19(3): 399–419.
- Marshall, C.S. and Rossman, G.B. (1989) *Designing Qualitative Research*, Sage Publications: Newbury Park, California, USA.
- Mason, J. (1996) *Qualitative Researching*, Sage: Thousand Oaks, California, USA and London, UK.
-
- Mathieson, A. and Wall, G. (1982) *Tourism: Economic, Physical and Social Impacts,* Longman Scientific and Technical: Harlow, UK.
- Mayo, E. (1973) Regional images and regional behaviour. In *TTRA Fourth Annual Conference Proceedings*, TTRA: Sun Valley, Idaho, USA, pp. 211–218.
- Mayo, E. and Jarvis, L. (1981) *The Psychology of Leisure Travel*, CBI: Boston, Massachusetts, USA.
- McClinchey, K. and Carmichael, B.A. (2006) Rural images and implications for sustainable rural tourism. In *37th Annual TTRA Conference Proceedings: New Frontiers in Global Tourism: Trends and Competitive Challenges*, Jennings, G.R. and Beeton, S. (eds.), TTRA: Dublin, Ireland, pp. 23–32.

- McDaniel Jr, C. and Gates, R. (1993) *Contemporary Marketing Research*, 2nd edn, West Publishing Company: St. Paul, USA.

- McGuckin, M. and Demick, D.H. (2000*)* Northern Ireland's images – Platform or pitfall for gaining the competitive edge? In Ruddy, J. and Flanagan, S. (eds.), *Tourism Destination Marketing – Gaining the Competitive Edge*, Tourism Research Centre, Dublin Institute of Technology: Dublin, Ireland, pp. 395–409.

- McKay, K. and Fesenmaier, D. (1997) Pictorial element of destination in image formation, *Annals of Tourism Research*, 24: 537–565.

- Meitzner, D. and Reger, G. (2005) Advantages and disadvantages of scenario approaches for strategic foresight, *International Journal of Technology Intelligence and Planning*, 1(2): 220–239.

- Mertens, D.M. (2003) Mixed methods and the politics of human research: The transformative-emancipatory perspective. In Tashakkori, A. and Teddlie, C. (eds.), *Handbook of Mixed Methods in the Social and Behavioural Science*, Sage Publications: Thousand Oaks, California, USA.

- Middleton, V.T.C. and Clarke, J. (2001) *Marketing in Travel and Tourism*, 2nd edn, Butterworth-Heinemann: Oxford, UK, pp. 133–337.

- Middleton, V.T.C and Hawkins, R. (1998) *Sustainable Tourism-A Marketing Perspective*, Butterworth-Heinemann: Oxford, UK.

- Miles, M.B. and Huberman, A.M. (1994) *Qualitative Data Analysis: An Expanded Sourcebook*, 2nd edn, Sage Publications: Thousand Oaks, California, USA.

- Miles, M.P., Munilla, L.S. and Darroch, J. (2006) The role of strategic conversations with stakeholders in the formation of corporate social responsibility strategy, *Journal of Business Ethics*, 69(2): 195–205.

- Milman, A. and Pizam, A. (1995) The role of awareness and familiarity with a destination: The central Florida case, *Journal of Travel Research*, 33(3): 21–27.

- Ministry of Tourism (2003) *Overview of the Tourism Industry*, Wellington: Ministry of Tourism, http://www.tourism.govt.nz (accessed 10/05/2009).

- Mintel (2003) *Film Tourism – International* (October), Mintel: London International Group: 1–21.

- Mintzberg, H. (1973) *The Nature of Managers' Work*, Harper and Row: New York, USA.

- Mishra, S., Kulshreshtha, S., Dixit, S., Bansal, S.P. and Grover, J. (2006) Impact of movies and television tourism. In *The International Conference on Impact of Movies and Television on Tourism Conference Proceedings*, Chon, K. and Chan, A. (eds.), The Hong Kong Polytechnic University: Hong Kong, China, pp. 82–96.

- Mitchell, R. (1998) Field of dreams. An experiential perspective on the influence of major motion pictures on perceptions of destinations and tourism experiences, Unpublished Working Paper, La Trove University: Melbourne, Australia.

- Mordue, T. (1999) Heartbeat Country: Conflicting values, coinciding visions, *Environment and Planning*, 31: 629–646.

- Mordue, T. (2001) Performing and directing resident/tourists cultures in Heartbeat Country, *Tourist Studies*, 1(3): 233–252.

- Morgan, D.L. (1998) Practical strategies for combining qualitative and quantitative methods: Applications to health research, *Qualitative Health Research*, 8(3): 362–376.

- Morgan, N. and Pritchard, A. (1998) *Tourism, Promotion and Power: Creating Images, Creating Identities*, John Wiley and Sons: Chichester, UK.

- Morgan, N.J. and Pritchard, A. (1999) Building destination brands. The cases of Wales and Australia, *Journal of Brand Management*, 7(2): 102–119.

- Morgan, N.J. and Pritchard, A. (2002) Contextualizing destination branding. In Morgan, N.J., Pritchard, A. and Pride, R., *Destination Branding: Creating the Unique Destination Proposition*, Elsevier Butterworth-Heinemann: Oxford, UK, pp. 11–41.

- Morgan, N.J. and Pritchard, A. (2004) Meeting the destination branding challenge. In Morgan, N.J., Pritchard, A. and. Pride, R., *Destination Branding: Creating the Unique Destination Proposition*, 2nd edn, Elsevier Butterworth-Heinemann: Oxford, UK, pp. 59–78.

- Morgan, N.J., Pritchard, A. and Piggott, R. (2002) New Zealand, 100% pure. The creation of a powerful niche destination brand, *Journal of Brand Management*, 9(4–5): 335–354.

- Morgan, N.J., Pritchard, A. and Piggott, R. (2003) Destination branding and the role of the stakeholders: The case of New Zealand, *Journal of Vacation Marketing*, 9(3): 285–299.

- Morgan, N.J., Pritchard, A. and Pride, R. (2002) *Destination Branding: Creating the Unique Destination Proposition*, Elsevier Butterworth-Heinemann: Oxford, UK.

- Morgan, N.J., Pritchard, A. and Pride, R. (2004) *Destination Branding: Creating the Unique Destination Proposition*, 2nd edn, Elsevier Butterworth-Heinemann: Oxford. UK.

- Morris, T. and Wood, S. (1991) Testing the survey methods: Continuity and change in British industrial relations, *Work Employment and Society*, 5(2): 259–282.

- Morse, J. (2001) The Sydney 2000 Olympic Games: How the Australian tourist commission leveraged the games for tourism, *Journal of Vacation Marketing*, 7(2): 101–109.

- Morse, J.M. (1991) Approaches to quantitative–qualitative methodological triangulation, *Journal of Nursing Research*, 40(1): 120–123.

- Murphy, C. (2006) Nationality and Ireland's tourism destination imagery. In O'Connor, N., Keating, M., Malone, J. and Murphy, A. (eds.) *Tourism and Hospitality Research in Ireland – Concepts, Issues and Challenges*, Waterford Institute of Technology: Ireland, pp. 147–169.
- Murray, D.M. (1982) *Learning by Teaching: Selected Articles on Writing and Teaching*, Boyton/Cook: Montclair, New Jersey, USA.
- Nasser, N. (2003) Planning for urban heritage places: Reconciling conservation tourism and sustainable development, *Journal of Planning Literature*, 17(4) (May): 467–479.
- National Park (2008) Frequently asked questions – What are National Parks for? http://www.nationalparks.gov.uk/learningabout/faqs.htm (accessed 08/01/2008).
- National Trust (2007) Not ours – but ours to look after, http://www.nationalparks.gov.uk/aboutus.htm (accessed 27/07/2007).
- Neale, S. (1994) Tom Kershaw: Everyone knows his name, *Boston Business Journal*, 14(22): 8.
- Neuman, W.L. (2000a) *Social Research Methods: Qualitative and Quantitative Approaches*, 4th edn, Ally and Bacon: Boston, Massachusetts, USA.
- Neuman, W.L. (2000b) *Social Research Methods*, 2nd edn, Allyn and Bacon: London, UK.
- New Zealand Institute of Economic Research (2002) Scoping the lasting effects of the *Lord of the Rings: A Report to the New Zealand Film Commission*, Thorndon: Wellington, New Zealand.
- Newman, I. and Benz, C.R. (1998.) *Qualitative and Quantitative Research Methodology: Exploring the Interactive Continuum*, University Press: Carbondale, Southern Illinois, USA.
- Nielson, C. (2001) *Tourism and the Media – Tourism Decision Making*, Hospitality Press: Melbourne, Australia.
- NWRDA (2008) *Who We Are*, http://www.nwda.co.uk/who-we-are.aspx (accessed 08/01/2008).
- *Observer* Newspaper (1996) 11 August.
- O'Connor, N. and Flanagan, S. (2000): The sociocultural impacts of *Ballykissangel* on the Village of Avoca, County Wicklow. In *Dublin Institute of Technology/University College Dublin – Sustainability in Tourism Development Conference Proceedings*, Andrews, N., Convery, F., Flanagan, S. and Ruddy, J. (eds.), Dublin Institute of Technology: Dublin, Ireland, pp. 255–265.
- O'Connor, N. and Flanagan, S. (2001) The effect of television induced tourism on the Village of Avoca, County Wicklow. In *ATLAS* (Association for Tourism and Leisure Education) *Conference Proceedings, Ireland: Innovation, Tourism and Regional Development*, Andrews, N., Flanagan, S. and Ruddy, J. (eds.), Research Centre, Dublin Institute of Technology: Dublin, Ireland, pp. 145–159.

- O'Connor, N., Flanagan, S. & Bayliss, D. (2002): The importance of integrated tourism planning in reducing the sociocultural impacts of movie induced tourism: *XVI AESOP (Association of European Schools of Planning) Congress – Tourism Planning*, Volos, Greece;

- O'Connor, N., Flanagan, S. and Gilbert, D. (2006) The importance of destination branding in movie induced tourism locations. In *Cutting Edge Research in Tourism – New Directions Challenges and Applications Conference Proceedings*, Papageorgiou, G. (ed.), The School of Management, University of Surrey: Guildford, UK, pp. 1–17.

- O'Connor, N., Flanagan, S. and Gilbert, D. (2008) The integration of film induced tourism and destination branding in Yorkshire, UK, *International Journal of Tourism Research*, 10(5): 423–437.

- O'Connor, N., Flanagan, S. and Russell P. (2005) Tourism planning and the impact of filming on the branding of a tourist destination. In *University of Ulster Conference Proceedings, Tourism and Hospitality Research in Ireland: Exploring the Issues*, Boyd, S. (ed.), University of Ulster: Portrush, Northern Ireland, pp. 1–23.

- O'Regan, M. (2000) The use of image in tourism destination marketing. In Ruddy, J. and Flanagan, S. (eds.), *Tourism Destination Marketing – Gaining the Competitive Edge*, Tourism Research Centre, Dublin Institute of Technology: Dublin, Ireland, pp. 410–425.

- OECD (2003) *OECD Economic Surveys: New Zealand*, Organisation for Economic Cooperation and Development, Paris.

- OECD (2008) About the OECD, http://www.oecd.org/pages/0,3417,en_36734052_36734103_1_1_1_1_1,00.html (accessed 24/01/2008).

- Oxford Economic Forecasting (2005) *The Economic Contribution of the UK Film Industry*, Supported by the UK Film Council and Pinewood Shepperton PLC (20 September, 2005).

- Palmer, A. (2004) The internet challenge for destination marketing organisations. In Morgan, N.J., Pritchard, A. and. Pride, R., *Destination Branding: Creating the Unique Destination Proposition*, 2nd edn, Elsevier Butterworth-Heinemann: Oxford, USA, pp. 128–140.

- Patton, M. (1990) *Qualitative Education and Research Methods*, 2nd edn, Sage Publications: Newbury Park, California, USA.

- Pearce, D. (1988) *The Ulysses Factor*, Springer-Verlag: New York, USA.

- Pearce, D. (1989) *Tourist Development*, 2nd edn, Longman Scientific and Technical Publishers: New York, USA.

- Pearce, P. (1982) Perceived changes in holiday destinations, *Annals of Tourism Research*, (9):145–164.

- Pelegrino, D.A. (1979) *Research Methods for Recreation and Leisure*, William C. Brown Co: Dubuque, Iowa, USA.

- Pendreigh, B. (2002) *The Pocket Scottish Movie Book*, Mainstream Publishing: Edinburgh, Scotland.

- Perry, M, Izraeli, D. and Perry, A. (1976) Image change as a result of advertising, *Journal of Advertising*, 16(1): 45–50.

- Philliber, S.G., Schwab, M.R. and Samsloss, G. (1980) *Social Research, Guides to a Decision Making Process*, Peacock: Itasca, Illinois, USA.

- Pictures of England (2009) http://www.picturesofengland.com/mapofengland/regions.html (accessed 06/05/2009).

- Piggott, R., Morgan, N. and Pritchard, A. (2004) Brand New Zealand: Leveraging public and media relations. In Morgan, N.J., Pritchard, A. and Pride, R., *Destination Branding: Creating the Unique Destination Proposition*, 2nd edn, Elsevier Butterworth-Heinemann: Oxford, UK, pp. 207–225.

- Pike, S. (2004) *Destination Marketing Organisations*, Advances in Tourism Research Series, Elsevier: Oxford, UK.

- Pike, S.D. (2002) Destination image analysis: A review of 142 papers from 1973–2000, *Tourism Management*, 23(5): 541–549.

- Pilling, M. (2004) Movie set tourism. Film fans flock to locations, *The Gold Coast Bulletin*, B-Main, 4 December.

- Pizam, A. (1978) Tourism's impacts: The social costs to the destination community as perceived by its residents, *Journal of Travel Research*, 20: 8–12.

- Pizam, A. (1994) Planning a tourism research investigation. In Ritchie, B.J.R and Goeldner, C.R. (eds.), *Travel, Tourism and Hospitality Research: A Handbook for Managers and Researchers*, 2nd edn, John Wiley and Sons: New York, USA, pp. 91–104.

- Preston, P. (1999) Branding is cool, *The Guardian*, 15 November.

- Proctor, T. (2005) *Essentials of Marketing Research*, 4th edn, Pearson Education: Harlow, Essex, UK.

- Punch, K.F. (1998) *Introduction to Social Research*, Sage Publications: London, UK.

- Ratcliffe, J. (2002) Scenario planning: Strategic interviews and conversations, *Foresight, Journal of Future Studies, Strategic Thinking and Policy*, (4): 19–30.

- Reddy, A. (1989) Reducing healthcare costs by de-marketing benefits, *Health Marketing Quarterly*, 6(4): 137–145.

- Reeves, T. (2003) *Worldwide Guide to Movie Locations*, Titan Books: London, UK.

- Reilly, M.D. (1990) Free elicitation of descriptive adjectives for tourism image assessment, *Journal of Travel Research*, 28(4): 21–26.
- Reinhardt, C.S. and Rallis, S.F. (1994) *The Qualitative-Quantitative Debate: New Perspectives*, Jossey-Bass: San Francisco, USA.
- Riggin, J.C. (1997) Advances in mixed methods evaluation: A synthesis and comment. In Greene, J.C. and Caracelli, V.J. (eds.), *Advances in Mixed Methods Evaluation: The Challenges and Benefits of Integrating Diverse Paradigms*, Jossey-Bass: San Francisco, USA, pp. 87–94.
- Riley, R.W. and Van Doren, C.S. (1992a) Movies as tourism promotion: A pull factor in a push location, *Tourism Management*, 13(3): 267–274.
- Riley, R.W. and Van Doren, C.S. (1992b) The Crocodile Dundee paragon: Justifying a film commission's existence, *Locations*, (Fall): 14–19.
- Riley, R., Baker, D. and Van Doren, C.S. (1998) Movie induced tourism, *Annals of Tourism Research*, 25(4): 919–35.
- Riley, R.W. (1994) Movie-induced tourism. In Seaton, A.V. (ed.), *Tourism. The State of the Art*, John Wiley and Sons: West Sussex, UK.
- Robson, C. (2002) *Real World Research*, 2nd edn, Blackwell: Oxford.
- Roesch, S. (2009) *The Experiences of Film Location Tourists*, Aspects of Tourism, Channel View Publications: UK.
- Ross, G.F. (1993) Destination evaluation and vacation preferences, *Annals of Tourism Research*, 20(3): 477–489.
- Ross, J. (2003) Clearances could bring thousands in, *The Scotsman*, 6 December.
- Ruddy, J. and Flanagan, S. (eds.) (2000) *Tourism Destination Marketing – Gaining the Competitive Edge*, Tourism Research Centre, Dublin Institute of Technology: Dublin, Ireland.
- Ruler, J. (1984) Where to see those famous views, *The Scotsman*, 27 February.
- Safari Kinkead, N. (2002) The influence of movies on tourists travel decision making, Unpublished M.Sc. Dissertation, University of Surrey, Guilford, UK.
- Sarantakos, S. (1998) *Social Research*, 2nd edn, Macmillan: South Melbourne, Australia.
- Sargent, A. (1998) The Darcy effect: Regional tourism and costume drama, *The International Journal of Heritage Studies*, 4(3/4): 177–186.
- Saunders, M., Lewis, P. and Thornhill, A. (2003) *Research Methods for Business Students*, 3rd edn, Prentice Hall: Harlow, UK.
- Saunders, M., Lewis, P. and Thornhill, A. (2007) *Research Methods for Business Students*, 4th edn, Pearson Education: Essex, UK.
- Schama, S. (1996) *Landscape and Memory*, Fantana Press: London, UK.

- Schlosser, A.E., Mick, D.G. and Deighton, J. (2003) Experiencing products in the virtual world: The role of goal and imagery in influencing attitudes, *Journal of Consumer Research*, 30(2): 184–198.

- Schofield, P. (1996) Cinematographic images of a city, *Tourism Management*, 17(5): 333–340.

- Schuman, H. and Presser, S. (1981) *Research Methods: Questions and Answers in Attitudes Surveys*, Academic Press: New York, USA.

- Screen Yorkshire (2008) What we do, http://www.screenyorkshire.co.uk (accessed 08/01/2008).

- Screentourism (2008) About Screentourism.com, http://www.screentourism.com/index.html (accessed 08/01/2008).

- Seaton, A. and Hay, B. (1998) The marketing of Scotland as a tourist destination 1985–1996. In MacLellan, R. and Smith, R. (eds.), *Tourism in Scotland*, International Thompson Business Press: London, UK, pp. 209–240.

- Seaton, A.V. and Bennett, M.M. (1996) *Marketing Tourism Products: Concepts, Issues and Cases*, International Thompson Business Press: London, UK, pp. 127–134.

- Selby, M. and Morgan, N.J. (1996) Reconstructing place image: A case study of its role in destination market research, *Tourism Management*, 17(4): 287–294.

- Selltiz, C., Wrightsman, L.S. and Cook, S.W. (1976) *Research Methods for Social Relations*, 3rd edn, Holt, Rinehart and Winston: New York, USA.

- Sharp, J. (2000) Towards critical analysis of fictive geographies, *Area*, 32(3): 327–334.

- Sharp, J.A. and Howard, K. (1996) *The Management of the Student Research Project*, 2nd edn, Gower: Aldershot, Hampshire, UK.

- Sheldon, P. and Var, T. (1984) Resident attitudes to tourism in North Wales, *Tourism Management*, 5(1): 40-48.

- Sieber, S.D. (1973) The integration of fieldwork and survey methods, *American Journal of Sociology*, 78(6): 1335–1359.

- Singapore Tourist Board (2008) Introduction, http://app.stb.gov.sg/asp/abo/abo.asp (accessed 27/02/2008).

- Singh, K. (2006) Lived experiences of a screened location: An exploratory case study approach. In *Council for Australian University Tourism and Hospitality Education (CAUTHE) 2006 Conference Proceedings*, Melbourne, Australia, pp. 1330–1334.

- Singh, K. and Best, G. (2004) Film-induced tourism: Motivations of visitors to the Hobbiton movie set as featured in *The Lord of the Rings*. In the *International Tourism and Media Conference Proceedings*, Frost, W., Croy, G. and Beeton, S. (eds.), Tourism Research Unit, Monash University: Melbourne, Australia, pp. 98–111.

- Slater, J. (2004) Brand Louisiana: Capitalising on music and culture. In Morgan, N.J., Pritchard, A. and. Pride, R., *Destination Branding: Creating the Unique Destination Proposition*, 2nd edn, Elsevier Butterworth-Heinemann: Oxford, UK: 226–241.

- Smith, J.K. and Heshusius, L. (1986) Closing down the conversation. The end of the qualitative–quantitative debate and educational enquiries, *Educational Researcher*, 15: 4–12.

- Smith, M.C. and MacKay, K.J. (2001) The organization of information in memory for pictures of tourist destinations: Are there age-related differences? *Journal of Travel Research*, 39(3): 261–266.

- Springpoint (1999) *UK Voices of our Times: Contemporary Values, Regional and National Identity and their Impact on Communication*, (February): Springpoint.

- Stake, R.E. (1995) *The Art of Case Study Research*, Sage Publications: Newbury, Park, California, USA.

- Stanley, L. and Wise, S. (1990) Method, methodology and epistemology in feminist research processes. In Stanley, L. (ed.) *Feminist Praxis: Research Theory and Epistemology in Feminist Sociology*, Routledge: London, UK, pp. 20–60.

- Stern, L.W. (1988) *Marketing Channels*, Prentice-Hall: Englewood Cliffs, New Jersey, USA.

- Stewart, M. (1997) The impact of films in the Stirling area – A report. *Scottish Tourist Board (STB) Research Newsletter* (July) 12: 60–61.

- Strauss, A. and Corbin, J. (1998) *Basics of Qualitative Research*, 2nd edn, Sage Publications: Newbury Park, California, USA.

- Swan, H. (2003) Business braced for new park challenges, *Strathspey and Badenoch Herald*, 8 December.

- Tashakkori, A. and Teddlie, C. (1998) *Mixed Methodology: Combining Qualitative and Quantitative Approaches*, Sage: Thousand Oaks, California, USA.

- Tashakorri, A. and Teddlie C. (eds.) (2003) **Handbook of Mixed Methods in Social and Behavioural Research,** Sage: Thousand Oaks, California, USA

- TAT (2008) About TAT – TAT history, http://www.tourismthailand.org/about-tat/about-tat–47–1.html (accessed 24/01/2008).

- The Travel Industry Association of America (2003) State tourism office budgets down 8% for 2002–2003, Press Release, 2 June.

- TIL (2008) Tourism agencies – Who does what? http://www.tourismireland.com/Home/about-us/who-does-what.aspx (accessed 24/01/2008).

- Tooke, N. and Baker, M. (1996) Seeing is believing: The effect of film on visitor numbers to screened locations, *Tourism Management*, 17(2): 87–94.

- Torchin, L. (2002) Location location location: The destination of the Manhattan TV tour, *Journal of Tourism Studies*, 2(3): 247–266.

- Tour2Korea (2006a) Korean movies [On-line, Chinese]. http://big5.chinese.tour2korea.com/02Culture/Movies/movie_01.asp?konum=subm11&kosm=m 2_4 (accessed 14/08/2006).

- Tour2Korea (2006b) Korean TV ministeries [On-line, Chinese]. http://big5.chinese.tour2korea.com/02Culture/TVMiniseries/synopsis_location.asp?kosm=m2_5 (accessed 14/08/2006).

- TNZ (2002) Regionalrap, 24 October, http://www.tourismnewzealand.com/tourism_info/fms/Tourism_Info/Publications/Regional%20 Rap/Regional%20Rap%20October%202002.pdf (accessed 28/05/2009).

- TNZ (2008) Corporate Overview, http://www.tourismnewzealand.com/tourism_info/about-us/corporate-overview/corporate-overview_home.cfm (accessed 24/01/2008).

- Trow, M. (1970) Comment on participant observation and interviewing: A comparison. In Filstead, W.J. *Qualitative Methodology*, Markham: Chicago, Illinois, USA.

- Tull, D.S. and Hawkins, D.I. (1984) *Marketing Research Measurement and Method*, 3rd edn, Macmillan Publishing Company: New York, USA.

- Turner, C.F. and Martin, E. (1984) *Surveying Subjective Phenomena*, Russell Sage: New York, USA.

- UK Film Council (2008) About the Film Council, http://www.ukfilmcouncil.org.uk (accessed 08/01/2008).

- UK Film Council (2009) Funded partners – Regional Screen Agencies, http://www.ukfilmcouncil.org.uk/fundedpartners (accessed 28/05/2009).

- Urry, J. (1990) *The Tourist Gaze: Leisure and Travel in Contemporary Societies*, Sage Publications: London, UK.

- Uysal, M., Chen, J.S. and Williams, D.R. (2000) Increasing state market share through a regional positioning, *Tourism Management*, 21(1): 89–96.

- van der Heijden, K. (1996) *Scenarios: The Art of Strategic Conversation*, John Wiley and Sons: Chichester, West Sussex, UK.

- Veal, A. (1992) *Research Methods for Leisure and Tourism: A Practical Guide*, Longman: Harlow, Essex, UK.

- Veal, A. (1997) *Research Methods for Leisure and Tourism: A Practical Guide*, 2nd edn, Pearson Professional: London, UK.

- Vellas, F. and Bécherel, L. (1999) *The International Marketing of Travel and Tourism: A Strategic Approach*, Palgrave Publishing: Basingstoke, Hampshire, UK, pp. 190–192.

- VisitBritain (2005) London on film, http://www.visitbritain.com (accessed 05/01/2005).

- VisitBritain (2008) Welcome to VisitBritain, http://www.visitbritain.org (accessed 08/01/2008).

- VisitScotland (2008) About us, http://www.visitscotland.org/about_us/faqs/faqs-the_organisation.htm (accessed 24/01/2008).

- Ward, S.V. (1998) *Selling Places: The Marketing and Promotion of Towns and Cities, 1850–2000*, Routledge: London, UK.

- Ward, D. (2001) Island life through a lens boosts bookings, *Travel Trade Gazette*, 9 July: 40.

- Weaver, D. and Oppermann, M. (2000) *Tourism Management*, John Wiley and Sons: Brisbane, Queensland, Australia.

- Weber Shandwick (2005) Weber Shandwick embarks on destination entertainment marketing to put the travel and tourism industry in the spotlight, http://www.webershandwick.com (accessed 15/01/2005).

- Weber Shandwick (2008) About us, http://www.webershandwick.com/default.aspx/aboutus (accessed 15/01/2005).

- Woodside, A. and Lysonski, S. (1989) A general model of traveller destination choice, *Journal of Travel Research*, 27(4): 8–14.

- Woodward, I. (2000) Why should the UK's tourism industry be interested in Bollywood' films? *Insights*, 12: 23–26.

- WTO (1979) *Tourism Images*, WTO: Madrid, Spain.

- WTO (2006) *Tourism Highlights*, 2005 edn, WTO: Madrid, Spain.

- WTO (2008) About UNWTO, http://www.unwto.org/aboutwto/index.php (accessed 24/01/2008).

- Xiang, R.L. (2006) A proposed conceptual framework for tourists' destination brand knowledge and loyalty. In *37th Annual TTRA Conference Proceedings: New Frontiers in Global Tourism: Trends and Competitive Challenges*, Jennings, G.R. and Beeton, S. (eds.), TTRA: Dublin, Ireland, pp. 37–43.

- Yin, R.K. (1984) *Case Study Research – Design and Methods*, Applied Social Research Methods Series, vol. 5, Sage Publications: Beverley Hills, California, USA.

- Yin, R.K. (1989) *Case Study Research – Design and Methods*, Applied Social Research Methods Series, vol. 5, Sage Publications: Newbury Park, California, USA.

- Yin, R.K. (1993) *Applications of Case Study Research*, Applied Social Research Methods Series, vol. 34, Sage Publications: Beverley Hills, California, USA.

- Yin, R.K. (1994) *Case Study Research – Design and Methods*, 2nd edn, Applied Social Research Methods Series, vol. 5, Sage Publications: Thousand Oaks, California, USA.

- Yin, R.K. (2003a) *Case Study Research – Design and Methods*, 3rd edn, Sage Publications: Thousand Oaks, California, USA.

- Yin, R.K. (2003b) *Applications of Case Study Research*, 2nd edn, Applied Social Research Methods Series, vol. 34, Sage Publications: Thousand Oaks, California, USA.

- Yorkshire Forward (2009) Homepage, http://www.yorkshireforward.com (accessed 28/05/2009).

- Youell, R. (2003) *Complete A–Z Travel and Leisure Handbook*, 2nd edn, Hodder and Stoughton: London, UK.

- YTB (2001/2002) *Yorkshire On Screen Film Trail*, YTB: York, Yorkshire UK.

- YTB (2003) *Tourism TIC: Volume and Value*, 2002, YTB: York, Yorkshire UK.

- YTB (2006) *YTB Market Intelligence Manual: Tourism Structure – Key Relationships and Market Intelligence Product Information*, Unpublished Report, York City Council: York, Yorkshire UK.

- YTB (2008) YTB's role, http://www.ytb.org.uk/about/index.shtml (accessed 08/01/2008).

- Zikmund, W.G. (1997) *Business Research Methods*, Dryden Press, Harcourt Brace College Publishers: Orlando, Florida, USA.

- Zukowski, H. (2003) Outtakes from middle-earth, *Westworld*, November: 50–53.

APPENDIX 1

Tourist Attitude Survey

This survey is being completed as part of a Ph.D. academic study through Dublin Institute of Technology, Ireland.

Private and Confidential: Tourist Attitude Survey

PART I

Question 1: Personal details

Survey Number		Location	
Male		Female	

Question 2: Where do you live?

UK		Rest of Europe	
Where exactly? _____		Where exactly? _____	
North America (USA and Canada)		Other	

Question 3: What is your occupation? _____

Question 4: Whom are you travelling with?

Alone		With children	
With other adults		With partner	
With partner and children		Other	

Question 5: Is this your first time in Yorkshire?

Yes		No	

If no, when was your first visit? _____

Question 6: What is your main reason for visiting Yorkshire?

Business / work		Visiting friends and/or relatives	
Day trip		Shopping	
On holiday		Other	

Question 7: Are you travelling independently or as part of a package?

Independently		Package	

Question 8: How did you book your trip?

Directly with accommodation provider		Staying with friends and/or relatives	
Directly with transport provider		Tour operator	
Directly with Yorkshire Tourist Board		Travel agent	
Did not book		Other	

Question 9: Where did you obtain your information about Yorkshire?

Internet		Recommendation (Friend/relative)	
Newspaper / magazine advert		Previous visit	
Newspaper / magazine article		Guidebook	
Radio		Live in Yorkshire	
Regional leaflet at accommodation		Signposting	
Television		Tourism Information Centres	
Other			

Question 10: When did you arrive in Yorkshire? _____

Question 11: How long are you staying in Yorkshire? _____

Question 12: What type of accommodation are you using?

B & B / Guesthouse		University / college	
Friends and relatives		Second home	
Hostel		Caravan / camping	
Hotel		Self catering apartment / house	

Question 13: Is this your main holiday or just a short break?

Main holiday		Second Holiday		Short break	

Question 14: When you arrived in Yorkshire, where did you source your tourist information from?

Friends and/or relatives		Tourism Information Centre	
Accommodation provider		Guidebook	
Local tourism website		Didn't source any	

Question 15: Which of the following activities if any, have you done or will you take part in on this visit to Yorkshire?

Go on an organised tour		Visit local village and/or market	
Go out in the evening to a pub or restaurant		Visit historic house, monument, museum or gallery	
Go shopping		Visit zoo, farm, wildlife, leisure, theme park or garden	
Go to a local cultural or sporting event e.g. theatre or horseracing		Walk, hike, cycle, go to the beach or other such activity around the area	

Question 16: How satisfied are you with your experience so far in Yorkshire?

Very satisfied		Satisfied		Neither satisfied or dissatisfied		Dissatisfied		Very dissatisfied	

Question 17: Before taking your first holiday in Yorkshire did you have any image of what the place would be like?

Yes		No	

If yes, what was this image?

_____

_____

_____

Question 18: How was that image of Yorkshire formed?

Books		Television		Pictures		Friends & relatives		Other	

Question 19: Is Yorkshire different from what you thought it would be like?

Yes		No	

Please give reasons for your answer

_____

_____

_____

Question 20: Has any of the tourism information that you have received mentioned the region's association with television and/or film?

Yes		No	

If yes, please state the tourism information sources and also which television and/or films were actually mentioned;

_____

_____

_____

Question 21: How important was the television association of Yorkshire a factor in your decision to visit the area?

Very important		Important		Neither important or unimportant		Unimportant		Very unimportant	

Question 22: Were any of the following television series' actually filmed in Yorkshire?

All Creatures Great and Small		Heartbeat	
Brookside		Hollyoaks	
Coronation Street		Last of the Summer Wine	
Eastenders		Peak Practice	
Emmerdale		The Royal	

275

Question 23: How often would you watch any of the following series'?

All Creatures Great and Small

Every week		Once a month		Every 6 months		Never	

Emmerdale

Every week		Once a month		Every 6 months		Never	

Heartbeat

Every week		Once a month		Every 6 months		Never	

The Royal

Every week		Once a month		Every 6 months		Never	

Last of the Summer Wine

Every week		Once a month		Every 6 months		Never	

PART II

Question 24: What image do you think the following Yorkshire based television series' portray?

All Creatures Great and Small

_____

_____

Emmerdale

_____

_____

Heartbeat

_____

_____

The Royal

_____

_____

Last of the Summer Wine

_____

_____

Question 25: Do you feel that Yorkshire is promoted well?

Yes		No	

Question 26: Are you aware who promotes Yorkshire?

Yes		No	

If yes please name the organisation; _____

Question 27: Have you read anything in the tourism literature e.g. guidebooks, brochures about the following areas?

	Yes	No
Heartbeat Country		
Herriot Country		
Summer Wine Country		

Question 28: Have you seen any signage relating to these areas while in Yorkshire?

Yes		No	

Question 29: Could you tell me where in Yorkshire 'Heartbeat Country' is located?

Yes		No	

If yes: Please describe_____

Question 30: Could you tell me where in Yorkshire 'Herriot Country' is located?

Yes		No	

If yes: Please describe_____

Question 31: Could you tell me where in Yorkshire 'Summer Wine Country' is located?

Yes		No	

If yes: Please describe_____

Question 32: What would you say was the highlight of your visit to Yorkshire?

_____

_____

_____

Question 33: What would you say if any was the disappointing aspect of your visit to Yorkshire?

_____

_____

_____

Question 34: Are you likely to return to Yorkshire again in the future?

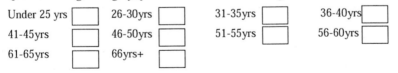

Definitely will visit again		Probably will visit again		Uncertain		Probably will not visit again		Definitely will not visit again	

Question 35: Age Category; please tick one of the following:

Under 25 yrs ☐   26-30yrs ☐   31-35yrs ☐   36-40yrs ☐

41-45yrs ☐   46-50yrs ☐   51-55yrs ☐   56-60yrs ☐

61-65yrs ☐   66yrs+ ☐

Thank You for Your Time and Co-Operation

APPENDIX 2

Sample strategic conversation

Strategic Conversations
Marketing Manager

Introduction

1. Most Destination Marketing Organisations have very limited budgets and yet they have to market globally competing not just with other destinations. Discuss.

_____

_____

_____

Imagery

1. In tourism, while factors such as cost of travel, convenience and quality of facilities are important, the strongest motivator is "the destination brand image". Discuss.

_____

_____

_____

2. Despite the undeniable power of film and television, visual images or symbols also play a role in promoting a destinations image such as the Eiffel Tower (Paris/France). Discuss.

_____

_____

_____

3. Television can directly influence the tourism image through the broadcast of tourism commercials. Discuss.

_____

_____

_____

4. If more people are exposed to increasing amounts of visual media one might assume that popular images portrayed in films plays an important role in shaping images and determining traveller's expectations of a particular destination. Discuss.

_____

_____

_____

5. The development of a strong image whether visual, vocal, personal, film or television is the key to success but the brand must reflect the destination. Discuss.

_____

_____

_____

6. The need for destinations to create a unique image and brand to differentiate themselves from their competitors is more critical than ever. Discuss.

_____

_____

_____

7. For destination management, the image portrayed is very important and therefore should be given special attention in destination management planning. Discuss.

_____

_____

_____

8. Are the images of the rural idyll, small villages and community life, the images, which are seen in many of the television series' filmed in Yorkshire and form part of the brand, the actual images that the Yorkshire region in general wants to portray?

_____

_____

_____

9. Do you feel that Yorkshire is presently portraying a strong image? Why? How?

_____

_____

_____

10. Do you think that Yorkshire's television series have been successful in changing the image of the region?

_____

_____

_____

Branding

1. Tourism destinations are probably one of the most difficult products to market involving large numbers of stakeholders and a brand image over which a destination marketing manager typically has very little control. Discuss.

_____

_____

_____

2. Destination marketers need valid and reliable research from which to make branding decisions. How do you do this?

_____

_____

_____

3. The challenge for destination marketers is to find the best ways to use images stories and emotions to capture the consumer's attention and build the destinations brand. Discuss.

_____

_____

_____

4. Destinations cannot afford to ignore branding as it offers an innovative and effective tool with which managers can establish emotional links with the consumer. Discuss.

_____

_____

_____

5. Its takes patience to establish brand reputations and building a powerful destination brand is a long term effort. Discuss.

_____

_____

_____

6. A destination brand can be developed in a variety of ways e.g. direct marketing, personal selling on websites; how have you done this?

_____

_____

_____

7. VisitBritain stated that the Yorkshire brand is the 3rd most recognisable tourism brand in England. How have you achieved this?

_____

_____

_____

8. Has VisitBritain been involved in the development of the Yorkshire brand?

_____

_____

_____

9. Have the Yorkshire Tourist Board monitored the strength of the Yorkshire brand?

_____

_____

_____

10. Has the brand been effective to date?

_____

_____

_____

11. Have you looked at any best practice examples while designing your brand campaign?

_____

_____

_____

12. Are the media brands (*Heartbeat Country*, *Herriot Country* and *Summer Wine Country*) the most effective brands to use in branding Yorkshire?

_____

_____

_____

Film Induced Tourism

1. The phenomenon of film induced tourism will continue to grow as films are internationally distributed and viewed. Discuss.

_____

_____

_____

2. It has been suggested that as people read less, what is shown in films, videos and television will become even more important. Discuss.

_____

_____

_____

3. The limited research that has been published to date shows that film induced tourism can add significant benefits to the development of a destination. Discuss.

_____

_____

_____

4. Films and television series are widely recognised as a stimulus that can induce people to visit destinations. Discuss.

_____

_____

_____

5. What do you feel are the drawbacks of film induced tourism to a destination, if any?

_____

_____

_____

6. Displacement in the film induced tourism context refers to the aspect of a film being shot in one place but in reality representing somewhere else entirely. Have you encountered this?

_____

_____

_____

7. Film enables destinations to boost their tourism potential, has this happened?

_____

_____

_____

8. Recognising that films can enhance awareness of places and affect decision-making processes, marketers are increasingly working with film producers to promote their destinations as possible film locations. Has this happened?

_____

_____

_____

9. The emergence of movie maps has only occurred in recent years. Discuss their role.

_____

_____

_____

10. An influx of visitors is not always advantageous with many towns unsuited to supporting tourism growth because of their limited infrastructure, facilities and services. Has this occurred Yorkshire?

_____

_____

_____

11. The influence of filming re-imaging rural areas has proven to be extremely important as illustrated by *Heartbeat* in Goathland and *The Lord of the Rings* in New Zealand. Discuss.

_____

_____

_____

12. Would you agree that television series' tend to have a greater impact than films due to their longevity e.g. *Last of The Summer Wine* v.'s *The Full Monty*? If not what evidence is there to support this?

_____

_____

_____

13. If there are reruns of the show or a further series is filmed the image will remain longer as has happened with *Ballykissangel* and *All Creatures Great and Small*. Discuss.

_____

_____

_____

Stakeholder Involvement

1. There is a major buy in from the national tourist organisation's to the association with a film or television series, the results can be very effective. Discuss.

_____

_____

_____

2. It has become increasingly evident that some agencies are over using the film or television imagery in destination promotion. Discuss.

_____

_____

_____

3. It is crucial that film/television is incorporated into tourism/destination marketing planning, especially in small communities that are most sensitive to development. Discuss.

_____

_____

_____

4. For any real maximisation of potential, the tourist and film stakeholders should work together and the tourist stakeholders in particular have to take a more active strategic approach to the concept. Can you please discuss this relationship?

_____

_____

_____

5. Can you please highlight how your current Tourism Marketing strategy intends to build on the strength of the Yorkshire Brand?

_____

_____

_____

6. How has your current Tourism Marketing Strategy incorporated Yorkshire's role as a film induced tourism destination? Has it been successful?

_____

_____

_____

7. Do you plan to use the Yorkshire brand as an umbrella under which destinations can grow and develop?

_____

_____

_____

8. Which stakeholders did you consult with when devising your Tourism Marketing Strategy 2006-2010?

_____

_____

_____

9. Some communities have been able to prevent negative film images of their neighbourhood but until tourism stakeholders financially contribute to filming they will not have any rights to control how these images are portrayed in media such as films. Discuss.

_____

_____

_____

10. Planning needs to adopt a long term consideration to the image of film. How can stakeholders carry out this?

_____

_____

_____

11. Can you please expand on your relationship with the other tourism stakeholders?

_____

_____

_____

Any Other Comments

_____

_____

_____

_____

APPENDIX 3

FMAP – Issues, Strategic Interventions, Actions and Responsibility

Table 6.3b

FMAP – Issues, Strategic Interventions, Actions and Responsibility

Issue	Strategic Intervention	Action	Responsibility
	Before	Release planning	
Marketing			
Devoted websites	Do not underestimate the importance of designing a devoted media related website.	Update any media related website prior to the film and/or television series release.	RSA
Electronic links	Work with the Screen Commissions to design an online link to the destination.	Create links to the filming destination via the film and/or television series and the film studios website.	RSA/RTA
Media feature	Decide if a 'making of the film or television series' feature would be a viable investment.	Produce a 'making of the film or television series' feature to entice tourists to the destination.	RSA/RTA
Promotional value	Contemplate the promotional value of a film or television series.	Evaluate the film's financial worth in terms of its promotional value, which will be difficult to quantify.	RSA/RTA
Film incentives	Investigate the feasibility of using film incentives.	Financially support the film and/or television series directly through sponsorship.	RTA
Filming credits	Support the use of end credits for the film and/or television series.	Agree on the end credits for the destination.	RSA/RTA
Other tourism sectors	Develop linkages with other tourism sectors.	Propose regional activities to promote other tourism sectors e.g. food and wine.	RTA
Scouting services	Propose effective scouting services.	Formulate a scouting service programme to lobby prospective film studios.	RSA
The travel media	Formulate a list of the travel media.	Invite the travel media to the filming destination.	RTA

Issue	Strategic Intervention	Action	Responsibility
	After release	Maximize (Positive impacts)	
Marketing			
Recognition of the importance of destination planning	Establish a planned approach to tourist management.	Identify the importance of integrating tourism into sustainable destination planning.	NPA/RTA
Facilities and services	Draw tourists to the destination by providing many facilities and services.	Provide high quality facilities and services at the destination by supporting quality standards throughout the destination.	NPA/RTA
Good for tourism	Cultivate the value of the domestic market.	Encourage domestic tourists to visit the destination in the off peak/shoulder season through assertive marketing.	NTA/RTA
Increase in economic activity	Exert a pull on high yield tourists.	Supply money spinning facilities and services.	RTA
Infrastructural improvements	Improve infrastructure to achieve standards of excellence.	Secure funds and grants for infrastructural development.	LA
Brand marketing			
Brand research	Brand the destination as a film induced tourism destination.	Commission brand research on film induced tourism.	RSA/RTA
Priority target markets	Position the brand as a destination brand of choice for priority target markets with respect to key competitors.	Achieve measured increases in awareness of key sub-regional destinations brands through examining their importance	RTA
Official branding material	Official branding material is important for those destinations which have little awareness in the market place.	Adopt the official branding material to continue to raise regional awareness.	NTA/RTA
Brand hierarchy	A meaningful brand hierarchy and structure needs to be acknowledged.	Focus on the perceptions and aspirations of the tourists to the destination in any marketing research activities.	NTA/RTA

Issue	Strategic Intervention	Action	Responsibility
Co-operative marketing			
Market focus	Better integrate the destination through co-operative marketing.	Contrive promotional strategies of different segments of the tourism industry at national and regional levels.	NTA/RTA
Corporate brands	Review corporate brands.	Use corporate brands in partnership with industry communications.	RTA
Cross-boundary marketing	Look at cross-boundary marketing and communications.	These should be agreed in context of the marketing strategies.	RTA
Inbound tour operators	Evaluate the viability of integrated marketing activity with inbound tour operators.	Partake in integrated marketing activity with inbound tour operators to the destination.	RTA
Local industry PR	Highlight the opportunities for the private sector from training to quality development and business supported local industry PR.	Strengthen the role of the private niche product marketing groups e.g. major sporting events by incorporating them into destinational PR.	RTA
Partner Travel Trade Marketing	Foster relationships with retailers through event sponsorship.	Sustain a high profile at conferences and events. Link with tour operators to formulate an annual activity plan.	RTA
Marketing campaign			
Displacement	Consider the displacement factor.	Factual marketing material and movie maps will alleviate this issue.	RSA/RTA
Film and television merchandise	Assess the importance of using merchandise as a marketing tool for the destination.	Build exhibitions of film and television series memorabilia and sell related merchandise.	RTA/LA
Destination interpretation	Create signage and tourism related interpretation for the destination.	Put relevant signage and interpretation in place at the destination.	RTA/NPA
Destination message	Refresh the destination message.	Portray a complimentary destination message to the prospective tourist.	RTA/NPA
Destination PR	Create a PR plan for internal and external stakeholders' role in the brand.	Disseminate its key message. Seek, broadcast, explore and boost the glossy publication contact database and maximize exposure.	RTA
Destination profile	Build a profile of the destination.	Raise the profile of the destination as a luxury location with a continued presence at international trade shows.	NTA
Holiday guides	Deliver a holiday and accommodation promotional toolkit for all markets.	Strengthen the main holiday and accommodation guides for duplication / collaboration.	NTA
International and domestic campaigns	Construct international and domestic campaigns.	Showcase international and domestic campaigns via the internet.	RTA

Issue	Strategic Intervention	Action	Responsibility
Marketing research			
Guide strategy and service development	Carry out market research of the current network requirements.	Use research to guide strategy and service development. Monitor this research and also economic impact modelling.	RTA/NPA/LA
Research findings	Collect data about the tourism industry.	Disseminate (e-newsletter, stakeholder forum) research findings and market intelligence to the tourism stakeholders.	RTA
Research needs	Identify research needs and gaps in current knowledge of the destination.	Authorize brand tracking international research for markets and online research.	NTA/RTA
Market intelligence	Commission appropriate market research and intelligence to meet activities.	Review the *Anholt GMI National Brand Index* regularly to measure brand perceptions.	NTA/RTA
Product marketing techniques			
Accommodation	Identify accommodation outlets used for filming.	Endorse these outlets in any destination promotional material.	RTA
Existing events and activities	Endorse existing programme of events and activities.	Progress cross-cutting themes including e.g. Walking and cycling routes.	NPA/RTA
Extend the tourism season	A specific campaign to extend the tourism season and range of tourism associated events will ease the seasonality problem.	Joint advertising, direct mailing, brochures and website co-ordination across the main stakeholders in the destinations will reduce seasonality.	RTA
High profile events	Ascertain high profile events and cultural activities.	Subsidize high profile events and cultural activities.	NTA
Local produce	Acknowledge any local produce.	State the role of local produce in supporting the marketing of the destination and vice versa.	RTA
Media signage and promotion	Choose the media signage and promotion	Reduce litter and visual promotion by being selective when using media signage and promotion	RTA/LA
Off season campaigns	Implement off season campaigns in key markets.	Launch a *Short Breaks* and a *Touring* campaign in the short haul markets.	NTA/RTA
Outdoor Adventure	Make a transformational change in the nature and perception of the destination as both a tourist destination and place to live and work.	Operate with stakeholders to advance product marketing and outdoor activities.	NPA/RTA
PR calendar	Contrive a PR calendar of activity	Implement the PR calendar of activity	RTA
Promotional activity	Sustain a promotional activities framework.	Operate with brands that will provide the framework for all promotional activity across the destination.	RTA
Regional and national messaging	Incorporate regional and national messaging.	Integrate regional and national messaging into the destinations marketing activity to provide a more informative product/service.	RTA
Tourist stay	Extend the tourist stay.	Package attractions and activities to reduce the seasonality problem.	NPA/RTA
Trade and consumer sales platforms	Take on new integrated trade and consumer sales platforms in key destinations.	Attend trade shows and other events and/or exhibitions.	NTA

Issue	Strategic Intervention	Action	Responsibility
Online marketing			
Communications strategy	Assemble a communications strategy.	Create an events and networking programme to disseminate knowledge and provide opportunities for co-learning and collaboration.	RTA
Destinational events data base	Create a destinational events data base.	Organize dissemination through print, electronic formats, press and the media.	RTA
Development programme	Maximize the use of ICT.	Develop a programme with the industry to maximize the use of ICT for marketing and CRM.	All
E-commerce applications	Effective use of customer friendly e-commerce applications.	Support the ongoing introduction and development of effective customer friendly e-commerce applications.	RTA
Film and television tours	Undertake ad-hoc research into film and television tours.	Advertise website links to film tours organized by local tour operators.	RTA
High-tech marketing activities	Carry out high-tech marketing activities to effectively target the potential tourist.	These activities may include blogs, podcasts, photos and virtual opportunities.	RTA
Increase web traffic	Increase web traffic by running pay-as-per click campaign with Google for example.	Negotiate online distribution deals with major tourism stakeholders and news websites.	RTA
New CRM system	Work with technology to build a new CRM system.	Improve functionality of the new CRM system and use control measures to monitor its viability.	RTA
On-and-off line campaigns	Increase market based trade in all of the on-and-off line campaigns.	Work out the content for the current website. Schedule and commission content liaise with third parties (internationally).	RTA
Online ecommerce shops	Compare the roll out of online e-commerce shops.	Install effective reporting mechanisms for the online e-commerce shops.	RTA
Publishing	Utilize new distribution/sales channels.	Ensure good representation of the destination in the online shops.	All
The internet	Ensure that tourists make the best use of the tourist information on offer via the internet.	See if the destination requires an effective Destination Management System (DMS).	RTA
Virtual marketing toolkit	Continue to develop a virtual marketing toolkit to help run campaigns.	Make available audio CD's and MP3's which can be downloadable from the destinations website.	RTA
Website assessment	Annually assess the functionality of the website.	Maximize traffic on website by running innovative features.	RTA

Issue	Strategic Intervention	Action	Responsibility
Relationship management			
Quality and depth of information	Further enhance the quality and depth of information held on the database.	Acquire new customers and capture marketing research data into prospective markets.	NTA/RTA
World class experience	Develop a world class experience for tourists which will consistently exceed all expectations.	Continue to collect international survey results to initiate this (FECTO/WTO/WTTC surveys).	NTA/RTA
Behavioural targeting	Invest in behavioural targeting.	Effectively optimize online media investment opportunities which may arise.	RSA/RTA
Service strategy	Adopt a customer service strategy.	Align the customer service centre with online service activity.	RTA
International tourists	Draw a greater proportion of international tourists, while seeking to nurture the return from the core domestic market.	Target high value tourists through a focused marketing campaign.	NTA/RTA

Issue	Strategic Intervention	Action	Responsibility
	After release	MinimiZe (Negative impacts)	
Residential dissatisfaction	Minimize residential dissatisfaction.	Community involvement at all stages of the planning process will help counteract any residential dissatisfaction though loss of privacy and small town atmosphere.	NPA/RTA/LA
Residential exploitation	Recognize the needs of the community.	The community should be considered a stakeholder for any tourism and/or filming plans to be employed at a destination.	NPA/RTA/LA
Support major initiatives	Build up the primary niche segments.	Implement cooperative campaigns to sustain major initiatives in niche markets.	RTA/SA
Tour groups	Relieve congestion at peak times.	Assign alternate times for bus tour groups.	NPA/LA

Issue	Strategic Intervention	Action	Responsibility
De-marketing strategies			
Business			
Business engagement	Engage all businesses from across all the sub-sectors of the tourist economy.	Promote good balance with all stakeholders from hospitality to the tourist attractions.	NTA/NPARTA
Proactive supportive polices	Defend the industry by creating proactive supportive polices.	Aid industry by using these polices in collaboration with the tourism stakeholders.	All
Strategic partnerships	Sustain the drive for better strategic partnerships at all levels.	Encourage better cohesion and engagement between local, regional and national tourism stakeholders through the forum.	All
Tourism Advisory Service	Offer special support for tourism business start ups.	Install a project to link local environmental resources, skills and products with new style business developments in land use and tourism.	LA
Web portal	Design a web portal.	Give advice for the stakeholders.	All
Annual forecast	Produce an annual inbound forecast for the destination.	Propose a mid-year update of the annual inbound forecast.	NTA/RTA
Business advice and support services	Integrate business advice and support services.	Give specific help on business planning and investment funding.	NTA
Centralized coordination	Continue to build on the destination relationships with strategic partners.	Provide centralized coordination and communication services.	All
Event expertise	Provide event expertise and management.	Offer expertise and management for events, conferences and receptions.	NTA
Industry relations	Create a strategy for effective engagement with industry.	Implement the strategy.	LA
Non-traditional partners	Work with the non-traditional partners to promote the destination.	Instigate a cruise and travel trade strategy to facilitate a developmental strategy.	NTA/RTA
Prioritization framework	Plan a prioritization framework for all new activities.	Keep in mind both the consumer stakeholder and corporate needs.	All

Issue	Strategic Intervention	Action	Responsibility
Economic			
Business performance	Incorporate tourism into the overall economic strategy.	Create opportunities to form cross sector initiatives e.g. with festivals and creative industries.	All
Cost management	Boost the industry's cost management capabilities.	Utilize specific training supports to enhance the industry's capability in cost management.	NPA/RTA/LA
Economic impact assessment	Identify the feasibility of using film induced tourism to market a destination.	Use a consistent economic impact assessment to Identify the feasibility of using film induced tourism to market a destination..	NTA
Maximize economic impact	Encourage additional visits	Increase the value of each visit and promote additional visits particularly at shoulder and off-peak times to lessen congestion.	NPA/RTA
Product investment	Initiate product investment.	Maintain product investment through events programming, joint ticketing and packaging of offers.	NTA/RTA
The multiplier effect	Create local support for the film induced tourism phenomenon.	Inform locals of the positive economic impacts of such tourism to the community.	RTA/LA
Additional investment	Co-ordinate and expand existing activity.	Assemble niche markets across the sub-region in cities e.g. events and themed itineraries.	RTA
General price increase	Repeat tourists should be encouraged.	They should not incur unrealistic prices.	LA
Longer stays	Encourage economically viable stays.	Increase longer stays by giving local guided tours to attractions and activities that are both time consuming and economically viable yet interesting.	NPA/RTA
Park and ride	Potential income generation.	Support a park and ride system, which will create income for the regional transport providers.	LA
Purchase items	Have high yielding souvenirs on sale.	Encourage the purchase of lucrative souvenirs.	NPA/RTA
Sales and promotion costs	Calculate the cost of sales and promotion.	Decrease sales and promotion costs through using more electronic promotional material and less print material.	NTA/RTA

Issue	Strategic Intervention	Action	Responsibility
Environmental			
Local tour guides	Promote a sustainable product.	Educate and certify local guides to promote a sustainable tourism product.	RTA
Preservation protection plan	Conserve the landscape, including the towns and villages, and their special qualities	Create and implement a preservation protection plan.	NPA
Transport strategy	Plan a tourism and public transport strategy.	The tourism and public transport strategy should include interchangeable ticketing, tourist tickets, marketing and service development.	RTA/LA
Access paths	Diminish litter pollution on access routes.	Place rubbish bins on all access routes.	LA
Accessibility to the tourism product	Design a tourism product that is accessible to all.	Make the countryside and leisure facilities accessible for the disabled.	LA
Closure of roads and paths	Protect any damaged areas.	Interim closure of roads and paths at peak times.	NPA/LA
Footpaths and trails	Examine tourist footpaths and trails.	Enhance the 'right of way' network, footpaths and trails.	LA
Quality			
Delivery of services	Add value to the delivery of services.	Increase the value of the delivery of services through a reduction in duplicated activity and a minimization of overheads.	LA
High quality packages	Create new high quality packages for the tourist.	The high quality packages should relate back to the marketing plan.	NTA/RTA
Infrastructure standards of excellence	Encourage improvements in infrastructure to achieve market standards of excellence.	Standards of excellence in the planting of floral displays, the maintenance of public toilets, the cleaning standards of litter bins, the interpretation in town centres and the design of street furniture.	LA
Businesses participation	Pinpoint the barriers to businesses participating in quality assurance schemes.	Evaluate the strength of the barriers to businesses (marketing research), participating in quality assurance schemes.	All
Quality of services	Improve the quality of services which affect the tourist economy.	Oversee the successful implementation of common standards.	LA
Tourism product and service	Increase participation of quality by focusing on the benefits and by adding value services and strategic partnerships.	Compete strongly in an international market, provide the highest standards of customer service and surpass the expectations of its tourists.	NTA
Value of quality assurance schemes	The necessity and value of quality assurance schemes should be reviewed.	Advance the use and value of quality assurance schemes.	All

Issue	Strategic Intervention	Action	Responsibility
Social			
Banned activities	Ascertain any prohibited activities.	Advise tourists of prohibited activities at the information gathering stage.	NTA/NPA/RTA
Best times to holiday	Decrease congestion at popular parts of the destination.	Inform tourists of best times to holiday in the destination	NTA/NPA/RTA
Council services	Maintain council services.	Increase the regularity of council services e.g. refuse collection, road maintenance.	LA
Day visits	Clarify the percentage of day visitors who arrive by public transport.	Encourage day visits by bus and train.	LA
Destination Marketing Strategy (DMS)	Develop a DMS for the destination which will compile and update a comprehensive database of tourist information.	Provide for the DMS by printed material, training for local businesses, appropriate direction signage and interpretation to provide a complete guide for visitors.	NPA/RTA/LA
Natural audience peak	Monitor a films natural peak.	Host events that prolong the films initial pull beyond its original release.	RSA/RTA/LA
Promotional literature	Both tourists and the media should be aware of acceptable behaviour, while at the destination.	Educate tourists concerning suitable behaviour in the promotional literature prior to their arrival.	NTA/NPA/RTA
Tourist numbers	Use the principles of carrying capacity management.	Restrict tourist numbers at peak times.	NPA/RTA
Destination activities	Assess the carrying capacity of destinational based activities	Help the destinational based activities which have the carrying capacity to facilitate them.	NPA/RTA
Entry fees	Use entry fees as a means of alleviating congestion.	Introduce or even increase entry fees at destination attractions.	NPA/RTA
Law enforcement	Appraise the level of police presence in the destination	Increase the level of police presence through constant liaising with the local force.	NPA/RTA/LA
Organization of large groups	Control large groups.	Large groups should be individually organized to reduce congestion.	NPA/RTA
Pedestrian crossings	Research the need for pedestrian crossings.	Acquire funding to build more pedestrian crossings as and when required.	LA
Picture taking areas	Lessen the pressure of picture taking in popular areas.	Create areas within the destination for appropriate picture taking.	NPA/RTA/LA
Picture taking protocol	Set up a picture taking protocol plan.	Inform tourists' of the picture taking protocol while in the destination, by displaying it in the relevant areas.	NPA/RTA/LA
Private areas	Restrict the use of private areas	Devise access paths to avoid private areas.	LA
Public toilets	Consider the available grants to supply public toilets.	Increase the number of public toilets particularly in busy areas.	LA
Safety	Safety and security at the destination is of the utmost importance.	Improve regional safety and security by being observant and working with the police service.	LA

VDM publishing house ltd.

Scientific Publishing House

offers

free of charge publication

of current academic research papers, Bachelor´s Theses, Master's Theses, Dissertations or Scientific Monographs

If you have written a thesis which satisfies high content as well as formal demands, and you are interested in a remunerated publication of your work, please send an e-mail with some initial information about yourself and your work to *info@vdm-publishing-house.com*.

Our editorial office will get in touch with you shortly.

VDM Publishing House Ltd.
Meldrum Court 17.
Beau Bassin
Mauritius
www.vdm-publishing-house.com